# Phenomenology and Literature

# Phenomenology and Literature

## An Introduction

### by
### Robert R. Magliola

1977
*Purdue University Press*
*West Lafayette, Indiana*

*Second printing, April 1978*

© 1977 by the Purdue Research Foundation
Library of Congress Card Catalog Number—76-21584
International Standard Book Number 0–911198–46–6
Printed in the United States of America

## dedicated

*to my wife*
Rosa

*to my children*
Lorinda-marie
Jon-carlo
Clara-marie

*and to my parents*
Florence and
Hugo Magliola

# contents

# preface

Part One of this book is intended as an introduction to phenomenological literary criticism. Its audience will include, I hope, specialists in American and English literature who want to learn more about Continental letters. To the best of my knowlege, Part One is the only attempt in English to describe phenomenological criticism (both French and German) in synoptic terms. Thus I believe it holds interest too for specialists in European criticism. In her book on the Geneva School, entitled *Critics of Consciousness* (Cambridge: Harvard University Press, 1968), Sarah Lawall gives an account of Genevan practice, but does not focus on the relevance of phenomenological philosophy and esthetics to this practice. Furthermore, she does not include writers who are phenomenological in the Genevan sense, but not members of the school. Nor does she consider German phenomenology.

My Part Two, on phenomenological literary theory, fills another need of the academic community—the need for English-language commentaries on Roman Ingarden and Mikel Dufrenne. I examine *The Literary Work of Art* (*Das literarische Kunstwerk*) and *The Phenomenology of Aesthetic Experience* (*Phénoménologie de l'expérience esthétique*), respectively. Part Two assays this function and parallels it with evaluation and comparative analysis. Ultimately, the second part is a comparative study of four phenomenologists, Edmund Husserl, Roman Ingarden, Mikel Dufrenne, and Martin Heidegger, and one non-phenomenologist, E. D. Hirsch, included because his work bears so heavily on the topics in point. Hirsch, Husserl, and Heidegger are addressed specialized questions; Ingarden and Dufrenne are asked the same questions *en passant,* as part of the more global treatments of their respective books. The questions are crucial ones for any theorist of literature. What is meaning? When a text can present several senses, which is the valid sense? What does one do in the face of multiple meanings? What if a word projects contradictory senses? Moreover, the phenomenological answers to these questions are often different from those of the Anglo-American community. Some while ago the editors of the

*London Times* described the rift between the Continental and Anglo-Saxon literary establishments:

> English literary scholars and critics—and, in some spheres, their counterparts across the Atlantic [Americans]—have held firm in late years to certain hard-headed ideas about the value of literature, and given short shrift to any others. But on the Continent many distinguished critics expound, with enthusiasm and eloquence, points of view that to the well-indoctrinated English student are likely to seem little short of disreputable. The right response to such a situation is surely neither to feel that the bulk of English criticism today is absurdly over-confident or one-sided; nor to support that "England's thinkers, as ever, point the one way to reason. . . ."[1]

I hope my book abets the cause of mutual understanding. For some, understanding can convert uninformed hostility into informed disagreement; for others, it can encourage a backing away from rigid *parti pris;* for still others, it can disclose parallels between the two critical camps. In any case, there is in my project an element of chance. I close this preface with the appropriate words of Mallarmé—*"Toute pensée émet un coup de dés";* that is, "All thought emits a throw of the dice."[2]

# acknowledgments

Thanks to the Purdue Research Foundation for its financial support.

Quotations from Martin Heidegger's *Being and Time,* translated by John Macquarrie and Edward Robinson, copyright 1962, have been printed by permission of Harper and Row, New York and Evanston.

The fourteen lines of poetry from *The Complete Poems of Hart Crane,* edited and with an introduction by Waldo Frank, copyright 1933, 1958, and 1966, appear with the permission of the Liveright Publishing Corporation.

Excerpts from Roman Ingarden's *The Literary Work of Art,* translated by George Grabowicz, copyright 1973, have been quoted by permission of Northwestern University Press, Evanston.

Quotations from Edmund Husserl's *Logical Investigations,* 2 vols., translated by J. N. Findlay, copyright 1970, appear with the permission of Humanities Press, Inc., New York.

Excerpts from Mikel Dufrenne's *The Phenomenology of Aesthetic Experience,* translated by Edward S. Casey, Albert A. Anderson, Willis Domingo, and Leon Jacobson, copyright 1973, have been quoted by permission of Northwestern University Press, Evanston.

Quotations from Martin Heidegger's *Poetry, Language, Thought,* translated by Albert Hofstadter, copyright 1971, appear by permission of Harper and Row, New York, Evanston, San Francisco, and London.

Substantial portions of Part One, Chapters One and Two, derive from my article, "The Phenomenological Approach to Literature: Its Theory and Methodology," *Language and Style* 5, no. 2 (Spring 1972), and appear through the permission of E. L. Epstein, editor, who holds the journal's copyright.

Likewise, substantial portions of Part One, Chapter Four, borrow from my article, "Parisian Structuralism Confronts Phenomenology; The Ongoing Debate," *Language and Style* 6, no. 4 (Fall 1973), and appear through the permission of the same editor.

# part 1

# Phenomenology and Literary Criticism

# chapter 1

# Philosophical and Linguistic Background

The ontology of the literary work as understood by most phenomenological theorists depends on certain basic principles of phenomenological epistemology. This epistemology first appears in a fully developed sense in the philosophy (or, more appropriately, in the "phenomenology") of Edmund Husserl (1859–1938). Every discussion of Husserl must pause for a moment at the term *phenomenology* itself, so entrammelled is the word's history, and so prolific its use over the last several decades. *Phenomenon* for Kant meant the appearance of reality in consciousness, as opposed to *noumenon,* or the being of reality-in-itself (and unknowable by man). In Hegel, phenomenology has a historical perspective: for him it is the "science" describing the development which natural phenomenal consciousness undergoes by way of science and philosophy toward the absolute knowledge of the Absolute. When the early Husserl takes over the term, he renounces what he calls the "dualism" between phenomenon and noumenon posited by Kant, and the "constructionism" whereby Hegel dialectically moves from phenomena to the Absolute Mind they supposedly manifest. Husserl agrees with them in asserting that only phenomena are given, but he claims that in them, and only in them, is given the "essence" of that which is. Since by Husserl's time the philosophy of Hegel had already been tagged with other labels, Husserl felt he could legitimately appropriate the word *phenomenology* for his own philosophical approach. Thus, as Joseph Kockelmans puts it, "when contemporaries speak about phenomenology, the name that arises spontaneously is that of Edmund Husserl."[1]

The early Husserl claims that contemporary epistemology is at an impasse. His disciples often interpret him to mean that since Descartes, thought and world have been falsely dichotomized, and that such a dichotomy results from regarding consciousness as self-enclosed (that is, as thought knowing itself, not knowing the outside). Consciousness is wrongly considered a faculty for being conscious instead of an act of being conscious. The idealist, emphasizing subjectivity (and its priority, spontaneity, and activity), maintains that subject actively projects object. Indeed, so much is this the case that the trend of the Idealist Movement is to eliminate the world as a source of knowledge. The empiricist, on the other hand, stresses the passivity of consciousness. The empiricist maintains there is a reflecting image, or impressed species, lodged in the knower. The impressed species has been imprinted by physical reality and (as a "double" of reality-in-itself) becomes the immediate object of knowledge. Though opting for opposite horns of the subject-object dilemma, both idealist and empiricist agree there is no bridge between thought and world.[2]

The early-phase Husserl rejects both these epistemologies because they fail to understand consciousness as a unified intentional act. Consciousness for Husserl at this time is not a Cartesian knowing of knowledge but a real intercourse with the outside. Consciousness is an act wherein the subject intends (or directs himself towards the object), and the object is intended (or functions as a target for the intending act, though the object transcends this act). The subject intending and the object intended are reciprocally implicated (and, it should be added, the subject is real and the object is real, that is, truly emanating from the outside). Following the lead of several historians of philosophy, I shall call this epistemological formula "Husserlian Neo-Realism." Phenomenology thus believes it can get at reality through a recognition of "essences" revealed in consciousness.

In his later phases Husserl becomes progressively appreciative of Descartes and Kant. In what is often called his "idealist" period, Husserl makes subjectivity constitutive of objectivity. Unsympathetic critics lambaste this move as a "retreat to Kant." In any case, it is the earlier Husserlian formula ("the mutual implication of subject and object," or neo-realism) that comes to influence both the Geneva School and the Heideggerians (and both of these literary schools I consider phenomenological). The influence of Husserl's later phase on literary theory and criticism has been much weaker. The outstanding exception is its impact on Maurice Natanson, who has brilliantly applied the notion of Husserl's "transcendental subjectivity" to literature and all the arts.[3]

After Husserl, phenomenological epistemology undergoes meaningful changes at the hands of Martin Heidegger, Jean-Paul Sartre, and Maurice Merleau-Ponty. Whereas Husserl brackets the question of existence so that he can better isolate the essence of the intentional act, Heidegger, radicalizing the Husserlian definition of consciousness, declares consciousness should be grasped not as a static but as a dynamic action, and indeed, as existence itself. In his own words, "the essence of human being lies in existence." The whole human being is "Being-in-the-world" (*in der Welt sein*), a reciprocal relation of subjectivity and world. The human being "is there" (*Dasein*) in the world, and feels thrown there (thus experiencing *Geworfenheit,* or a sense of "thrownness"). Human being is a movement towards future possibility, a "falling back into" the past, and a "falling for" the present. Because temporality and death are threatening, and man as act is fearful, the fundamental structure of human being is Care (*Sorge*). While Husserl's stress is on rational acts of consciousness, Heidegger's emphasis is on Care and the "moods" (*Stimmungen*). Thus the effect of Heidegger's monumental book *Sein und Zeit* is to shift focus from intellect-consciousness to a more radical emotion-consciousness. Heidegger also charts the "field of consciousness" according to various systems of meaning, such as the generalized "other" (impersonal people or *das Man*), and the world of physical objects experienced as either "present-at-hand" (*Vorhandenheit*) or "ready-to-hand" (*Zuhandenheit*).

As we shall see, Heidegger's focus on temporality, the non-rational modes of consciousness, and regionalization in the field of consciousness all influence the Geneva School in due time. After *Sein und Zeit,* Heidegger fixes a more direct gaze on "Being," and his philosophical approach becomes, in the eyes of orthodox Husserlians, more and more disreputable (though they had already been somewhat dissatisfied even with *Sein und Zeit*). To understand this rift between Heideggerians and Husserlians, perhaps some description of the Husserlian reaction to Heidegger is in order. Husserl believed that the metaphysics of his day, and for decades to come, was doomed to failure. He argued that philosophy had first to become a "basic transcendental science"; it had, in short, to master its own methodology. Instead of "seeing" meaning *in* experience as it should, traditional metaphysics had illegitimately imposed meaning *on* experience. Husserlian phenomenologists (and especially those who borrow heavily from their master's early or more "descriptive" phase) have thus tended to see their task as description (the phenomenological objective) rather than elaborate hypothesis (in their eyes, the *modus operandi* identified with metaphysicians). Thus most Husserlians call themselves "descriptive phenomenologists" and treat the "hermeneutical phenomenology" of Heidegger with disdain. Though Heidegger would demur vigorously (in fact, he rejects traditional metaphysics completely and calls his enterprise the "Thought of Being"), the Husserlians consider Heideggerian hermeneutics a premature and presumptuous indulgence in metaphysics.

Herbert Spiegelberg, the historian of the Phenomenological Movement and a Husserlian at heart,[4] considers *Sein und Zeit* a kind of bastard phenomenology and most of Heidegger's later writings not phenomenological at all. Spiegelberg also supports the argument that Heidegger undergoes a "reversal" in thought after *Sein und Zeit,* though here again Heidegger denies this is the case. *Sein und Zeit* was about human *Dasein,* says Heidegger, but only because *Dasein* allows the philosopher to wedge his way into the realm of Being. The hermeneutical enterprise from the very beginning, says Heidegger, has been the study of ontology, not of existential anthropology. (Husserlians oppose *Sein und Zeit* even as existential anthropology, however, because the latter is for them "psychologistic.")

As I shall explain further on, I personally consider enough of Heidegger (both early and late) phenomenological so that I can call him a phenomenologist. I might add that Being in the early Heidegger has sinister and negative overtones, and in the later Heidegger, metamorphoses itself into a benign presence. In this Part One, I am first treating the Geneva School, which practices a kind of phenomenological literary criticism that shares views analogous to those of Husserl and Merleau-Ponty. It is interesting in this connection that Spiegelberg no doubt criticizes Merleau-Ponty, but tends to recognize him as a much more legitimate phenomenologist than Heidegger. I have already indicated above the selected notions from Heidegger's *Sein und Zeit* that the Geneva School assimilates, and I shall soon do the same for its occasional borrowings from Sartre. In the third chapter of this part, I shall describe briefly that Heideggerian literary criticism which draws from *Sein und Zeit,* and does so much more than the Geneva School does; and I shall describe at length Heidegger's own literary criticism, which appears exclusively in his later phase (when he has no discernible impact at all on the Geneva School).

Taking a cue from Husserl (and from many others whom I shall duly acknowledge), the phenomenologist of the Geneva School has been particularly adamant about "metaphysical" neutrality. Attempting to remain metaphysically neutral and to merely experience and explicate what is in the literary work itself, the Geneva critic distinguishes this approach from "metaphysical" literary criticisms which interpret literature in the light of a critic's own *Weltanschauung*. (If there be any talk of *Weltanschauung* for the Geneva critic, it must be of the author's own *Weltanschauung* as incorporated in the literary structure.) When Heidegger interprets a poem in terms of what a Husserlian would consider purely hypothetical "Being," "Earth," "Holiness," and the like, Heidegger is practicing (in the eyes of the Geneva critic) an aprioristic, and consequently non-phenomenological, criticism. By "aprioristic," the Geneva critics mean here that Heidegger has "metaphysical" expectancies prior to his encounter with the text, and willy-nilly jams the text into these "extrinsic" categories.

Apparently René Wellek agrees with the Geneva School and considers the Heideggerian approach metaphysical. In his article on *Ästhetik* in the German *Lexicon der Weltliteratur im 20. Jahrhundert*, Wellek distinguishes between phenomenological (Husserlian) aesthetics and metaphysical aesthetics. Phenomenological aesthetics "brackets the reality of the object and inquires only after aesthetic value, in so far as it is given as phenomenon." On the other hand, Wellek tells us that statements in the tradition of metaphysical aesthetics "find their foundation and ground in an ontology or metaphysic."[5] In *Concepts of Criticism,* Wellek goes on to disparage the "eccentric interpretations of poems by Hölderlin and Rilke" one finds in Heidegger's literary criticism.[6]

I believe it is in this same anti-metaphysical spirit that the Geneva critic Jean-Pierre Richard warns, "The greatest danger here is heaviness, that is to say, the forced imposition of a dogmatic edifice on a work. . . ."[7] Likewise, Roland Barthes (of all people!) in his *Essais critiques* opposes positivistic *"critique universitaire"* to *"critique idéologique,"* but then bifurcates the latter into extrinsic criticism and *"critiques d'interprétation."* Lucien Goldmann (a Marxist) and Charles Mauron (a Freudian) are singled out as exemplars of extrinsic criticism (in Husserlian parlance, "metaphysical" criticism); Georges Poulet and Jean-Pierre Richard (Geneva critics) are named as representatives of *critique d'interprétation.* The former two critics refer literature to "something external"; the latter two "bring a new kind of criticism into view: it is completely or

almost completely immanent."[8] On the one hand, the Geneva critics
are correct: Heideggerians are certainly not "neutral" when they
interact with a literary text; indeed, Heidegger's whole notion of
"forestructure" denies the possibility of neutrality (thus he disagrees
with the "transcendental, suppositionless" stance aimed at by
Husserl). On the other hand, the Geneva critics do good Heideggerian critics an injustice: though hermeneuts bring forestructures to
the "world" of the literary work, those forestructures permit to the
literary work both autonomy and an epiphanic singularity (for a
discussion of forestructure, see my Part Two, Chapter Four).

It might be significant to add here, too, that good Heideggerian
criticism is in large measure a kind of poetic serendipity. In this
matter, Heideggerian hermeneutics is much less methodical than
the cerebral calculation of Husserl, or the "poetic" methodology of
the Geneva School (for I shall argue that the Geneva critics practice
a methodology—be it conscious or unconscious—though certainly
it is not the conceptual calculation of a Husserl). Nor are
Heideggerian terms such as "Being," "Earth," and the "Holy"
intended to be hypostatic; in fact, Heidegger's great crusade is
against hypostasis in philosophy.

Another bellwether of the Heideggerian approach (I use the
word *approach* loosely: Heidegger would cringe at the notion of a
"school" of criticism) is its "metapersonal" vision. Imaginative
literature for the Heideggerian is an "unconcealment" of Being, and
Being is the "presence" which mysteriously "grounds" all *Seienden*
(things-in-being). At times, Heidegger says that the author's personality is absent from the literary work, and when Heidegger so
speaks, he sounds strangely like the Parisian Structuralists (with
whom phenomenologists of whatever stripe are usually at violent
odds). At other times, Heidegger implies that the author's personality is present in the work, but is a mere conduit whereby Being can
reveal itself. In either case, Heideggerian theory maintains the
personal life-world of the author is relatively unimportant. For the
Geneva School, however, the experiential world of the author as
enverbalized in the text is all-important: as we shall see, it is the
"center" and *foyer* of the text, and ultimately imparts whatever
meaningful coherence the poetic text displays. At bottom, I surmise
most Geneva critics avoid metapersonal criticism simply because it
entails (according to them) a commitment to metaphysics. To "live"
(vicariously) the subjective life-world of an author as it is present in
poetic language and to describe it are relatively secure operations:

one need only describe the "subjective truth" of that author (that is, describe what truth-to-the-author happens to be). But to describe, without regard for the author's subjective truth, the success with which Being is revealed by a given poem is to engage in metaphysical judgment: one must measure the poem against what Being really is (in short, one must gauge "objective truth"), and such a project requires an ideological commitment. I must remind the reader, however, that the above version of personal versus metapersonal criticism I impute to the Geneva School alone. Certainly Heideggerians disagree with the above argument from beginning to end.

The next issue I would like to consider is "psychologism," the *bête noire* which Husserlian phenomenologists attack with a passion. For the early Husserl, psychologism meant the "erroneous" theory that logic is reducible to neurology, that is, the psychological mechanisms of mind. Hence Husserl's insistence that intended object transcends intending act. In Husserlian theory, represented largely by Roman Ingarden (though the latter often disagrees with his mentor), psychologism is identified with theories of *Einfühlung* ("empathy") which equate the literary work with the psychic experiences of author and reader. Most phenomenologists working squarely in literary theory and aesthetics (Roman Ingarden and Mikel Dufrenne are good cases in point) take great pains to avoid psychologism, although their success in doing so can be disputed. However, my main task in this essay is to infer the literary theory and critical methodology which characterizes practicing phenomenological critics. Heidegger's own practical criticism (which is a product of his later phase) avoids psychologism to a greater or lesser extent, depending on one's interpretation of what his criticism is actually doing. But the Geneva School regards the *moi profond* of the literary text to be that of the author (or, to be more accurate, of that aspect of the author which "crosses over" into poetic language). And the reader's task is to "live" the experience of this *moi profond* as it is inviscerated in the text. As I shall explain later, this practice of the Geneva School derives largely from the influence of Schleiermacher and Dilthey (who represent a tradition of "objective hermeneutics" very different from the "non-objective hermeneutics" of Heidegger).

The first generation of Geneva critics is especially influenced by the objective hermeneutical tradition, and the practice of the Geneva School can be described as a transvaluation of Dilthey through the

lens of a Husserlian optic. The situation is further complicated by
the practical borrowings of the Geneva School from phenomenological psychology. Ironically, these borrowings are from Heideggerian
psychiatrists such as Ludwig Binswanger and J. H. Van Den Berg,
but the latter two men derive their theories from the early Heidegger,
the Heidegger of *Sein und Zeit,* and *Sein und Zeit* (which occurs, of
course, before the alleged "reversal") was labeled from the very
beginning as "existential anthropology" by the Husserlians, and
therefore as "psychologistic." The upshot of all this is that the
borrowings from Heideggerian *Daseinanalyse* (the "psychological
analysis of Dasein" identified with Binswanger) makes the Geneva
School appear even more psychologistic. In *Concepts of Criticism,*
René Wellek accuses Georges Poulet and J. Hillis Miller (both
Geneva critics at the time, though Miller has now changed) of an
extrinsic approach.[9] By "extrinsic," Wellek apparently means here
that Poulet and Miller both refer the literary text to the consciousness of the author, and hence are "psychologistic." In his *Theory of
Literature* (with Austin Warren as co-author), Wellek attacks not
only mechanistic psychology (an attack in which all phenomenologists would join), but all psychological approaches.[10] In the same
book, Wellek rejects the notion "that the genuine poem is in the
total experience, conscious and unconscious, during the time of the
creation [of the literary work]."[11]
     Actually, the critical practice of the Geneva School does not
trace the poem back to the author's original experience, or the "total
experience" of the author at the time he creates his work. The
school's approach is much more sophisticated and focuses only on
that aspect of the author's consciousness which has transferred itself
into the literary work, and indeed, is now and forever present in the
work. Thus Geneva critics insist their approach is immanent and
intrinsic. Even Dufrenne, the phenomenological aesthetician,
makes this point: he distinguishes between the author's "phenomenological ego," immanent in the work, and his "actual ego,"
which is deemed inaccessible. Anyway, by all the above I simply
wish to make clear that the Geneva critics, often quite faithful to
Husserl (whether they know it or not), do seem to flirt with
psychologism, and, to the extent they do, behave in an "un-
Husserlian" manner. When I review Merleau-Ponty and his theory
of language the reader may notice that the same charge of
psychologism can be made against him, but I will not advert to the
matter at the time. It suffices to say now that the Geneva School's

alleged psychologism may be reinforced through Merleau-Ponty's example.

After Heidegger, the next philosopher to influence the Geneva critics is Jean-Paul Sartre, who was already studying Husserlian thought in Germany at the age of twenty-three. It is clear, furthermore, from an early essay of Sartre that the latter was most impressed by the younger Husserl,[12] who still saw consciousness as "a real intercourse with the outside." Two motifs of Sartrean thought have special impact in terms of the Geneva School. The first is the identification of a given individual's intentionality with that individual's "fundamental choice." The intentional acts of an individual imply his unique way of "living" life; they constitute, in short, his "forward throw" or *projet*.

The second motif concerns the nature of the work of art. Sartre discusses this theme in various portions of his books *L'Imagination* (1936), *L'Imaginaire* (1940), and *Qu'est-ce que la littérature?* (1948). The various theories of the literary imagination proposed in the first two books have had, in my opinion, little influence on practical criticism. However, in *Qu'est-ce que*, Sartre's distinction between prose-art and poetic-art can be used to help explain the ontology of the poetic work as Geneva critics conceive it. *Qu'est-ce que* intends to apotheosize prose-art, since only prose (according to Sartre) can produce a literature of social engagement. But what Sartre says about poetic-art in this same book places him in the tradition of phenomenological esthetics, and develops very effectively certain ideas already present in *L'Imagination* and *L'Imaginaire*. According to Sartre, the poet treats language as an image of the world, and the prose artist treats language as a sign. Sartre tells us "the poetic word is a microcosm," and that in the poetic word "Emotion has become thing. . . ."[13] The affinity between such statements and the assumptions of the Geneva School will become obvious shortly.

The time has once again come, however, to make the distinction implied in the occasional theoretical statements and the consistent critical practice of the Geneva School. And here again I am representing the views of the Geneva critics, not necessarily my own. Much as was done with Heidegger, Jean-Paul Sartre as phenomenologist is to be distinguished from Sartre as metaphysician. Herbert Spiegelberg, the orthodox Husserlian, complains that "Sartre's phenomenology is certainly not free from [metaphysical] preconceptions."[14] Another of Spiegelberg's paragraphs *re* Sartre is worth quoting in its entirety:

The danger to phenomenology comes chiefly from the peculiar methods preached and practiced by some of the existentialists. Sartre maintains at least the principle of a description based on intuition. However, in trying to incorporate in it a hermeneutic method of deciphering, he not only introduces interpretations of the sense of the phenomenon which run far beyond the direct evidence but are even apt to interfere with the unbiased description of the directly accessible phenomena.

When Jean-Paul Sartre criticizes *The Sound and the Fury* because Faulknerian man is "a sum total without a future,"[15] and when Sartre follows this with a sermon on "authentic man,"[16] the Geneva critic would claim Sartre is here performing metaphysical, and therefore not "immanent," literary criticism. The orthodox Husserlian usually consigns Sartrean talk of "bad faith," the "hateful stare," and man as a "useless passion," to the realm of fanciful thinking. For the Husserlian, Sartre's "careless" philosophizing is "existentialist philosophy" (as opposed to essentialist phenomenology, and even existentialist phenomenology). Where the same Sartrean talk of "bad faith" and the like appears in literary criticism, the Geneva critic would consign it to the realm of ethics (that is, metaphysical problems), and not intrinsic literary criticism. (Of course Sartre can answer in defense that he intends his criticism of imaginative literature as philosophical, not as literary.)

Personally, I do not consider Sartre's practical criticism phenomenological, because I am not convinced he really sees the ethical essences involved; rather, he speculates about them. Consequently, except for isolated phenomenological passages, I shall not treat his literary criticism at all. I am not suggesting that Sartre's criticism and his literary theory, too, are not eminently worthwhile. I am just saying they are not phenomenological. Furthermore, so rapidly did Sartre's fame spread some years ago that his aesthetic has been if anything overtreated. Besides, Eugene Kaelin's brilliant book, *An Existentialist Aesthetic,*[17] seems to me the definitive English work on the subject, and has long been available. Before I pass on to a brief review of Merleau-Ponty (whom Kaelin has also treated exhaustively), I add one more qualification. I know full well that Heideggerians, Sartreans, and a score of others can claim the Geneva School is every bit as "metaphysical" as they are, and perhaps sinfully so because blindly so. Sartre may be able to say, ironically, that those who discredit the notion of "bad faith" are themselves *in* bad faith. These matters I shall evaluate when in an upcoming section I deal with phenomenological method.

The third major philosopher who contributes to phenomeno-logical epistemology is Maurice Merleau-Ponty. He not only re-asserts that subject and object are reciprocally implicated, but carries Husserl's original theory of intentionality a momentous step fur-ther by claiming subject and object are analytically inseparable. Through so monistic an epistemological formulation, he hopes to transcend the subject-object issue once and for all. All conscious-ness, according to Merleau-Ponty, is a unified subject-object re-lation. Claiming he derives the idea from what were the un-published manuscripts of Husserl, he also expands the definition of intentionality to include the individual's whole experiential world (or *Lebenswelt*).

It is especially in the area of linguistics, however, that Merleau-Ponty provides needed theoretical support for the practice of the Geneva School. The theory of intentionality he used to transcend the idealism-empiricism dilemma is put to very similar uses in his treatment of language. Merleau-Ponty regards language as an in-tentional act, thus rejecting on one hand the American structuralist theory (Bloomfieldian) that language is autonomous and in-dependent of the speaker (so its meaning is self-generated) and, on the other hand, the behaviorist and idealistic theories, both of which see language as a mere sign for the speaker's mental activities (in the case of behaviorism, language is a sign for the speaker's neurologi-cal impulses; in idealism, it is a sign for the speaker's thought; in both cases the sign does not "have" meaning but "points to" the meaning in the speaker's mental processes). Language as intention-al act is for Merleau-Ponty a gestural action; it is not a sign for meaning, but an embodiment, an "incarnation" of meaning. Embodiment is densest and richest in poetic language because in it conceptual and non-conceptual elements *(sens emotionnel)* play roles approximating their importance in the total life of the human being (for language that expresses concretely instead of just con-ceptually, Merleau-Ponty reserves the term *la parole)*. The theory of *parole* thus strikes a balance between language understood as sign and language regarded as autonomous. It answers the former by saying that words are gestural embodiments of meaning: thus one cannot abandon the language-structure and find meaning elsewhere. It answers the latter by saying that precisely because language-structure as embodiment of meaning is gestural—is an action—language-structure must be interpreted as a speaker's expression. Since language is a unified action linking subject and object ("object" here can be either that which is talked about, or it can be the reader/listener), language cannot be arbitrarily isolated from its origins.

Merleau-Ponty, in short, focuses his attention upon the meaning immanent in the language-structure, but interprets this immanent meaning in the light of its true nature as expression. According to Merleau-Ponty, the various modes of consciousness in the human person are unified into a fundamental "project" (*projet*, the word also used by Sartre), and *parole* at its best can embody this single "life-style," integrate its various levels of meaning (*couches de signification*) accordingly, and manifest in its own total "style" the experiential unity of the speaker. Merleau-Ponty has, of course, much more to say about the ontology of language: sections of his work treat the internal dynamism of words, their capacity to shape as well as be shaped by what the speaker intends, and even their equation with thought, since our silent thoughts do not precede language (in this case, a silent "inner language") but come to birth in and with language.[18]

Before moving on to a discussion of neo-Kantianism, I close this brief review of phenomenological epistemology with the already promised remarks on "objective" versus "Heideggerian" hermeneutics. I have already mentioned the phenomenological formula which most influences phenomenological literary criticism: a person's *Lebenswelt*, or experiential world, is a mutual implication of "selfhood" and the "world" (or "outside"). Merleau-Ponty's theory of language goes on to conclude, then, that an author's *parole* "embodies" some of an author's "self-world" relations (be they imaginative, or whatever). But what about the literary critic's "relation" to the author's *parole?* When the critic is conscious of a literary work, isn't this activity a case again of a subject (the critic) interacting with an object (the literary work)? And, in order to be consistent, must we then not conclude that interpretation is a "mutual implication" of critic and text? And if this is so, isn't "objective interpretation" an impossibility? Here, precisely, is the question of questions for the phenomenological critic: it places him at a *bifurcation du chemin* from which there is no turning back. And at this inexorable fork in the road the Heideggerian critic takes one path, and the Geneva critic the other.

The Heideggerian critic considers literary interpretation to be the description of a meaning which arises from a unitary phenomenon: an engagement of critic and text in which the critic actively contributes to the overall meaning. I refer the reader to my Part Two for a precise explication of "meaning" in terms of the Heideggerian scheme. The Geneva critic, while he in general accepts the same formula of mutual implication, assumes (much more than Heidegger) that the degree of implication can and should be strictly controlled by the critic. One can never be perfectly objective, but one can be more or less objective according to his chosen epistemological stance. Spontaneous "life as it is lived" is naive[19]: that is, there is no effort to assume an objective position. When I, as a typical human being, look at the ocean (for example), I ordinarily make no effort to analyze what part of the generated "meaning" issues from me, and what part from the ocean itself. If I almost drowned in the ocean as a young child, I may fear the ocean, and the overall meaning which arises from this later encounter with the same ocean may therefore include the quality of fear. But if I am a scientist (and therefore not "naive"), I strive for an objective vision, and separate out as best I can the subjective quality of fear from, say, such an objective quality as the temperature of the water. The author of a literary work ordinarily enverbalizes spontaneous "life as it is lived." If the author fears the ocean, he or she will allow this subjective "input" to operate within the total meaning of ocean as he or she describes it.

A human being's *Lebenswelt* is normally naive, so that its self-world relations are monistic (as Merleau-Ponty suggests). Now, it is ordinarily the author's task to enverbalize the spontaneous mutual implications of his *Lebenswelt*, without scientific regard for subjectivity and objectivity as such. In other words, the mutual implications found in a literary work usually involve inextricable and therefore highly ambiguous interactions of self and world. Elements of meaning may issue from subject and object respectively, but these origins remain undifferentiated. The Heideggerians insist that not only the author's epistemology, but the critic's epistemology as well (in order to be legitimate), must be naive. (In fact, I might add that even at the scientific level, Heideggerians downplay objectivity, because of their notion of "forestructure.") In contrast, the Geneva critics maintain that there is a distinction to be made between the epistemologies of author and critic. Whereas the author's epistemology is naive, the critic's must be relatively objective (as indicated earlier, the objectivity can be only one of degree: perfect objectivity is the ideal, but is an unattainable goal). Thus the Geneva critics speak again and again of the "passive receptivity" which characterizes good interpretation. The critic is to divest his ego of its own trappings, so it can "live" the *moi profond* of the author. Actually, the criticism of the Geneva School seems to involve two stages: first, a poetic and vicarious experience of the author's phenomenological ego (that is, the ego enverbalized in the literary work), and second, a description of this experience (so the description becomes the "interpretation" proper). While the practice of the Geneva School is eminently poetic rather than scientific ("passive receptivity" is more a discipline of the heart than the mind), the school's stress on sophisticated control of epistemological field is very Husserlian.

Despite the distinction between the author's empirical ego and the text's phenomenological ego, the latter is still reducible to an aspect of the author's psychology which has been duplicated in the literary text. This remnant of psychologism appears in the Geneva School largely through the influence of old Germany's "objective hermeneutics." Richard Palmer, in his book *Hermeneutics*,[20] has already given the English-speaking world an account of objective hermeneutics, associated formerly with the two great German theorists, Schleiermacher (1768–1834) and Dilthey (1833–1912), and currently with an Italian, Ugo Betti. As opposed to the "new hermeneutics" identified with Martin Heidegger and his disciple, Hans-Georg Gadamer, traditional German hermeneutics called for "historical objectivity," and demanded interpretations which could be proven "objectively valid." In Schleiermacher, interpretation was openly psychologistic: it was an act whereby the critic reconstructed the mental processes of an author.

Towards this end, the early Dilthey permitted the use of biographical and other extrinsic evidence, but in his later phase, he limited himself (much like the Geneva School) to only that part of an author's experience which is "objectified" in the text itself (he moved, in other words, from extrinsic to intrinsic criticism). Dilthey argued that in the literary work the "heightened experience" (*Erlebnis*) of the author is duplicated: the *Erlebnis* becomes the "inner center" of the literary work, with the result that the work is an "expression of heightened experience" (*Erlebnisausdrück*). The interpreter, then, through the artful use of "understanding" (*Verstehen*), repeats the author's original *Erlebnis*. Through such a formula, and its stress on the immanence of meaning in the text, Dilthey attempted to transcend the manifest psychologism of Schleiermacher: few contemporary historians of philosophy feel he succeeded.

Kurt Müller-Vollmer, in his book *Towards a Phenomenological Theory of Literature: A Study of Wilhelm Dilthey's Poetik*,[21] presents Dilthey as a proto-phenomenologist and cites what was a fertile exchange of ideas between Husserl and Dilthey. Müller-Vollmer successfully exonerates Dilthey from the abuses perpetrated in his name by the *Geistesgeschichtliche* critics. And Müller-Vollmer proves as well that Dilthey's significant contribution to aesthetics appears in the *Poetik* and not in *Das Erlebnis und die Dichtung* (which is really an exercise in intellectual history and popularizes the notions of *Zeitgeist* and *Weltanschauungen*). In any case, the Geneva critic's aspiration towards "objectivity," and his lapse, if any, into psychologism, come in large part by way of Schleiermacher and Dilthey, mediated (among others) through two critics working in the French tradition, Albert Béguin and Marcel Raymond.

Neo-Kantianism presents a final problem. In the classroom I have found students often confuse phenomenological criticism with the work done by the Marburg School, and specifically by Ernst Cassirer and Susanne Langer. I surmise this confusion is quite universal among beginners, and thus deserves some attention here. Again, the reader must keep in mind that by phenomenology I mean at this point the epistemological theory of mutual implication, and I thus exclude from it the idealism of the late Husserl. If one remembers this, the distinction between neo-Kantianism and neo-realist phenomenology should clarify at once. Neo-Kantians assert that form emanates entirely from the side of the subject and that only undifferentiated sense-data issue from the side of the outside object. For the phenomenologist (to use one of Husserl's famous slogans), knowledge is the grasp of an object that is simultaneously gripping us; for the neo-Kantian, knowledge is not the grasp but the construction of an object. The neo-Kantian does not grant Being exists in its own right; rather, Being for him is a creation of thought. Furthermore, there is in neo-Kantianism nothing which corresponds to phenomenological knowledge of contents and essences.

Ernst Cassirer has developed some theories which are both alike and different from those of phenomenological aesthetics. Parts of his *Philosophie der symbolischen Formen,* and his *Language and Myth,* argue that art activity is a special kind of symbolic form that "shapes" sense-data in a way no other symbolic form can. But because Cassirer's "symbolic form" issues solely from the subjectivity of the author (understood in a Cartesian sense), it has been a favorite target for phenomenological attack. Thus the phenomenologist Marvin Farber, in his *The Aims of Phenomenology,* claims that Cassirer "confuses the relationship between knowledge and reality." Cassirer falsely argues "as though it [the given] were posited by thought itself and begotten by means of its constructive conditions."[22] Cassirer's likenesses and differences in relation to neo-realist phenomenology stand out in bold relief in the following quotation from *Language and Myth:* we are told that the world of poetry is "a world of illusion and fantasy—but it is just in this mode of illusion that the realm of pure feeling can find utterance, and can therewith attain its full and concrete actualization."[23] Most phenomenologists would agree that the realm of feeling finds utterance in the poem, and therein attains a full and concrete actualization. They would deny, however, that the feeling is "pure" in the Kantian sense; rather, they would see it as at least in part formed and organized by the outside world. The author's feeling is a mutual implication of his selfhood and the outside.

As for Susanne Langer, the neo-Kantian author of *Philosophy in a New Key* and *Feeling and Form,* the same phenomenological critique applies. When Langer declares that "although a work of art reveals the character of subjectivity, it is itself objective; its purpose is to objectify the life of feeling,"[24] the "life of feeling" which is objectified receives its orchestration from subjectivity alone.

# chapter 2

# The Geneva School and its Accomplices

## Phenomenology and the Geneva School

René Wellek, in the essay on *Ästhetik* in the *Lexicon,* designates the literary theories derived from Husserlian thought as "phenomenological." The term *phenomenology* or *phenomenological* is applied by the following sources to the kind of practical criticism I am about to treat: Mikel Dufrenne, Jean-Pierre Richard, Paul de Man, Vernon Gras, Robin Magowan, and (more ambiguously) Roland Barthes.[1] As already indicated, Sarah Lawall's book on the Geneva School, *Critics of Consciousness,*[2] gives an account of Genevan practice, but does not focus on the relevance of phenomenological philosophy and aesthetics to this practice. Nor does she include writers who are phenomenological in the Geneva sense, but not members of the school.

Some of the critics I shall treat have been called (or have called themselves) "genetic critics," "thematic critics," and "critics of consciousness." It is my own position throughout this essay that essentialist and existentialist phenomenology are ultimately the most important formative influences on the critics in question, and that consequently the label "phenomenological" is best applied to them. I shall now review in summary fashion the critics associated with Genevan practice. Marcel Raymond and Albert Béguin constitute the first generation of the Geneva School and are treated first. Because of reasons to be offered shortly, I consider both of them proto-phenomenologists rather than phenomenologists, properly speaking. Next comes Georges Poulet, who figures as the important link between the first and second generation of the school; his practice, in my opinion, is rightly called phenomenological. I shall next review the "second generation" of the Geneva School: Jean-Pierre Richard, Jean Rousset, Jean Starobinski, and J. Hillis Miller. Finally come those critics who are not members of the school, but who are rightly called "accomplices" because they practice the same kind of criticism (in at least some phases of their careers). I include in this category Emil Staiger, the late-phase Gaston Bachelard, the early Roland Barthes, and the American, Paul Brodtkorb.

Marcel Raymond was born at Geneva in 1897 and taught at the universities of Basel and Geneva. Though Sarah Lawall mentions the influence of phenomenology on Raymond,[3] she is correct in saying that he, along with Albert Béguin, is a transitional figure:

> The Geneva perspective forms a definite historical pattern of dis-covery and related theories from Raymond to Poulet to J. Hillis Miller. Raymond and Béguin are the historical forerunners of this theory, but they show it emerging from traditional ways of thought rather than give a coherent philosophy of literary existentialism. It is with Georges Poulet that this perspective takes on its full philosophical significance and influences the work of Richard, Starobinski, Rousset, and Miller.[4]

There is still simply too much of the nineteenth-century academic critic, still too much of *Lansonisme,* in Raymond's *De Baudelaire au Surréalisme* (1933). Raymond writes some brilliant phenomeno-logical pieces, but is in the main non-phenomenological. From the 1950s, and in the collection *Vérité et poésie* (1964), Raymond becomes what I have called an ideological critic: he only approves of literature which measures up to his personal conception of the Divine.

Albert Béguin was born in 1901 and died in 1957. Also of Swiss origin, he studied both at the Faculté de Lettres of Geneva and at the Sorbonne. In time, he accepted the chair of French literature at Basel, and became the editor of *Esprit*. He was also a famous *Germaniste,* and on this account probably knew Husserl's work well. Béguin's *L'Ame romantique et le Rêve* (1937) delivers broadsides against old French positivism, but retains many of the techniques associated with traditional scholarship. Very early in his publishing career he became a Catholic (1940), and the predomi-nance of his work is firmly ideological. Good examples of his Catholic criticism are *L'Eve de Péguy* (1952) and *Poésie de la présence* (1957). When I say Béguin is not phenomenological in our sense, I mean only that his criticism demonstrates great selectivity (he eventually limits himself to Catholic authors), and that his criticism makes the literary text subservient to a "higher truth" (that is, Catholicism). The phenomenological approach, as I understand it, is universal (at least in principle), so that someone like Georges Poulet can treat any author and any literary period; and the phenomenological approach is non-ideological, so that the literary text is not subordinate to a developed philosophy. That Béguin was empathetic and sensitive to the literature of his own choosing I do not in the least deny. In fact, I have great admiration for him as critic and scholar.

Georges Poulet, born in Belgium (1902), taught at the University of Edinburgh and at Johns Hopkins, and now teaches in Zurich. He began to publish considerably after the writing careers of Raymond and Béguin were well-established. His most famous works comprise *Etudes sur le temps humain* (first volume published in 1949), *Les Métamorphoses du cercle* (1961), *L'Espace proustien* (1963), *Trois Essais de mythologie romantique* (1966), *Qui était Baudelaire* (1969), and *La Conscience critique* (1971). In the words of Sarah Lawall: "Georges Poulet is the first critic to develop Raymond's and Béguin's concept of experience in literature as a systematic tool of analysis." He "cuts their last ties with the formal and historical approach." and "he is the first critic to propose analytic coordinates for the human experience in literature"[5] (coordinates we shall call the "modes and contents of consciousness").

Poulet refuses to identify himself exclusively with Romantic literature, and he forbids the use of extrinsic ideology. Indeed, in many places he argues that the critic should not judge the philosophy of a literary work. Sarah Lawall indicates Poulet is a phenomenologist because he "belongs to a school of thought that recognizes as valid the author's relationships with reality, and builds systems of existence only upon these integrated perceptions."[6] Vernon Gras in *European Literary Theory and Practice* uses Poulet as exemplar of the phenomenological approach,[7] and Paul de Man does likewise in the *Encyclopedia of Poetry and Poetics.*[8] Yet in a private letter to J. Hillis Miller, quoted first by Miller and then by Lawall,[9] Poulet insists he is a Cartesian. Thus we find ourselves confronted with a not uncommon state of affairs in the history of literary criticism: there is a considerable divergence between how the critic sees himself and how other critics see him.

Poulet's last word on the matter comes in *La Conscience critique,*[10] where he distinguishes among three kinds of epistemology found in the literary work. The first epistemology is clearly phenomenological: "There is in the work an element which is properly called mental, deeply engaged in the objective forms which at the same time reveal and dissimulate it"(298). Somewhat earlier, Poulet says the critic should relive the author's enverbalized epistemology, and "go from the subject, across objects, and back to the subject again"(297). The "consciousness inherent in the work . . . is in direct rapport with a world which is its world, with objects which are its objects"(285,286). Poulet endorses the phenomenological approach of Jean Rousset, who "climbs back to the interior of the work, from the perception of objective elements which are intelligibly arranged, to a certain unifying will inherent in the work, as if the latter revealed itself endowed with an intentional consciousness determining its own dispositions"(295,296).

In the following chapter, when he describes the *Cogito,* Poulet offers the most phenomenological formula of all: ". . . it seemed to me that the whole *Cogito* I was surveying comprised in the indissolubility of one and the same act a total presence of self to self and a total presence of the world to self." Like a Leibnizian monad, says Poulet, the *Cogito* "is conscious at the same time of itself and of the whole environment. There can't be one without the other"(310). After finding the phenomenological epistemology, the critic should ascend to a second kind of epistemology operative in the literary work: "There is still a different, more elevated plane in the work: abandoning its forms, the consciousness reveals itself to itself by transcending all that is reflected in it"(298). This formula is undoubtedly Cartesian, and, I might add, sounds much like the late-phase Husserl (who, you will recall, abandoned a neo-realist phenomenology and began to talk much like an idealist). What resembles the idealist Husserl more than this passage from Poulet?—"Therefore, all critical method has for its express mission to make me recognize the primacy of subjective consciousness" (298). Finally, Poulet says the critic should find a third epistemology, one which resembles Zen Buddhism more than anything else: "At last there is a point when it [consciousness] reflects nothing, when, always in the work and nevertheless above the work, it is content to exist. Then all that one can say of it is what exists there of consciousness. At this point, no object can any longer express it, no structure can any longer determine it, it uncovers itself in its ineffability, in its fundamental indetermination"(298, 299).

My own assessment of all this can be reduced to the following. Keep in mind that I am more concerned with Poulet's critical practice than with his account of the practice (which may be misguided). Or it may even be the case that what Poulet calls Cartesianism can be absorbed into our more specialized definition of neo-realist phenomenology as such. Poulet's practice remains phenomenological, in that it describes a life-world which is a mutual implication of self and outside. Take up any sample of Poulet's criticism you wish. You will find that it repeats and describes the imagery characteristic of a phenomenological ego. Poulet may consider this ego Cartesian, in that (according to his opinion) it has appropriated the images of world, and, tearing these images away from their customary values, has revalued them in terms of subjective consciousness. But my point is that no matter how much a subject attempts to do this, part of the resultant symbol has come from the outside. An author may appropriate the image "green tree," and treat it as a symbol of "hopeful desire," say. But the appearances of a green tree still maintain their literal value because green things, and trees, issue in part from the world. In fact, even hopeful desire emanates in part from the outside, since it can arise as a value only through intersubjectivity. This is the case even when an author's epistemology, in Poulet's words, "reveals itself to itself by transcending all that is reflected in it."

In his critique of Maurice de Guérin, Poulet sees just such a Cartesian epistemology operative in Guérin's writing. Guérin situates himself at a *punctum saliens* which, "detached from nature, detached from his own life," is "pure consciousness and pure existence." But when Poulet quotes the passages from Guérin representing this rarified state, he quotes lines heavily laden with images. In Guérin's words (quoted by Poulet), the *punctum saliens* is like "lightning that quivers on the horizon between two worlds"; it is the place "where one sees the sources re-enter earth's breast."[11] Clearly, the appearances of "lightning" and "earth's breast" rebound from the outside. Poulet is here a phenomenologist without knowing it. As for Poulet's third epistemology, wherein "no object can any longer express . . ., no structure can any longer determine" consciousness, this formula by definition excludes literature. Here Poulet must speak of it in purely abstract terms (or at least in terms he considers abstract). As soon as he quotes literary passages, the supposedly formless consciousness re-engages itself with the world, and Poulet disproves what he is proving. That Poulet is out to prove anything at all raises another question, of course—one that I can only mention here. Sarah Lawall rightly points out that he seems to assume the ideal experience for man is one of coherence. Doesn't this assumption convert Poulet into an ideological critic? I answer that it does not, since the assumption is not ideological in the strict sense. The problematic of ideological criticism will be reviewed in the upcoming treatment of metaphysics and the Geneva School.

Jean-Pierre Richard, Jean Starobinski, and Jean Rousset are professedly phenomenological, so I shall limit myself here to a few words on each: all I say elsewhere in this chapter is isomorphic with their critical theory and practice. Jean-Pierre Richard, born in 1922 at Marseilles, has taught in London and Madrid. His criticism includes *Littérature et Sensation* (1954), *Poésie et Profondeur* (1958), *L'Univers imaginaire de Mallarmé* (1961), *Stéphane Mallarmé et son fils Anatol* (1961), and *Onze études sur la poésie* (1964). Strongly influenced by Merleau-Ponty, Richard weighs the balance of intentionality in favor of the outside world (though, unlike Merleau-Ponty, Richard often stresses things over people). For Richard, the privileged modes of access to the world are sensation and emotion, but he often uses specifically linguistic traits to infer these.

Jean Starobinski, born in 1920, teaches in his native Geneva. Author of *Montesquieu par lui-même* (1953), *Jean-Jacques Rousseau, la transparence et l'obstacle* (1957), *L'Oeil vivant* (1961), and *L'Invention de la liberté* (1964), he has demonstrated conclusively that phenomenological criticism can deal as effectively with neo-classical literature as it can with the Romantic and post-Romantic. Unlike Richard, Starobinski's main concern is intersubjectivity, the intentional field generated between person and person, not person and thing. Starobinski specializes in the modal awareness initiated by reason and will, and is the most methodological member of the Geneva School. His dependence on Husserl is widely acknowledged, and his theoretical essay "Le Voile de Poppée"[12] is grounded securely on Husserlian principles.

Jean Rousset, author of *La Littérature de l'âge baroque en France* (1953) and *Forme et Signification* (1962), was also born at Geneva (1910), and has taught at the university there. His first book displays the proper universality of phenomenological criticism, since the book treats sixteenth- and seventeenth-century literature. To be a comprehensive hermeneutic, phenomenological criticism must interpret form as well as theme: Rousset's second book, the influential *Forme et Signification*, accomplishes this task with a fierce passion. In the face of Parisian Structuralism, Rousset shows that phenomenology too can account for structure, and account for it in precisely phenomenological terms.

J. Hillis Miller (born 1928) has taught at the Johns Hopkins University, and now teaches at Yale University. His phenomenological period comprises three books, *Charles Dickens: The World of His Novels* (1959), *The Disappearance of God* (1963), and *Poets of Reality* (1965). As a disciple of Poulet, whom he knew at Johns Hopkins, Miller echoed the theoretical sentiments of his mentor. Miller's phenomenological work applies Genevan practice to English and American literature, and this is its great contribution. Miller ranks among the foremost of America's literary scholars, and he has won for the Geneva School an audience it might not have otherwise had.

Emil Staiger, born in 1908, is a professor of German literature at Zurich (where Poulet also teaches). In the *Lexicon der Weltliteratur*, René Wellek singles out Staiger as a prime exemplar of the phenomenological approach. Staiger's early works, *Zeit als Einbildungskraft des Dichters* (1939), and *Grundbegriffe der Poetik* (1946), are heavily influenced by the Geneva School, but remain metapersonal and existentialist in some of their objectives. Staiger's metapersonal interests are illustrated in *Grundbegriffe der Poetik*, where he imposes on genre study (in apriori fashion) the three temporal ecstasies suggested by Heidegger's *Sein und Zeit*. His later works, *Die Kunst der Interpretation* (1951) and *Stilwandel* (1963), operate purely in the Geneva tradition. In a late essay, "Time and the Poetic Imagination," Staiger poses a rhetorical question. What can account for the unity of a piece by Goethe, for example? Staiger continues, "The unprejudiced reader will say that the whole poem is unambiguously informed by Goethe's individuality. We agree without hesitation, but the question is: what is meant by individuality?" After rejecting positivist psychology and Freudian psychoanalysis as clues to an answer, he explains that individuated rhythm accounts for individuality: "It is rhythm, it is 'time' as inner gravitation and tension, which is the underlying unity sustaining the complexity of a work of art."[13] He goes on to show that an author's time is unique and intensely personalized, so that the literary work is a symbol of experiential pattern. This formulation is isomorphic with that of the Geneva School.

Gaston Bachelard (1884–1962) acted as an extremely potent influence upon most literary criticism contemporary with and

subsequent to his own publication. His relation to the Geneva
School is complicated, since he assisted at the school's provenance
but was in turn influenced by the school in his later years. As a
young philosopher of science, Bachelard was first interested in the
"obstacles" to abstract scientific thinking posed by man's persistent
emotive attachment to things, to the "world." In order to expose the
roots of this pre-scientific and concrete involvement with world,
Bachelard "psychoanalyzed" various phenomena (such as earth, air,
fire, and water) as they *appear* in the human imagination. In what
amounts to one of the most triumphant (and I think amusing) of
conversions, Bachelard was seduced by the very beauty of his
"obstacles," and became a fervent esthetician. Through a description of the connotative values phenomena bear in imaginative
literature, he claimed to expose the non-conceptual but psychologically vital values of collective human consciousness. For much of his
career Bachelard discussed these values in terms of Freudian
psychoanalysis or a Jungian archetypal system. For example,
authors were classified according to four cosmogonies, orbiting
around earth, air, fire, and water respectively. These four categories
were adjudicated as real, and as embedded in psychic structure much
like Jungian archetypes.

In his later career, Bachelard abandons the collective consciousness for individual consciousness. He puts aside any dependence on
Freud or Jung, and becomes unabashedly phenomenological in the
Genevan sense. Eva Kushner, a Bachelard specialist, witnesses to
this second conversion: "In Bachelard's most recent books, *Poétique
de la rêverie* [1960] and *Poétique de l'espace* [1957], phenomenology
is the key word because the author has come to realize more and
more clearly the impossibility of applying ready-made categories of
aesthetics to the study of poetry."[14] Small wonder that Poulet says of
Bachelard's approach, ". . . the method of Bachelard is of infinite
fecundity not only in its exploration of consciousness by consciousness, but also in that it constitutes . . . a marvelous application of
phenomenology to literature."[15]

Born at Bayonne in 1915, Roland Barthes studied at the
University of Paris, and eventually joined the prestigious Centre
National de la Recherche Scientifique. At present he is Directeur
d'Etudes in the sixth section of the Ecole Pratique des Hautes
Etudes. So famous is he now as a Parisian Structuralist that his early
period is at worst neglected, and at best interpreted only in the light
of his later evolution. In actuality, two of Barthes's books, *Michelet*

(1954) and *Sur Racine* (1963), can stand as works written in the Geneva tradition. Richard places *Michelet* in a phase he calls *"le complexe homme-oeuvre,"* and opposes the latter to *"le complexe homme-oeuvre-époque,"*[16] a phase wherein Barthes evolves towards pure structuralism. The early Barthes correlates both imagery and linguistic data to the phenomenological ego of the text, and thus employs two techniques of the Geneva School. More profitable is it by far to read *Sur Racine* in this light, rather than to ferret out seminal signs of what is to become his structuralist method.

Paul Brodtkorb (born 1930), an American presently teaching at Hunter College, C.U.N.Y., has contributed to our domestic criticism an outstanding treatment of Melville's *Moby Dick*. Entitled *Ishmael's White World: A Phenomenological Reading of Moby Dick* (1965), the book is written *à la manière de Genève,* and is a very good specimen of its kind. In his introduction, Brodtkorb declares: "My reading of Moby Dick will differ from other readings chiefly in its focus on the Ishmaelean consciousness through the medium of a methodological discipline specifically adapted to comprehend subjectivity, a discipline some sixty years old, and some thirty years—in France, at least—readily available—namely, phenomenology."[17] The introduction proceeds to a very reasonable statement of the phenomenological approach, and constitutes an *apologia* I would recommend to even the most xenophobic of our compatriots.


## A Programmatic Description: The Geneva School's Ontology of the Literary Work


The Geneva School is for the most part a group of practicing critics rather than of theorists, though most members of the school in one form or another have given accounts of their theoretical assumptions. It remains true despite the latter that any comprehensive ontology of the literary work must be extrapolated from the school's critical practice, and this has been no easy task. The Geneva critics are as at variance with each other as a John Crowe Ransom is with a Cleanth Brooks in American "New Criticism." But just as Ransom and Brooks hold a set of bedrock principles in common, and thus can present a common front against a "neo-Aristotelian" such as R. S. Crane, so too can it be said that the various Geneva critics, with some important reservations, "agree on the basics." In general, the Geneva School and its allies accept the description of human consciousness we have already encountered in our survey of phenomenological epistemology. Human consciousness is a massive self-world relation, a *Lebenswelt* or network of personal experiences. The author of a literary work becomes, then, one whose imagination selects and transforms elements of his or her *Lebenswelt* and creates out of them a fictive construct, a fictive "universe." Thus the phenomenologist Fakhir Hussain tells us "that the artist chooses among diverse characteristics of the real, which he puts in relief by comparison and contrast. In other words, the artist chooses some meaningful aspect of the world in which he lives, and places it under a new light in association with other aspects of this world."[18] The creative writer develops and embodies this "fictive universe" in and through language. Jean-Pierre Richard, when speaking of that "universe," declares it is the critic's job to analyze the "fibers of the work" (*fibres de l'oeuvre*). The "fibers" consist of the work's "verbal tissue" (*tissu verbal*) and "imaginative substance" (*substance imaginaire*).[19] It is of interest to note that the metaphoric language Richard uses to describe literature suggests an organism, and adumbrates the upcoming theory of "embodiment" or "incarnation." If they wish, the Geneva critics can at this point invoke the support of Roman Ingarden, the great phenomenological aesthetician who writes in the Husserlian tradition. In his monumental *The Literary Work of Art* (*Das literarische Kunstwerk*),[20] Ingarden describes the literary work as a structure of four strata which constitute a "polyphonic harmony." The four heterogenous yet interdependent strata are: (1) that of word sounds and higher phonetic formation, (2) that of meaning units, (3) that of "schematized aspects and aspect continua," and finally, (4) that of "represented objectivities." The fourth or climatic level is a fictive world which "unfolds" out of the preceding levels and includes them.[21]

The next phase of the ontological description, however, takes one a crucial step further. It states that precisely because language is gestural, is expressive, the literary work bears within itself the unique imprint of the author's own consciousness. The Geneva critic considers the author's unique imprint immanent in the literary work and critically available there. The Geneva School, with few exceptions, agrees that biographical criticism, or any critical system which treats the author's "self" in "disembodied form" (that is, as external to the work), is invalid.[22] Since phenomenological critics operate solely within the confines of the literary structure, they consider their approach intrinsic, a parameter of phenomenological method since Husserl's day. Probably on this account, among others, the critical writings of the early Georges Poulet and Emil Staiger disregard historical milieu. Their ahistorical attitude is beginning to reverse, however, and I shall, in due time, discuss this reversal. I might add here too a word of explanation for those who feel talk of an "author's imprint" comes perilously close to what is called in the Anglo-American world the "intentional fallacy." When the phenomenological critic refers to the author's "intentionality" enverbalized in the literary work, intentionality means the author's multi-modal interaction with world, and not just the conceptual interaction; the intentionality concerned is accessible only through internal analysis of the text. Furthermore, the author's concept of what the literary work is or will be does not necessarily identify with what of the self was actually put into the work. Intentionality in the phenomenological sense refers only to those interactions between the author's selfhood and world which actually appear in the work (whether the author knows he or she put them there or not). Thus the American "New Critical" admonition against "intentional fallacy" does not apply.

To bolster the claim that the author's intentionality is present in the work, the Geneva critic can cite the conclusions of the phenomenological aesthetician Mikel Dufrenne, who in his *Phenomenology of Aesthetic Experience* (*Phénoménologie de l'expérience esthétique*) avers that literature "exhibits" its author (the technical term *exhibition* is from Husserl). The "expressivity" of the work, says Dufrenne, renders the author present in the text: the aesthetic perceiver is to seek out the author's expressive *projet* in the text's "world."[23] In Roman Ingarden, the situation is more complicated. Only the "coming into being" of the literary work depends on the intentionality of the author, while the "completed" work has other ontic bases (namely, ideal concepts and word-signs). Nevertheless, for Ingarden the purpose of the aesthetic reader should be the "duplication" of the "sense-bestowing" acts of the author, so to this extent the author's intentionality still remains the arbiter of the reader's response.[24]

Though the Geneva School receives rather strong corroboration from Dufrenne, and even some indirect (but much weaker) confirmation from Ingarden, the school is much more vulnerable than they to charges of psychologism. The school speaks openly of the author's experiential patterns,[25] and the actual presence and operation of equivalent patterns in that author's literary work. To put it another way, his experiential patterns remain essentially the same, whether they appear in his personal *Lebenswelt* or in his imagination's finished product (the literary work). The experiential patterns are not "experiences," but literally "patterns of experience," and are thus latent in the author's experiential world. Experiential patterns are unique, and are the foundation of all of the author's enterprises, including imaginative ones. The patterns provide the unity characteristic of an author's whole life-style.

Most importantly for us, experiential patterns are precisely the means whereby something of the author's consciousness is present in the work. The patterns underpin the literary work itself, and are discoverable through "phenomenological scrutiny." In the introduction to his *L'Univers imaginaire de Mallarmé,* Jean-Pierre Richard tells us he seeks the *infra-langage,* that is, the *sous-jacence* of Mallarmé's poetry.[26] The *sous-jacence* is the latent zone where meanings are patterned; it reveals *how* the *conscience mallarméenne* experiences. Thus Richard's criticism is "a museum of the *imagination mallarméenne,*" a description of its "geology, botany, bestiary, and feminine typology."[27] The purpose is to expose the "essential attitudes" of Mallarmé's mental landscape and to provide a "concrete phenomenology" of Mallarmé's imagination, "through which a single *projet* is pursued." Richard attempts to locate "the psychological reality of the theme,"[28] and to echo Mallarmé's "act of consciousness"[29] as it appears in the poetry. J. Hillis Miller, in the introduction to his *Charles Dickens,* likewise talks of experiential patterns. Miller informs us that his objective is "to assess the specific quality of Dickens' imagination in the totality of his work, to identify what persists throughout all the swarming multiplicity of his novels as a view of the world which is unique and the same, and to trace the development of this vision of things from one novel to another throughout the chronological span of his career."[30]

Paul Brodtkorb, in *Ishmael's White World,* announces he is going to use "a methodological discipline specifically adapted to comprehend subjectivity . . . namely phenomenology. . . . Phenomenology applied to criticism assumes that arrangements of letters on a page express state of mind and thereby make manifest states of being."[31] In his famous essay on Marivaux, Georges Poulet claims to expose the "concrete form of the Cogito"[32] (what Sartre would call the "prereflexive Cogito"). And in one of his few ventures into practical criticism, Merleau-Ponty sums up the phenomenological notion of experiential pattern very well: "It is not the role of Stendhal to discourse on subjectivity; it suffices for him to render it present."[33]

At this juncture a possible difficulty intrudes. I have already attempted to make clear that the embodiment of intentionality in language is not an idealistic formula; the fictive universe which is the literary work does not refer to the relevant consciousness of the author, but rather, duplicates it.[34] But is the theory of embodiment idealistic in a second sense? Does it make the author's "thought" of the work precede a "transfer" of that thought into language? Merleau-Ponty again provides the answer of the phenomenologist. The thought was simultaneously language from the start (and a multitude of subject-object relations from the start), though an "inner language" not yet articulated externally through sounds or print ("the *Cogito* is a *loquor,*" says Dufrenne). It is interesting to note that Merleau-Ponty even argues that esthetic language confers *en-soi* existence on what is simultaneously a thought; he argues for that fusion of *en-soi* and *pour-soi* Sartre thinks forever and always impossible. (Mikel Dufrenne later develops this theory of "fusion" in his *Phenomenology of Aesthetic Experience.*) Other phenomenologists introduce more variations. In some of their theorizing, the creation of a literary work is not only the enverbalizing of intentionality, but an actual extension of the author's intentional field. Language causes the author to further apprehend the self, to further interact with the world, and in a sense to further build a personal being. Thus, in the "Avant-propos" to his *Littérature et sensation,* Richard declares, "Literary creation appears nevertheless as an experience, or even as a *praxis* of self, as an exercise of apprehension and of genesis in the course of which a writer tries at the same time to seize himself and build himself."[35]

Experiential patterns, I have said, are latent, and are unique to any given consciousness. They are, furthermore, the precise means whereby an author is "present" in his work. To resume the central thread of my programmatic description, let me develop my definition still more. Experiential patterns are fundamental self-world relationships which underlie their actualizations, real or imaginary. Though experiential patterns on a day-to-day basis can be considered constant, the Geneva critics do admit the possibility of change in these patterns. Patterns of self-world relationship can

change, but change in a factor so fundamental is equivalent to, or
rather, *is* a fundamental "depth-change" in the given individual's
consciousness; such a change often is, for better or for worse, a
turning point in his life. In *La Distance intérieure,* Georges Poulet
finds fundamental changes of this kind in the experiential patterns
of Stéphane Mallarmé. During one phase, Mallarmé's poetry is
characterized by a latent pattern which "blocks out" the Ideal; and
in another phase, by a pattern which stares the Ideal in the face.
Since neither pattern "works" for Mallarmé psychologically, his
whole personality undergoes a positional shift: it strikes a compromise with the Ideal. This compromise is one of "indirect
encounter," and is symbolized by a new pattern of "translucency"
(which has, of course, many actualizations: "fog" and "luminous
curtains" are two of them).

As already indicated, experiential patterns play another vitally
important role in human consciousness: they are the real cause of
unity in the human person. This being the case, the consequences
for literature are readily apparent. Experiential patterns unify the
imagination's fictive constructs, and the literary enverbalizations of
these constructs. The unity meant here is organic, or the wholeness
which is constituted by the relationships of parts to each other.
These relationships need not be ones of identity or analogy; they can
just as well be oppositional. Thus the Geneva critic can account for
schizophrenic patterns of experience and other abnormalities.
Furthermore, and this is of great significance to literary criticism,
since latent experiential patterns are omnipresent and related to
each other in dialectically unified ways, they constitute the factor
which unifies all the literary works of an author into a whole (and
dialectical unity can account for fundamental change and development). Because experiential patterns effect unity in an author's
collective works, J. Hillis Miller can say:

> Through the analysis of all the passages, as they reveal the
> persistence of certain obsessions, problems, and attitudes, the critic
> can hope to glimpse the original unity of a creative mind. For all
> the works of a single writer form a unity, a unity in which a
> thousand paths radiate from the same center. . . . The pervasive
> stylistic traits of a writer, his recurrent words and images, his
> special cadence and tone, are as personal to him as his face or his
> way of walking. His style is his own way of living in the world
> given a verbal form.[36]

Because experiential patterns are the source of a single literary work's (or a collective work's) "life" or being, their exposure and evaluation is the critic's ultimate task (though certainly not the only one). The "ultimacy" of this task acquires the force of a relentless critical imperative in the work of Emil Staiger. In his criticism, the experiential pattern which unifies the *corpus* of an author is specifically temporal. As Staiger tells us in *Die Kunst der Interpretation,* the pattern is a latent "rhythm":

> What do we observe when we first meet poetry? It is not only the full content which a fundamental reading first opens up. Nor is it only details, for a unity already imprints itself. There is a spirit which animates the whole, and which—though we feel it evident without being able to give account—proves itself in individual features. I call this feeling "rhythm."[37]

This rhythm controls the unified "sense" and beauty of the work:

> If our heart feels touched by the rhythm of a poem . . . even if the poem is otherwise dark but perceptibly determined in one sense, then we already perceive the poem's proper beauty.[38]

Staiger, in his essay "Time and the Poetic Imagination," credits Georges Poulet and two phenomenological psychologists, Eugène Minkowski and Ludwig Binswanger, for their pioneering work in the field of experiential time. Staiger's concern is for the unique way in which an author "times" his whole *Lebenswelt,* and therefore "times" his literature. Even the layman, says Staiger, must practice *Einfühlung,* or the empathetic experience of a poem's rhythm. This "quiet, selfless empathy, however, is only the first step." The ultimate task of the reader is to detect the temporal pattern which underlies the meter or "outer form": in Staiger's words, "Any critic aiming to make a more reliable statement than the gifted layman must try to see the rhythm clearly as an individual modification of 'time,' of the inner meaning."[39] The concepts of "inner and outer form" (which correspond to what I have respectively called "latent pattern" and "actualization"), and even the concept of experiential "unity," permit me to quote the following passage from Leo Spitzer: ". . . language is only one outward crystallization of the 'inward form,' or, to use another metaphor: the life-blood of the poetic creation is everywhere the same . . . Because I happened to be a linguist it was from the linguistic angle that I started to fight my way to his [Rabelais's] unity."[40] Spitzer is describing here what he calls the "philological circle": a tentative move from an author's style to that author's "psychological etymon," or "radix in his soul."[41] Spitzer is a German *Stilforschung* (or "style-investigation") critic, and the phenomenologist Jean Rousset acknowledges Spitzerian influence on his own work.[42] But for that matter, Spitzer himself affirms another acknowledgment made by a second *Stilforschung* critic, the great Erich Auerbach: Auerbach testifies that *Stilforschung,* or German *explication-de-texte,* is indebted in part to "Husserl's phenomenology."[43] All this suggests once again the tangled web of influences from which phenomenological criticism arises.

Now that I have described what the Geneva School considers literature to be, I can pass on to the more intricate issue of how they believe literature is what it is. There is every reason to believe that phenomenological critics have looked to the discipline of phenomenological psychology for some methodological insights. As already indicated, Staiger credits two phenomenological psychologists, Minkowski and Binswanger. Minkowski's classic work, *Le Temps vécu,* appeared in 1933 (and thus well before the phenomenological movement in literary criticism); the possibility of influence from him is therefore strong. Staiger's phenomenological literary criticism begins six years later in 1939, with *Die Zeit als Einbildungskraft des Dichters.*[44] And as late as 1965, the phenomenological literary critic Paul Brodtkorb is still crediting phenomenological psychology. In *Ishmael's White World,* he adopts the descriptive schemata devised by the Dutch phenomenological psychologist, J. H. Van Den Berg. However, no matter how weak or strong this influence (it varies from critic to critic), phenomenological psychology does provide us with a good way of describing the methodological assumptions of phenomenological criticism. Undoubtedly, such is the case because both the psychologists and critics in question describe consciousness, and do so in ways that are ultimately Husserlian. Thus, if we conduct our own "phenomenology" or "descriptive typology" of Geneva criticism, we find that the latter treats consciousness in terms of two categories: modes of consciousness, and contents of consciousness. Phenomenological critics do not regard these categories as real. The categories, no matter what the names they go by, are used solely to ensure that experiential patterns in the literary work are examined systematically and comprehensively. This is not to suggest that the Geneva critics are methodological in a scientific sense. But anyone who has read a critic like Jean-Pierre Richard can testify to the comprehensive nature of his criticism; and anyone who has met the rigorous dialectic of a Georges Poulet can notarize his systematization. The genius of these critics is their ability to achieve and organize poetic intuition, and phenomenology is admirably suited for the task.

Keep in mind that the "categories" of mode and content are artificial; they are just convenient ways of charting the field of consciousness. Perhaps for this reason the Geneva critic can rebut the charge that "psychological" assumptions render one as "metaphysical" and "extrinsic" as any Freudian. As if in anticipation of such a charge, Paul Brodtkorb is at pains to assure us his schemata are "just a way of ordering the description." The categories "overlap and parallel rather than strictly exclude each other." They "are used because collectively, with appropriate subdivisions, they can with some show of adequacy, comprehend a life-world."[45] The categories are not, in short, the Transcendental Forms of the Idealist. Neither are they apriori correlations, accepted as objectively real, of specific kinds of content and corresponding values. The Freudian critic normally presupposes that snake imagery bears a phallic value; the archetypal critic assumes that springtime ritual carries the value of spiritual resurrection; and the Sartrean Existentialist that images of viscosity represent the encroachment of *"l'être-en-soi."* In contradistinction, the Geneva critic claims to exclude such expectancies, and to merely describe the unique values of the author's enverbalized consciousness. Nor, finally, is it the case that modes of consciousness designate the subjective, and the contents of consciousness the objective. Needless to say, such a formulation would vitiate phenomenology's whole *raison d'être*. Rather, the modes designate the concretely differentiated functions of consciousness, and consciousness here means intentionality, the reciprocal implication of self and world.

The contents of consciousness are the quiddities of self and world involved in consciousness, that is, intentionality; contents too, then, are a reciprocal implication of subjectivity and objectivity. Thus, for example, when Paul Brodtkorb discusses the content category of "World,"[46] the constituent elements of "earth," "air," "fire," and "water" do not appear as passive recipients of the self's projected meanings; but neither do they behave as objects impinging on a neutral mind (a *tabula rasa*). The self experiences part of their meanings as coming from the outside, and part from the selfhood experiencing them. Likewise, in Roland Barthes's phenomenological work, *Sur Racine*, Racine experiences part of the meaning of *eyes* emanating from "eyes" themselves (and not exclusively from Racine's projected interpretation of them). For this reason, it can be said "Eyes are by nature light offered to shadow."[47] Yet the "nature" of eyes is not by any means considered pregiven by Barthes, since even eyes as "outside phenomena" *appear* differently to each perceiver, and thus the total meaning of *eyes* in a given author differs from that it may have in other authors. Yet on the other hand, the meaning of *eyes* is not purely objective, because Racine contributes to their meaning.

Though designations for the various modes of consciousness differ from phenomenologist to phenomenologist, the most sensible and thorough schema I have found classifies the modes into seven kinds: cognition, volition, emotion, perception, time (including memory), space,[48] and imagination.[49] Since we are concerned with literary works, products of the author's imaginative transformation of his *Lebenswelt*, the imaginative mode is understood to be the controlling mode—that mode which unifies the differentiated modal activities into a single, coherent consciousness.[50] Consequently, the Geneva critic believes that when studying the concretizations of the other six modes, he is really studying the author's imagination, and vice versa. As for the content categories of consciousness, the most representative schema divides into four designations: World (non-human entities), Happenings (events), Others (other human beings), and Self (selfhood as the content of one's own intentional act).[51] It should be evident at this point that Heidegger's emphasis on moods or *Stimmungen* helped inspire analysis of the non-rational modes. (Binswanger and other *Daseinanalyse* psychiatrists developed the implications of *Stimmungen* for psychiatry.) Another influence was Sartre's classification according to modal kinds, so one can speak of emotion-consciousness, pain-consciousness, and so on.[52] Apropos the rationale behind the literary critic's "content categories," Heidegger's division of the contents of consciousness into various systems of meaning (*Vorhandenheit, Zuhandenheit*, and so forth) can be seen as an important predecessor.

The next question that arises asks how the author's experiential patterns are embodied in the literary work. Thinking of this problem in terms of the modes of consciousness may help one to frame the question. That experiential patterns involving the cognitive mode (meaning here rational intellect, the faculty of conceptualization) find their expression in the conceptual layer of language is quite apparent. The difficult question asks how the non-conceptual modes are embodied in language. The answer can be found only in a theory of the symbol. The influences that converge on current phenomenological description of the symbol come from many directions. One recalls at once Sartre's "emotion" which becomes a poetic language-thing. Other influences include Karl Vossler and the Munich School (with its theory of "inner form" and "outer form"), Charles Du Bos, Marcel Raymond, Albert Béguin, Gaston Bachelard, and Jean Wahl; and antedating them, Sigmund Freud and Henri Bergson.

The German *Stilforschung* critics, and especially Leo Spitzer, constitute other important predecessors. The phenomenological theorist and critic Jean Rousset, in his *Forme et Signification*, acknowledges Spitzer's influence on correlations of mode and language. Spitzer correlates style and the author's radix of feeling, which he calls the "affective center of the author." The passage from Rousset reads:

> This great philologist [Spitzer] gives us some models of stylistic study established on the union of word and thought: a deviation, an accident of language, if it is well chosen, will betray an "affective center" of the author which is at the same time a principle of the internal cohesion of the work; all detail is homogenous in relation to the whole; "style and soul are two immediate *données,* and, at bottom, two aspects, artificially isolated, of the same interior phenomenon. . . ." The artist doesn't have a style, he IS his style. On this conviction rests the 'method' of Spitzer.[53]

Phenomenological description of the symbol has received definitive formulation at the hands of Merleau-Ponty, whose work we have already surveyed in brief. For Merleau-Ponty *la parole* is a concrete projection of the whole person.[54] *La parole's* articulatory and auditory styles constitute important ways that the non-rational elements of personhood express themselves.[55] Concrete expression involves the creative deformation of available meanings, or, in other words, metaphoric or other figurative language. Thus *la parole* is at its richest in poetic language.[56] All the above has two important implications for phenomenological criticism. The first is that the experience embodied in poetic language somehow represents all the modes of consciousness. If the experience embodied is primarily auditory, for example, somehow the participations of the emotive, volitive, cognitive, and other modes in this primarily auditory experience are also represented.[57] Second, the expressions of the nonconceptual modes receive their fundamental embodiment in rhyme, rhythm, and other phonemic values; in figurative language and all stylistic traits; and in the whole range of the connotative.

## A Programmatic Description:
## The Geneva School's Critical Methodology

We can now broach discussion of the methodology which undergirds the critical practice of the Geneva School. As already indicated, I do not mean to say that the school's methodology is scientific: all I mean is that a general typology of the school's practice does emerge when a historian of criticism examines that practice carefully. Although each Geneva critic develops a practical criticism which is unique, he or she does hold in common with other critics of the same school certain fundamental procedures, though the latter are sometimes conceptually premeditated and sometimes not. It is a thesis of this chapter that Edmund Husserl's phenomenology, *directe vel indirecte,* was "in the air" during the genesis and development of the Geneva School, and that his influence has a dominating effect on Geneva criticism. To document this influence in terms satisfactory to what Wellek calls "historical positivism" would require the exclusive attention of a book-length study. A chapter intended primarily as an introduction for generalists cannot mount such a campaign, so I shall content myself with a safer objective. I shall outline Husserl's phenomenological method *grosso modo,* and then indicate obvious parallels in the methodology of the Geneva School.

Husserl's phenomenological method, in its most developed form, involves two "reductions." "Reductionism" has a negative timbre in the Anglo-American world, since the latter tradition uses the term to mean an unwarranted narrowing of vision: in the face of facts which are by nature pluralistic, reductionism denies some relevant data in order to engineer a simplistic explanation. Husserl's reductions in the main do not deny data, but rather suspend or bracket out some considerations in favor of others. Thus the first, or phenomenological reduction (also called the transcendental reduction), brackets out consideration of actual existence so that "natural attitude" is suspended. In other words, the first reduction deliberately excludes from consideration the existence or non-existence of the phenomenon: the examiner is thereby unblinded so he can "see" the essential structure of the phenomenon before him. This "intuition of essence" parallels certain practices of the Geneva School, but I wish first to address two other functions of phenomenological reduction. Phenomenological reduction claims to suspend presuppositions and to disregard extrinsic (irrelevant) data. These two functions, when applied in an analogous way to literary criticism, demand the suspension of ideology, or what was called earlier metaphysical speculation. Hence the Geneva critic's already-mentioned aversion to metaphysics. He or she makes every effort to censor out bias towards a personal *Weltanschauung* when explicating literature. I can now proceed to a disquisition on the claimed neutrality of the Geneva School, and the counterclaim of Heideggerians that this neutrality is a stalking horse—that the Geneva School is as ideological as anyone else.

Let us begin with two characteristics of Geneva criticism. The first is description of consciousness in terms of intentionality. The Geneva critic can argue here that intentionality is an epistemological formulation, and not a metaphysical one. Intentionality concerns how one knows rather than what one knows, and only the latter falls within the purview of metaphysics. This distinction, however, I must deny. The mutual implication of "self" and "world" requires a being which is a self, and beings which are a world. Even if consciousness is an action, it is an action involving beings. Even Merleau-Ponty's monism requires a being, though it be a being which does not divide into subject and object. Husserl's first reduction may bracket out ontological questions, but Husserl's behavior rests on the principle that there is a "what" which is open to description. In fact, all epistemology rises out of a metaphysic, be that metaphysic implicit or explicit. Metaphysics is the study of being, and epistemology involves being(s). The case for an implied metaphysic becomes still more apparent when the Geneva critic speaks of latent experiential patterns in the author and in the literary work. Psychology of consciousness entails the way a human being is structured, and how he or she operates. As for the nature of literature, I had recourse earlier to the term *ontology of the literary work* simply because it was precisely the being of the work which was at issue.

Secondly, the Geneva critic in one way or another speaks of modes and contents of consciousness. Here he can argue that such schemata provide a convenient methodology, but do not harbor metaphysical pretensions. Self, Others, Happenings, and World may be "provisional" ways of charting the field of consciousness, but my point is that the critic considers them provisionally valid, and this literary description is useful in direct proportion to the metaphysical validity of these schemata. The critic distinguishes among Self, Others, Happenings, and World in terms of quiddity, or whatness (that is, in terms of metaphysics!). Nor do the modes of consciousness fare any better. Quiddities are in part defined by the modes which condition them. If the critic expects a *persona* to smell something, there is an odor to be smelled. If the critic expects a *persona* to see something, the critic implies there is a sight to be seen. So the critic has presupposed two metaphysical qualities which are ontological: odor in the first instance and color in the second. All methodology implies a metaphysic. The Geneva School, then, does bring to the literary work some fundamental presuppositions.

Having proven the above, however, does not in itself damn the practice of the Geneva School; much less still does it erase the great practical difference between criticisms called "immanent" and those called "extrinsic." As indicated earlier, any conscientious reader of criticism senses at once an enormous difference between the practice of a Geneva critic and that of a Freudian or Catholic or Marxist critic. Yet the opposition of "metaphysical" versus "neutral" criticism is on the face of it patently wrong. So we must redouble our efforts to locate the real nature of the difference. *Vive la différence, mais qu'est-ce qui est cette différence?* First, we must resurrect the validity of metaphysics in Husserlian terms. I have already said that Husserl considered the elaborate metaphysics of his day premature and illegitimate. Husserl wanted phenomenology to describe the simplest human experiences, and escalate towards more ambitious issues only very cautiously, and over many years. He did not by any means exclude metaphysical inquiry, as long as it "sees" the nature of Being concretely and *in* experience. Husserlians tend to feel that Heidegger and Sartre do not in fact do this, and are therefore speculative and non-phenomenological.

It is significant to note, however, that Heidegger and Sartre both claim to "see" their ontology in experience, so you and I as thinkers must judge for ourselves the phenomenological validity of their findings. My own opinion is that Sartre's ontology is speculative and eccentric. The task of the phenomenological philosopher is to find the essential structure of experience, that is, the structure which is common to all men. Sartre's ontology seems individuated and empirical; in other words, it bespeaks only his own empirical ego and the egos of a few people like him. In short, he does not perform what Husserl calls eidetic reduction and intuition (operations I shall soon discuss), nor does he perform the approximate equivalent of such operations. In contradistinction, I consider much of Martin Heidegger's work truly phenomenological. There is an important slogan in phenomenology: "Description is phenomenology's only verification." When confronted with another phenomenologist's description of essential experience, any given phenomenologist must "consult" his or her own experience and that of many others to verify the proffered description (of course, the consultation should exploit the reductions). For this reason, I think it is fair to say that phenomenology is a communal activity. In the seminars I offer in aesthetics, phenomenology, literature, and the like (often co-taught with other phenomenologists), the great majority of participants have repeatedly "verified" Heidegger's ontology (though not his practical criticism). Hence I conclude that many of his metaphysical insights (though Heidegger wouldn't use the term *metaphysics*) are phenomenological.

Recall, however, that the above discussion of a phenomenological metaphysics is intended to legitimatize the implied metaphysic of the Geneva School. Here the Geneva critic can say that in a truly phenomenological manner one "sees" intentional consciousness, and latent experiential patterns, and the nature of the literary work, and so on. Hence, though the critic's presuppositions when confronting a given literary work are metaphysical, they are themselves grounded in previous phenomenological discoveries, and are consequently valid.

At this juncture, the hydra rears another head. What phenomenologists see may not be what others see, and vice versa. It is a misnomer to think that a good Marxist critic or a good Catholic critic "imposes" a metaphysic on literature. On the contrary, the former invariably claims to "see" class dialectic in the literary work, and the latter claims to "see" Divine Providence in perhaps the same work. And each critic's "description" is usually confirmed by a community of people who see the same thing. What then is the tangible difference between Geneva critics, who we sense are "immanent," and these other critics, who are "extrinsic"?

I mentioned above a "community" which verifies or denies the critic's description. In the concept of community I think we find our tangible difference. That consciousness is an interplay of self and outside and that literature is an expression of consciousness, the vast proportion of mankind, or at least Western man, can accept. More importantly, the phenomenological schemata of modes and contents of consciousness are "lowest common denominators" which most can accept comfortably. That is, most people would agree that such schemata are valid ways of describing experiential consciousness. And if given individuals can't do this, they can at least agree to use these denominators tentatively, because they do some justice to the ontology of consciousness. Unlike more elaborate and therefore particularized metaphysics (which because of their particularization I call "ideologies"), the fundamental metaphysic of phenomenology can achieve quite universal acceptance. Most people can "see" the distinction between looking and touching (an example of modal distinction), and the distinction between person and thing (an example of content distinction). Much fewer can "see" premarital sex as disordered ontology (as a Catholic would), or private ownership as a disorientation of being (as a Marxist would). The usefulness of the phenomenological schemata, then, is in direct proportion to the extension of community accepting them.

Still, the most important point is yet to be made. It depends on a contrast mentioned earlier in this chapter: "personal" versus "metapersonal" criticism. By personal criticism I mean critical practice that describes a phenomenological ego, that is, the enverbalized consciousness appearing in a text. By metapersonal criticism I indicate critical practice that describes textual events in terms other than those of the phenomenological ego. Because, in the main, its metaphysical coordinates are so elemental, the Geneva School can accommodate and describe any phenomenological ego.[58] In other words, it can without elaborate ideological comment simply describe an author's enverbalized consciousness in the latter's own terms. If the Geneva School describes a Marxist novel, it describes the way a Marxist experiences life. If the school describes a Catholic poem, it describes the way a Catholic experiences life. And so on. The personal critic, in other words, describes a possible way of experiencing, be it a Marxist way, a Catholic way, or whatever. Thus what was earlier called immanent criticism is better translated into the term "personal criticism." Concomitantly, what was called extrinsic or metaphysical criticism translates into "metapersonal criticism." The ideological critic (that is, one with elaborate metaphysical convictions) becomes by necessity metapersonal. Whenever an author's enverbalized consciousness experiences life differently from the way the ideological critic does, the critic must re-interpret the text's *Lebenswelt* in terms other than its own. The ideological critic "cuts against the grain" of the author's personhood, and explains what is *really* happening. I conclude then that the Geneva School is not metaphysically neutral, so to this extent the Heideggerians and others are right. But the basic intuition of the school in this matter is also right: a chasm divides Geneva criticism from that of the Marxist, the Catholic, the Sartrean Existentialist, and other *idéologues.*

The later Geneva School is characterized by another practice analogous to Husserl's phenomenological reduction. Because Husserl called for a description of "things themselves" (*Zu den Sachen selbst* is yet another Husserlian password), he attempted to isolate these "things" from their previous histories, and from their existential ties with environment. Unlike Albert Béguin and Marcel Raymond, the later Geneva critics isolated literature from milieu. Emil Staiger, in his "Einleitung" to *Die Zeit als Einbildungskraft des Dichters,* rejected historical criticism,[59] and Roman Ingarden did the same in *Das literarische Kunstwerk.* In his *Etudes sur le temps humain,* Georges Poulet refused to acknowledge historical influence, or to draw cultural inferences from the *esprit* of a culture's literature. By the 1950s, the liabilities of so uncompromising an attitude begin to force a change. After all, without a consideration of literary history, how can one distinguish unique style from convention? Without reference to environment, how can one even understand those cultural elements which are embedded in literature? Poulet is pressured to concede "for each epoch a consciousness common to all contemporary minds. It is in this general consciousness that individual thoughts and sentiments would bathe." To be sure, Poulet (and all phenomenologists) will forever shun historical positivism like the proverbial plague. The above formulation is a throwback to *Geistesgeschichte,* if anything, but in terms of phenomenological criticism it represents a radical shift in posture. J. Hillis Miller, in an analysis of Poulet's critical evolution, explains:

> At any time each consciousness, however particular, participates in the general consciousness, its particularity consists in the unique version or organization it makes of ideas common to the age, not in its power to think ideas unheard-of in that time or place. This notion is, in Poulet's earlier books, present overtly only in the prefatory chapter to *Etudes sur le temps humain,* but *Métamorphoses du cercle* [published in 1961, and characteristic of Poulet's later phase] contains a number of chapters of a kind new in Poulet's criticism. . . . The presupposition of these chapters is that the consciousness of an age forms a closed unity, a crystalline

sphere much like that of a single mind. Such a collective mind can
be seized by the same consciousness of consciousness which grasps
the mind of a single author, and it can be followed through all its
structure by the same kind of dialectical route.[60]

Emil Staiger's *Die Kunst der Interpretation* (1955) and *Stilwandel* (1963) also show a postural readjustment.[61] In *Die Kunst,* after an
explication of a poem by Goethe, Staiger feels free to say: "In short,
as is here possible, I have observed the poem in the frame of the
whole Goethe era and also evaluated its stylistic unity in terms of
historical connections . . . We see with whom a poet is allied, and
also see in what ways he separates himself off from his relationships."[62] In my own opinion, the Geneva School can easily absorb
historical considerations without doing violence to itself or its
principles. The Geneva critic need only expand the field of vision, as
it were, so the frame accommodates both literature and literature's
essential contact with other phenomena. As long as he or she avoids
an apriori "theory of history," the critic can in good conscience
describe what is seen.[63] He or she has only widened the range of
phenomena described.

J. Hillis Miller said above that the particularity of an individual
consciousness is "in the unique version or organization it makes of
ideas common to the age." Many opponents of the Geneva School
maintain that the school's focus on individuality becomes useless in
the face of pre-modern literature, so a brief review of the school's
attitude towards this whole issue is in order. One must distinguish
at the outset between literature written by one person, and a folk
narrative composed by a whole culture. Though many specialists in
medieval and Baroque literature refuse to valorize the claim, the
Geneva School insists that a good author's individuality always
reveals itself. This is the case because a given individual is always
different from all other people (though only a "good" author knows
how to express this individuality: a poetaster uses hackneyed
language, and is thus untrue to his unique personality). When
working with sixteenth-century literature, the critic in search of
singularity assumes a formidable task. The master of discernment in
cases of this kind is (in my opinion) that old German polyhistor,
Leo Spitzer himself. Though of course not a member of the Geneva
School, he sets the best example for it. He penetrates into the past,
yet salvages singularity. I encourage the reader to scan Spitzer's
treatment of Joachim Du Bellay. Bellay's Sonnet 113 (from the
volume *L'Olive*) is a paraphrase of a poem written by the Italian

Petrarchist Bernardino Danello. Sonnet 113 is also dependent on
another French poem likewise derived from Danello. Besides all
this, the sonnet is highly stylized, and incorporates classical motifs
which are centuries old. Yet Spitzer demonstrates with a triumphal
adequacy that Bellay's poem is singular, and reveals the personhood
that is Bellay's alone.[64]

Of course, a *controversiste* may reply that other poets simply
express the collective spirit of their culture, and repress personal
uniqueness; and furthermore, that "hackneyed language" is a
modern and biased term. I think the phenomenologist can only
answer that such a writer is not an *auctor,* or "originator," but a
*conductor,* or "contractor," who contracts with society the expression of society's will. This is not to demean those who speak the
words of the tribe, but to distinguish their function from that of
authors as such. Finally, what about corporate authorship, the folk
narrative or medieval romance composed by many writers? I think
in this case the Geneva critic must adopt the notion of "collective
mind" found in *Les Métamorphoses du cercle.* A given culture
has its own uniqueness, expressed by a galaxy of *contractores.*
By bringing his consciousness of individual mind to a consciousness of collective mind, the Geneva critic even here can make a
contribution.

But now back to the plumb-line of our present discussion—the
methodology of Geneva criticism. Disposed for an empathetic
awareness of the literary work, the Geneva critic proceeds to the first
critical task, one shared in common with most literary exegetes. The
critic asks whether the "universe" (characters, theme, plot, etc.)
offered in the work is "made present" or vitalized through language
so it can "live" in the reader's imagination. If the universe is
"presenced" through language, the language is esthetically successful. The critic can determine whether or not the persons, things, and
events are vitalized only by checking them against his or her own
awareness of possible ways in which reality can be experienced
(imaginatively or otherwise). Here it is worth noting that one
cannot judge the absolutely "other." The literature of a Martian
would make no sense to us at all, or if it did make sense, that sense
would be in direct proportion to how much that life-world
resembles ours. Testing in the light of analogous experience, J.-P.
Richard reminds us, assumes for all men "a certain identity of
reactions when confronted with things and men."[65] For example,
though the critic may not personally think life is absurd, he or she

has experienced enough of absurdity to recognize life can be experienced as absurd by some people. And the critic must judge whether the literary work in question truly "presences" life-experienced-as-absurd. Far from being narrow in its approach, then, such a criticism appreciates the surrealist universe of a Kafka as much as the naturalist universe of a Zola.

The Geneva critic next undertakes the second critical task, one that is quite unique. Having described the work's experiential universe, he or she now describes the experiential patterns (of the author, but in the work) which coordinate and account for that universe. The first task did such things as describe the compassion of the hero, say, and the egotism of the antagonist. And it judged whether the work's language did justice to compassion and egotism, or, more accurately, whether it did justice to a possible way of imagining compassion and egotism. The second task seeks the underlying experiential pattern which can "type" and express reality in such wise. If one reads Geneva criticism at length, one finds the two tasks performed sequentially, or in reverse order, or in a kind of dialectical progression. If we take up Jean Rousset's essay on Flaubert (in *Forme et Signification*), for example, we find on page 120 a description of narrative modulations in chapter three, part two, of *Madame Bovary*. Rousset explains how Flaubert guides the reader from one point to another, from one circumstance in the plot to the next, with remarkable smoothness and certainty. Rousset first examines these stylistic *glissements* in terms of the plot and characters, that is, in terms of the experiential universe proffered by the novel. Then, on pages 121 and 122, Rousset discusses these *glissements* in terms of the author's consciousness, present in the same novel and organizing it "from below." Another example appears in Richard's critique of Stendhal (in *Littérature et Sensation*). Richard tells us (on page 78) that water signals an experiential pattern in Stendhal's literature. Water identifies with *"les tentatives de repli and de recueillement,"* and this association is characteristic of Stendhal's enverbalized consciousness. Then Richard shifts his gaze from experiential pattern to the universe arising therefrom. Water imagery is examined in relation to various plots and characters. The imagery appears in *Chartreuse de Parme* and *Le Rouge et le Noir*, and significantly shapes the experiential universes of these two novels. It affects the portrayal of Fabrice and Julien, and through them it comments on the nature of reality. The distinction between experiential universe and experiential pattern some Anglo-American critics find unnerving. Actually, the distinction can be also found in American New Critical theory, though it appears inchoate and unexploited in such a context. *Atmosphere* is defined by Brooks and Warren as "the general pervasive feeling aroused by the various factors in a piece of fiction, such as setting, character, theme, and the like." Atmosphere is to be distinguished from tone, they tell us, and they continue:

> Considerations of the metaphorical origin of the two terms, *atmosphere* and *tone*, may be helpful here. *Tone* is to be referred ultimately to the author's attitude (the tone of voice of a speaker as qualifying what he says) towards what is being presented, whereas *atmosphere* is to be referred to the general qualification provided by the materials themselves (an atmosphere of sunshine, of cheerfulness, an atmosphere of gloom, and the like).[66]

They define *tone* as "the reflection in the story of the author's attitude toward his material and toward his audience."[67] Atmosphere, then, is a constituent (among others) of what we have called the experiential world. Tone, on the other hand, is the reflection *in the story* of the *author's* attitude. Though the New Critics do not have by any means a developed theory of experimental pattern, their technical distinction between atmosphere and tone is generically the same as that made by the Geneva critics.

When examining the experiential patterns which control a literary work, the Geneva critic approximates Husserlian methodology in a broad sense. So that these parallels can be cited with some exactitude, a short explanation of Husserl's phenomenological method is in order. The phenomenological reduction I have already mentioned is either accompanied or followed in proper Husserlian method by phenomenological intuition (*Anschauung*). Phenomenological intuition is not mystical insight, as the word in English suggests, but the careful scrutiny or observation of the individual phenomenon so one "sees" or pinpoints its essential structure. The phenomenological intuition is followed or accompanied by phenomenological typology, which is the exhaustive description of the phenomenon, using the results of the phenomenological intuition as the rubric of classification. For some phenomenologists, description functions as the verification, and indeed the only verification, for the correctness of the intuition. Since phenomena are gradually "constituted within consciousness," and this constitution follows laws of development, Husserl speaks of *stages of crystallization* of the phenomena.

A comparison of these procedures with those of Geneva criticism reveals what are several analogous practices. When Geneva critics study a given literary work for experiential patterns, they expect these patterns to operate as an organic network responsible for the work's unity. This organic network of patterns I shall call a work's "ensemble of experiential patterns." The Geneva critics speak of "scrutinizing" or "intuiting" the literary work, and their purpose is to obtain an at least tentative grasp of the work's ensemble. What is of special import here is that they regard a given work's ensemble of experiential patterns as its *essential structure*. The notion of intense scrutiny, and specifically that of focus on essential structure, parallel Husserl's phenomenological intuition of essential structure to a remarkable degree. Jean-Pierre Richard, for example, says the critical task is to focus on "the same *projet* which emerges from a deep investigation of essences."[68] J. Hillis Miller says that "through the juxtaposition of passages from widely separated points" in an individual novel, he exposes "the pervasive presence of a certain organizing form."[69] This "organizing form" embodies the "original unity" of the author's "creative mind."[70] The Geneva critic follows this intuition of essential structure with a practice quite analogous to Husserl's phenomenological typology. The major elements of the individual literary work are described, and the essential structure is used as the rubric of descriptive classification. Richard speaks of "words of crystallization" which coordinate the various "silhouettes" or "profiles" of a poem. Words of crystallization are multi-layered packages of meaning which recapitulate and "crystallize" the dominant motifs of a poem into one word. Through their careful description of experiential ensemble, Jean Rousset, J. Hillis Miller, and Roland Barthes (during his phenomenological period) maintain respect for the integrity of the individual work. These critics do not normally describe patterns common to the whole body of an author's writings until they have described his works singly. Georges Poulet and Gaston Bachelard, on the other hand, begin at once with a collective description. Taking a *vue globale*, they only pursue experiential patterns that move horizontally through an author's whole literary corpus. On this account (perhaps with some justification), Poulet and Bachelard have been accused of insensitivity towards individuated literary structure.

At its best, the exegesis of the Geneva School moves from individual work to a collective interpretation, and then back again to the single work, by way of an *interpretative circle*. The mechanics of the circle are simple enough. As the Geneva critic proceeds from work to work, scrutinizing each for its essential structure, he or she finds that some latent experiential patterns recur with great frequency. The meanings of these patterns remain the same throughout the collected works, even though their relationships to other experiential patterns vary from work to work (thus ensuring that each work has a unique ensemble of experiential patterns). Each scheme of recurrences in the literary corpus of an author I shall call a "system of experiential patterns." As an author's system of patterning begins to crystallize for the critic, he may find it sheds light on a particularly obscure pattern in any one given work; it may, indeed, illuminate the obscure pattern's relationship to the unique ensemble of that work. For effective models of the interpretative circle, one can look to Richard's treatment of Mallarmé's "Cantique de Saint Jean," "Au seul souci de voyager," "Si génuflexion toute," "Ses purs ongles très haut," "Igitur," and "Hérodiade."[71] Richard circles out from these towards a collective description of nocturnal experience in Mallarmé, and in turn uses this gradually abuilding system of experiential patterns as a further comment on individual poems.

In all fairness, I must point out that the Geneva School's interpretative circle is only an adept application of Schleiermacher's "Circle of Understanding" (the actual term is Dilthey's). The members of the Munich School came to apply it to the dialectic between "inner and outer form"; Martin Heidegger uses it to explicate the "to and fro" movement between understanding and interpretation; and Gabriel Marcel applies it to the relation between "notion" and "pre-notion." Leo Spitzer baptizes his version of it as the "philological circle." In *Die Kunst der Interpretation,* Emil Staiger sums up the formula well: "We have long learned from hermeneutics,—that we know the whole through its parts, and parts through the whole. Thus the hermeneutical circle, which today we can no longer call 'vicious.' "[72]

What I have said about the interpretative circle does not indicate the precise nature of collective interpretation, so I turn to this issue next. How does the Geneva critic scrutinize and describe a collective work's system of experiential patterns? Again, the best approach is to survey Husserl's classic phenomenological method, and cite parallels in Genevan practice. According to Husserl, the phenomenologist should undertake *eidetic intuition* after the first attempts at phenomenological intuition and typology have been completed. Eidetic intuition is preceded or accompanied by *eidetic reduction,* the deliberate exclusion of whatever is peculiar to only one phenomenon among a set of phenomena. Eidetic intuition *(Wesensschau)* is the "seeing" or pinpointing of *general essences* within the structures common to all phenomena in the set. Eidetic intuition is followed by *eidetic typology,* which describes elements of the phenomena in terms of the general essence. The Geneva critic's description of systemic experiential pattern is analogous to these eidetic procedures. Husserl's eidetic intuition seeks the general essence, that which is common to all or most members of a set. The Geneva critic setting out to discover a system of experiential patterns practices a like operation: the locating of experiential patterns that recur throughout the author's collected works. When the Geneva critic discriminates between systemic patterns and patterns which appear in only one unit, he or she approximates eidetic reduction. Richard explains Genevan intuition of general essence in the following way: "The locating [*repérage*] of themes is most ordinarily accomplished according to the criterion of recurrence; the major themes of a work, those which form its invisible architecture, and which then must deliver to us the key of its organization, are those which are found developed most often,—those which are met with a visible and exceptional frequency. Repetition, here as elsewhere, signals obsession."[73] This repetition builds a "multiplicity of lateral relations which create here the *essence* of meaning"[74] (the emphasis is Richard's). Jean Rousset, when explaining his own phenomenological method, indicates he is in quest of the "common essence" or "spiritual essence" of an author's collected works.

Husserl attaches some further qualifications to eidetic intuition. For Husserl, essence is not equivalent to appearance (as is the case in "phenomenalist" theory), but is immanent in appearances. Appearances are the "slanted views" (*Abschattungen*) through which an identical thing makes itself known. Thus Husserl warns the phenomenologist to pay special attention to "modes of appearing." This Husserlian distinction between appearance and essence parallels certain differentiations made by literary critics who work in the phenomenological tradition. The phenomenological critic carefully discriminates between surface configurations (configurations of imagery, rhythm, sound, and the other elements which belong to the explicit, literal, immediately observable level of language), and underlying experiential patterns. A latent experiential pattern (analogous to Husserl's "essence") is actualized (made manifest on the surface level) by a surface configuration (analogous to Husserl's *Abschattung*). The phenomenologist hastens to add that not all recurrences of that same surface configuration automatically mean that the experiential pattern is being actualized. Rather, a particular example of a surface configuration usually associated with a certain experiential pattern may not be an actualization, or may even be an actualization of another pattern. Furthermore, a likeness between two (or more) surface configurations does not necessarily mean they share the same essence. The decisive factor to be consulted by the critic as he evaluates each possible actualization is the overall context of the ensemble.

Another pitfall, says the phenomenologist, is the assumption that a given experiential pattern only manifests itself through one surface configuration. Actually, the opposite is commonly true: an experiential pattern assumes many different surface configurations as its "modes of appearing," though of course they will have some common likeness that makes them suitable as manifestations. All these qualifications which the phenomenological critic attaches to *analyse globale* can be aligned with similar qualifications Husserl attaches to his phenomenological method. The distinction between latent essence and likenesses operative only on the surface level is discussed in Richard's theoretical introduction.[75] While recurrence on the surface level is often an important signal for the discovery of essence (as he said above), this is not always the case: "Furthermore, the criterion of frequency is not the only one which permits the disengagement of a work's dominant themes. For repetition does not always have significant value; or it does not always signify the essential."[76]

Richard goes on to oppose the case of superficial recurrence to the latent likenesses which constitute essential value, or essence. At this point, Richard calls essence "the topological quality." When we recall the scientific definition of *topology*, we find the word is a very fine synonym for *essence:* topology is the study of those factors in geometric form which remain invariant despite the form's transformation. Richard says that topological qualities "situate their life at some neurological points . . . of inner space," and that they "can therefore cause the same organizing rules to penetrate into very diverse fields of the lived [*le vécu*]." He then provides examples. One demonstration is by way of Mallarmé's "crucial image of nudity." In Mallarmé's work, images of nudity are surface configurations (or appearances) which actualize sometimes one essence, and sometimes another; at times the essence is eroticism, and at other times the essence is "esthetic and metaphysical dream."

Much like Husserl, the Geneva critic follows or accompanies eidetic intuition with eidetic typology. The critic describes the major features of an author's collective work in terms of systemic experiential patterns. Essential typology is the forte of Geneva critics, and examples are available everywhere in their writing. I here cite examples from Georges Poulet's *La Distance intérieure* and *Etudes sur le temps humain*. In the essay of *La Distance intérieure* devoted to Balzac, Poulet describes a pattern which equates "movement toward future" with "physical thrusts forward." This systemic experiential pattern helps towards the constitution of Balzac's work, and is actualized by several types of surface configuration. Some of these are flying, swimming, traveling, projecting, and rushing forth. It is to be noted that these actualizations are not identical, even denotatively, on the surface level: an observer does not immediately associate flying with swimming. Yet the actualizations are alike, in that they are all physical thrusts forward. They all conform to the rubric of the latent pattern which controls them. A second example is found in the appendix on "Time and American Writers" attached to the English version of Poulet's *Etudes*. A systemic experiential pattern identifies the "perpetual present" characteristic of time-in-dreams with "imagery of sunken things." Among the configurations in Poe which are said to actualize this pattern are sleep (a "sinking" into unconsciousness), submergence into water, the motif of the "sunken city," and nocturnal imagery (a "sinking" into darkness). Again, these otherwise diverse images conform to the latent rubric of "sunken things," and the meaning it carries.

One may next ask how the Geneva critic breaks into a network of experiential patterns. In short, where does the critic begin? And according to what does he or she monitor experiential patterns? Once patterns are discovered, how does one organize the presentation of these to the reader? We find our answers, as is likely enough, in the common practice of the Geneva School. A review of Geneva criticism reveals that three methods of entrée into experiential pattern occur most frequently. In the literary work, experiential patterns of the (1) modes and (2) contents of consciousness are embodied in (3) language. Thus, one method of entrée utilizes the modes, another the content-categories, and a third, linguistics.

The first method, entrée and classification by way of the modes of consciousness, usually applies the modal categories we have already encountered (cognition, volition, emotion, perception, time [including memory], and space). Experiential patterns of a cognitive nature, for example, find demonstration in Jean Starobinski's treatment of Montesquieu. Montesquieu's style, in its "discontinous rapidity," its "way of outrunning foreseeable connection, while giving to the unexpected the dignity of a logical result, and while conferring on rigorous deduction the charm of the unforeseen,"[77] is interpreted as symbolic of certain cognitive patterns characteristic of Montesquieu's thinking. The fulcrum of the French *philosophe*'s cognitive patterns is said to be "a certain number of values which serve as a center of equilibrium." Their "solidity . . . counterbalances the free movement of liberated intelligence." Starobinski maintains that the outstanding characteristic of Montesquieu's cognition is tension, a series of taut polarities. Richard is famous for his phenomenological descriptions of the emotional mode. His *Littérature et Sensation* examines "Sentiments," "Shame," "Melancholy," and "Joy" in Stendhal; and "Desire," "Frenzy," "Cruelty," and "Shame" in Flaubert. The same book diagnoses perceptual patterns which involve "Music," detected by the auditory sense, and "Pliability" and "Stiffening," both tactilely sensed. Volitional patterns are represented by treatments of "Determinism" in Flaubert and "Liberty" in Fromentin. The temporal mode, or how each author "times" experience in his literary work, receives the attention of Emil Staiger's *Die Zeit als Einbildungskraft des Dichters*. Here "flowing Time" is found to characterize Clemens Brentano; "the Moment," or "Duration amidst change," is associated with Goethe; and "peaceful Time" with Gottfried Keller. Good examples of spatial experiential pattern appeared in Bachelard's *La Poétique de l'Espace*.[78] His critique explores spatial dimensions such as "the miniature," "intimate immensity," and "the dialectic of outside and inside"; and spatial formations such as "corners" and "the phenomenology of roundness." Bachelard describes both what is unique to each author's experience and what of it he shares with others.

The second method effects entrée and classification by way of the content-categories (World, Happenings, Others, and Self). Emil Staiger, for example, examines World in Brentano through analyses of "Landscape" and "Vortex," and in Keller through "Light" and "River." Paul Brodtkorb, in *Ishmael's White World,* treats World as generated by experiences of earth, air, fire, and water. Gaston Bachelard, in *Lautréamont,* devotes a whole chapter to "The Bestiary of Lautréamont." The content-category of Happenings is exemplified by Richard's study of "the Glance,"[79] and of "Assimilation" and "Levitation."[80] The third content-category, the category of Others (that is, other human beings), is the focus of phenomenological description in Brodtkorb's critique of Melville (see the chapter appropriately entitled "Others" in *Ishmael's White World).* In his *Sur Racine,* Roland Barthes describes "Father-figures"; and in *Die Kunst der Interpretation,* Emil Staiger treats Conrad Ferdinand Meyer's experience of "the Mother." The last content-category is Self, meaning that experience of selfhood one may have (or think one has) either reflectively (by making the self or supposed self the object of one's own intentional act), or prereflectively (by sensing one's selfhood while that selfhood is intentionally involved with something else). Thus George Poulet's essay on Mallarmé (in *La Distance intérieure)* discusses that poet's "miracle of self" and "knowledge of self"; and J. Hillis Miller, in his book on Dickens, describes that novelist's changing experience of selfhood.[81]

The third method accomplishes entrée and typology by way of linguistics. Sometimes this method relates stylistic features, and at other times morphological features, to latent experiential patterns. Jean-Paul Sartre, in a phenomenological section of his essay "A propos de John Dos Passos," provides us an interesting instance. He discusses the thematic significance of Time in Dos Passos, then circles down to a morphological feature he considers expressive of this theme, and finds in this feature a symbol of experiential pattern. Dos Passos's predilection for compound sentences in lieu of complex sentences is deemed revelative of an experiential pattern wherein Dos Passos's experience of Time is embodied. Sartre says: "For Dos Passos, narrating means adding. This accounts for the slack air of his style: 'and . . . and . . . and . . .' The great disturbing phenomena—war, love, political movements, strikes—fade and crumble into an infinity of little odds and ends which can just about be set side by side."[82] The concatenation of conjunctions, in other words, is a symbol of Time as a neutral 'addition' of isolated moments. Marcel Raymond sets another good example in his book *Senancour.* Raymond finds a preponderance of preterite forms in the context of references to primitive society. This morphological feature, interpreted in the light of theme and other intrinsic values, is seen as a symbol of experiantial pattern: for Senancour, the rustic ideal is experienced as irrevocably past.[83]

The above adjudications between semantic and morphology are typical of sound phenomenological practice. Though I shall treat the differences dividing phenomenology and Parisian Structuralism later, I do have the opportunity now to indicate one very important contrast. The phenomenologist first describes the semantic level (including, of course, experiential patterns which constitute a "deep semantic"). Only when this task is accomplished does he examine the grammatical level, and, by matching morphological form to the deep semantic already discovered, expose experiential patterns operative in the morphology. Because the structuralist considers semantic dependent on morphology (and not the other way around), he normally begins at the phonemic and grammatical levels, and extrapolates from these morphological features to semantic. Roman Jakobson, the structural linguist, avers: "Briefly, equivalence in sound, projected into the sequence as its constitutive principle, inevitably involves semantic equivalence. . . ."[84] Most phenomenologists seem to consider the structuralist approach much too risky. A literary work's grammatical form can suggest so many alternative readings of the semantic level that the critic's selection can easily be one of caprice. By beginning with the semantic, and then unearthing morphological patterns which match it, the probability of a valid correlation of the two levels is much increased.[85]

The above treatment of the three methods of entrée rounds out our survey of Geneva criticism. In conclusion, I cite some features of the Geneva approach which distinguish it from the various Anglo-American criticisms. In the theoretical sector, the Geneva School explains the presence of the author in the work by way of a new formula, and this formula attempts to satisfy both the expressionist and the aesthetic formalist. The dilemma which on the American scene has pitted the "New Critic" against the psychological critic can perhaps find resolution in and through phenomenology. In the area of critical practice, several contrasts with Anglo-American criticism are quite apparent. First, while seeking out recurring elements, the Geneva critic tries to classify images according to the rubric of latent essence rather than surface likeness. His is a "deep reading" which his New World counterparts would tend to label as "subjective" or "free associationist" (though he insists his criticism is intrinsic and describes what is really in the text). The Freudian and archetypal criticisms of the American tradition also examine the submerged implications of imagery and other factors, but as already suggested, tend to be aprioristic and extrinsic in their evaluations. Second, the Geneva critic addresses a different set of questions to the literary work. He may ask, for example, how an author smells love, hears sorrow, "spaces" time, and "times" space. Non-phenomenologists sometimes ask these questions, but usually they do so only at random. The Geneva critic, on the other hand, often works his way through the modes and content-categories of consciousness in systematic fashion. The nature of this systematization is in turn responsible for a third contrast with Anglo-American criticisms. A phenomenologist usually produces an interpretation which accounts for an author's collective work; the elements of this work are arranged according to their "inner dialectic," and not the chronology of authorship or publication. In short, the critic who operates in the Genevan tradition attempts to turn the critical screw a notch deeper. In so doing, the critic no doubt becomes more vulnerable, running a greater risk of interpretative error. The claim, however, is that this approach aims at the heart of poetry, and that such an enterprise is worth the risk. Non-phenomenologists may respond to this approach with outright hostility, or a gentler skepticism, or with interest and even approval. The Geneva critic will in any case provoke—provoke through sheer intellectual force. And provocation is a business of both literature and its criticism.

# chapter 3

# *Heideggerian Hermeneutics*

### *The Early Heidegger*

The very general and derived influence of Martin Heidegger on Geneva criticism I have already indicated. Temporality, non-conceptual knowing, and the regionalization of consciousness, three motifs associated with the Geneva School, redound in part from Heidegger's *Sein und Zeit* (1927).[1] Much more direct is Heidegger's effect on what I have called existentialist literary criticism. Identified with critics such as Erik Lunding, Max Bense, and Ludwig Binswanger, the Heideggerian version of existentialist criticism is in practice thematic (though some of the critics concerned would remonstrate this is not at all the case). Heideggerian Existentialism draws in large part from Heidegger's early phase, that of *Sein und Zeit,* and thus weighs its interest in favor of *Dasein* ("the human existent") rather than *Sein* ("the ground which is Being"). The existentialists working in the Heideggerian tradition describe fundamental structures of human existence, and often judge these in ethical terms. The Husserlians consider such inquiry a species of existential anthropology, and Binswanger himself labels the artistic writer "a seer of anthropological forms."[2] The thematic parameters for the study of existence are the *existentialia,* such as the "they-self" (to be distinguished from authentic Self) and Care (*Sorge*). Since they constitute modalities of *Dasein,* the *existentialia* have contributed much to Ludwig Binswanger's psychology of *Daseinanalyse.* The more famous topoi of *Sein und Zeit* include "being-towards-death," "the self-disclosure of *Dasein,*" and man's radical "historicity." Even some of the German terms have been assimilated into English academic language. Words that spring to mind at once are

*Jemeinigkeit* ("existence is one's own"), the *Mitwelt* ("one exists with others"), *Angst* ("dread without particular cause"), and *Entschlossenheit* ("resoluteness in the face of dread"). Of special attraction to literary theorists is the idea of *Rede,* or discourse which preludes spoken words and reveals being-in-the-world. Heidegger further develops this theme in his later phase, and we shall have occasion to examine it.

Ludwig Binswanger, the doctor who fathered *Daseinanalyse* as a psychiatric method, has also turned a skilled hand to literary criticism. Inspired by *Sein und Zeit,* he has postulated an "experiential circle" which he names *koinonia,* and which he applies to literary texts (and to clinical patients as well). Binswanger's adaptation of Heidegger demonstrates existentialist criticism at its best, so I will devote several paragraphs to it here. For Binswanger, *koinonia* is a kind of consciousness. Since imagination discloses consciousness, and since imagination controls literature, the latter can be effectively evaluated in terms of the "experiential circle." As I explicate below the three functions of *koinonia,* I shall take the liberty of applying them to English and American authors, since Binswanger works with European examples. First, the experiential circle regards selfhood and the outside (be that "outside" another person or a world of things) as participations in the same unified ontological field. The healthy person in day-to-day activity does not dichotomize consciousness into subject and objects. Rather, he or she experiences *Weltbild* ("world-design") as Heidegger's hyphenated being-in-the-world. That is to say, such a person places self and world on the same circumferential line, effortlessly circling from selfhood to the outside and back without objectifying the outside (or subjectifying the self).

In my opinion, Wallace Stevens sometimes rises to this first kind of *koinonia.* In the climactic third section of his poem "The Rock," he says, "Turquoise the rock, at odious evening bright / With redness that sticks fast to evil dreams. . . ." The "rock" symbolizes the field of consciousness, constituted at one and the same time by "turquoise," or subjectivity, and "redness," or objectivity. Stevens goes on to say, "The rock is the habitation of the whole, / Its strength and measure, that which is near, point A / In a perspective that begins again / At B. . . ." The "whole," or *koinonia,* orchestrates the self, "that which is near, point A," and the outside, the perspective "that begins again / At B," so that the two perspectives are one. *Koinonia* functions in a second way. Binswanger, in his essay entitled "Heidegger's Analytic of Existence and Its Meaning for Psychiatry," affirms "that corporeality only becomes body via the *koinonia* that links 'the soul' with that which is corporeal." Thus Binswanger defines melancholia "as a disturbance of the *koinonia* between the bodily and mental being of the *Dasein*."[3] *In nuce*, the second function of *koinonia* is to lock body and spirit together in the same overarching circle of experience. Though all healthy human life requires the unity of body and spirit, in the Western tradition it seems to me that the Christ figure exhibits this type of experiential circle most perfectly. T. S. Eliot, in "The Dry Salvages," chants that "the hint half guessed, the gift half understood, is / Incarnation." And Gerard Manley Hopkins tells us that the spiritual Christ, at one with human souls, interpenetrates human bodies: ". . . Christ plays in ten thousand places, / lovely in limbs, and lovely in eyes not his / To the Father through the features of men's faces." Christ identifies with the souls of men, and these Christified souls radiate towards the Father through human corporeality. In this dynamic movement, the bodies and souls of men become one.

The third function of *koinonia* is temporal. Heidegger explains that the structure of *Dasein* is Care, and the "meaning" of Care is temporality. Heidegger follows this thesis with a thorough discussion of temporality as such. In *Sein und Zeit* he puts the matter this way:

> Only an entity which, in its Being, is essentially FUTURAL so that it is free for its death and can let itself be thrown back upon its factical "there" by shattering itself against death—that is to say, only an entity which, as futural, is equiprimordially in the process of HAVING-BEEN, can, by handing down to itself the possibility it has inherited, take over its own thrownness and can be IN THE MOMENT OF VISION for "its time." Only authentic temporality which is at the same time finite, makes possible something like fate—that is to say, authentic historicality.[4]

Binswanger, in his own treatment of temporality, follows the same path: "Corresponding to all that we know of its thrownness . . ., the being-in-advance-of-itself of the *Dasein*, its futurity, is through and through implicated with its past. Out of both these temporal 'ecstasies' the authentic present temporalizes itself."[5] *Koinonia* integrates movement towards future (*Zu-kunft*) and implication with the past (*Geworfenheit*), so that both belong to the same experiential circle.

The American poet Hart Crane achieves on occasion a pure
and authentic *Dasein:* he becomes a *Dasein* which can (to repeat
Heidegger's words) "take over its own throwness and be IN THE
MOMENT OF VISION for 'its time.'" Listen to the last stanza of his
poem "Legend":

> Then, drop by caustic drop, a perfect cry
> Shall string some constant harmony,—
> Relentless caper for all those who step
> The legend of their youth into the noon.

The past, "the legend of their youth," projects towards an ideal
future, "some constant harmony." Past and future converge on
blazing "noon," the moment of vision. Hear also Crane's paean to
the Bridge, image of ecstatic human experience:

> And Thee, across the harbor, silver-paced
> As though the sun took step of thee, yet left
> Some motion ever unspent in thy stride,—
> Implicitly thy freedom staying thee![6]

Foregrounded against the sun, a symbol of temporality, the Bridge
strides from past towards future. Yet freedom stays the experience, so
the Bridge rests in a poised present. These passages from Crane
illustrate *Dasein*'s authentic experience of time. The human being
can impede or shatter temporal *koinonia,* however, and then neurosis sets its blockade. For one, *Dasein* (and Binswanger again uses
Heideggerian terminology) can "fall for" (that is, become bogged
down in) a distracting present. In my opinion, Hart Crane
represents this "falling for" when he speaks in his verse of "the
stacked partitions of the day . . . the memoranda, baseball scores, the
stenographic smiles and stock quotations," and of "the year broken
into smoking panels."

Secondly, *Dasein* can "fall back" into an entrapping past. I
adduce as my example here a stanza from Hart Crane's "North
Labrador." At the beginning of the poem, time solidifies into an
eternal preterite:

> A land of leaning ice
> Hugged by plaster-grey arches of sky,
> Flings itself silently
> Into eternity.

Glacial ice suggests the fixity of a life paralyzed by the past. Hugged by a sunless sky, the glacier has no present, but inches along in a kind of prehistory. The same inertia appears in the poem "The Bridge," when the old sailor admits "I don't want to know what time it is—that / damned white Arctic killed my time. . . ."[7] Binswanger also discusses *Dasein* in terms of "being-toward-death" and "resolvedness," but my purpose—to provide a sample of existentialist criticism—is, I think, achieved.

Before passing on to Heidegger's later phase, which has produced what I shall call a phenomenological ontology of literature, I would like to alert the reader to the presence of section 32 (entitled "Understanding and Interpretation") in *Sein und Zeit*. As we have seen, the Geneva School considers mutual implication of subject and object to be operative within the phenomenological ego of the literary text. But the school does not apply the same theory of mutual implication to the encounter between critic and text. On the contrary, the school expects the critic to "hand over" his or her personality to the text, so that the text (or more specifically, the phenomenological ego of the text) can "live" within the critic. The Geneva critic attempts to efface his or her own, independently active personality, and to submit this "reduced" personality to the controls exercised by the text alone. We shall see that in his practical criticism (which belongs exclusively to his later phase), Heidegger contributes his active personality to the encounter with text. His criticism is not objective; his criticism becomes "discourse" or "meditation." But nowhere in his later phase does Heidegger explain precisely how "discourse" works, perhaps because by this time he has decided that the workings of meditation are ineffable.

I have found, however, that the description of "Understanding and Interpretation" in *Sein und Zeit* fits the bill perfectly—at least for me. Moreover, Heideggerian critics have not really tapped the energy reserved in section 32; they have not applied its relevance to the questions which plague modern criticism. Does intentionality confer meaning on a text? Is this intentionality subject to signals embedded in the text? Or is meaning itself "built into" the text, so that the reader merely submits to it? Can disparate, or what is more, contradictory interpretations stand as simultaneously valid? How does "mutual implication" fit in here? Because these questions can be understood only in the light of my Part Two, I reserve treatment of Heidegger's section 32 for that part. I proceed now to a general treatment of Heidegger's last phase, since the latter establishes German phenomenological criticism—our main concern at present.

## The Later Heidegger

For Heidegger, the word *phenomenon* means "that which shows itself in itself," and the preposition *in* has great import because it suggests that the phenomenon must be "raised up" or brought forth from hiddenness. The word *phenomenology*, says Heidegger, derives from the Greek *phainomenon* ("phenomenon") coupled to the Greek *legein* ("to let-something-be-seen," or "to uncover"). He advances still further to say that "the meaning of phenomenological description as a method lies in *interpretation*. The *legos* of the phenomenology of *Dasein* has the character of a *hermeneuein*, through which the authentic meaning of Being, and also those basic structures of Being which *Dasein* itself possesses, are *made known* to *Dasein*'s understanding of Being. The phenomenology of *Dasein* is a *hermeneutic* in the primordial signification of this word, where it designates this business of interpreting."[8]

Because phenomena are not immediately manifest, they demand interpretation, that is, hermeneutical activity. As a consequence, Heidegger's version of phenomenology comes to be called hermeneutical phenomenology. Note that the above quotation also declares that the "meaning of Being" is "*made known* to Dasein's understanding of Being." When one learns what Heidegger had said a few sentences earlier, that "phenomenology is the science of the Being of entities—ontology," his intention becomes very evident. Hermeneutical phenomenology is ontological. *Dasein* is to be interpreted as a privileged manifestation of Being (*Sein*), which is the ground of all things-in-being (*Seienden*). Heidegger argues that ontology is to be distinguished from ontic study, since the latter examines things-in-being as discrete entities, and not as revelations of the "ground." Heidegger's ontology is also to be distinguished from the "objective hermeneutics" identified with Schleiermacher, Dilthey, and Betti, since Heidegger's version is a mutual implication of the interpreter and the interpreted (and comes to be called the "new hermeneutic"). The definition of phenomenology utilized above derives from Heidegger's early period, and he does not frequent the word *phenomenology* after the writing of *Sein und Zeit*. He speaks rather of "the Thought of Being." However, since his purpose becomes (even more in the later phase than in the early) the "announcing" of a "proximate but reserved" Being, we can conclude that, according to his own definition, he still believes himself to be engaged in a phenomenological enterprise.

At this crossroad, we must cope with the most vexatious question of all—what entitles a literary critic to the adjective *phenomenological?* Here I reveal myself as a pluralist. In my opinion, most of the internecine skirmishes between descriptive and hermeneutical phenomenologists, and between Geneva critics and Heideggerians, have no bearing on the issue. I call "phenomenological" any literary theory or practice which is broadly in the neo-realist Husserlian tradition (and even Heidegger fits here), as long as the theory or practice adheres to the following two provisions. First, it must incorporate somehow an epistemology of mutual implication, and second, it must "see" the essence of Being and/or beings concretely, and in experience. Because both the Geneva critics and those I shall call phenomenological ontologists fulfill the above conditions, I have included them in my book. On the level of surface configuration, and on that of the phenomenological ego, the Geneva School postulates mutual implication of self and outside. Moreover, Genevan practice cultivates the concrete; it caresses the image, and cherishes sound. Though the Geneva School sometimes calls itself "thematic," this just means that Geneva critics unravel motifs and sort them out (dialectically) in terms of what we have technically called "modes" and "contents." The school's preference for non-conceptual modes of consciousness secures appreciation of the concrete, since "abstract" patterns of experience belong to the conceptual mode alone. Genevan practice interlards commentary with passages quoted directly from the literary work under study, so that the poetic sensibility of critic and reader luxuriate in the form and language of the original text. And the techniques of phenomenological and eidetic intuition "take the sight" of experiential essence. The school's one shortcoming, as I have said, is its failure to apply neo-realist epistemology to the relationship between critic and text. Though demonstration would require a separate book-length treatment, I am convinced that Genevan appreciation of the text's "deep self" could be preserved while admitting true "discourse."

As for the Heideggerian approach, or rather the Heideggerian approaches, to literature, I must circumscribe in a general way what are several operating sectors, sometimes mutually exclusive and sometimes not. In the case of *Sein und Zeit*, the proposed *existentialia* are in my opinion speculative and non-phenomenological, so I would apply to them what I said earlier about Sartrean Existentialism. Other parts of *Sein und Zeit*, especially those which deal with hermeneutical theory (such as section 32) are really adduced from concrete experience, and are, according to my lights, genuinely phenomenological.

Unfortunately, the German literary critics who derive from *Sein und Zeit* use its non-phenomenological sequences. These critics even misconstrue Heidegger's professed intention, which in *Sein und Zeit* is to gain access to Being through *Dasein*. Instead, the critics tend to fabricate a *homo existentialis* who is isolated from Being and environment. What is more, these critics are "thematic" in the bad sense: they manipulate abstract labels, and disregard verbal texture. Heidegger's later phase is marked by a more direct encounter with Being as such: the existential structure of *Dasein*, even understood as a revelation of Being, no longer plays a dominant role. The description of *Dasein* yields place to the charting of ontological structures which transcend the human. In *Sein und Zeit*, Heidegger sketches the coordinates of human existence, with the purpose of adducing Being through them (though this purpose never achieves fulfillment; mysteriously, the second half of *Sein und Zeit* is never written). In his later period, Heidegger sketches the coordinates of Being, and *Dasein* becomes a transparent space.

In my opinion, parts of the late phase are phenomenological, and parts are not. The reader will have to decide whether language bespeaks Being more than it does the individual ego, and whether elemental forces such as Sky, Earth, Divinities, and Mortals can in fact "chart," with a show of adequacy, the concrete and experiential. Heidegger at his best during this period does emphasize the experiential "presence" and particularity of literature and its unique "workly being." Formulations such as these are clearly phenomenological. Sadly, the above emphases appear in his theoretical sequences, but not in his practical criticism. The closer Heidegger moves to the actual criticism of a text, line by line, the further he removes from a successful implementation of his theory (as we shall see). Hölderlin and Rilke may be phenomenological "seers," but Heidegger cannot in practice "call forth" the Being which "presences" in their poetry. At times the later Heidegger is a brilliant literary theorist; he is seldom an effective practical critic. The German critics who best apply his phenomenology are those I call the phenomenological ontologists—Theophil Spoerri and Johannes Pfeiffer. Spoerri shows how a *given text* is sentient, and how it is an event. And he shows, *textually*, how Heidegger's notion of "strife" is a kind of mutual implication, an "opening up" of concreteness. Pfeiffer, the least thematic of critics, treasures the phonic and formal elements of the literary work; he rightly criticizes the conceptuality of Heidegger's practical criticism, and replaces it with a *Wesensblick* (insight into Being) that is truly sensual.[9]

I proceed now to a programmatic description of Heidegger's literary theory. My synthesis of the theory will be brief, because the American audience already has at its disposal several good books and articles on the subject.[10] The import of Heidegger's own critical practice, however, has received little attention, probably because the aforesaid commentaries have been written by aestheticians rather than critics. Analysts have not interrogated the results (at Heidegger's hands, anyway) which issue from all this theory, and they have not asked whether the results are different from those afforded by more conventional approaches. Hence I append a section which attempts to close this lacuna. For the convenience of the English-speaking reader, I have limited my references to those essays of Heidegger which are available in translation, and which bear most directly on literary study. Two of the essays, "Remembrance of the Poet" and "Hölderlin and the Essence of Poetry,"[11] appear in Werner Brock's *Existence and Being* (a collection of translations from Heidegger, augmented by commentary).[12] Seven of the essays appear in Albert Hofstadter's *Poetry, Language, Thought,*[13] and are entitled "The Thinker as Poet," "The Origin of the Work of Art," "What are Poets For?," "Building Dwelling Thinking," "The Thing," "Language," and ". . . Poetically Man Dwells. . . ."[14]

We begin by opposing the theory of "representational truth" (truth as "correspondence") to that of "commemorative truth." The first theory, associated with traditional Western metaphysics, divides the epistemological field into subject and object, so that truth is a correlation of an idea in the subject's mind and a *donnée* belonging to the object. When Heidegger declares his "discourse" with literature does not contribute to "research in the history of art and to aesthetics" (B232), he means discourse does not treat the literary work as object. "Commemorative thinking" is a poetic and concrete disclosure of Being, and Being manifests itself in a pre-objective experience, that is, an experience which antedates the Cartesian split. Truth for Heidegger is not *veritas,* or a correspondence of subject and object, but *aletheia,* the "unconcealment" of Being. Being is the "ground" of beings, or better yet, the Being of beings. Since it cannot be adequated by conceptual terms, Heidegger studiously avoids a rigorous "definition." He does remind us, however, that "presence" is the "ancient name of Being"(H93). Later, in a meditation on Rilke's poetry, he says "only Presence itself is truly present—Presence which is everywhere as the Same in its own center . . ."(H123). Elsewhere, Heidegger calls the Being of beings the *vis primitiva activa* (the "primordial and active force"). Thus, when we think of Being we must expect not a hypostatic essence, but force "at work." I might add that the English language too preserves this insight, since the word Being is Be-ing, a gerundive and therefore verbal (and active) form. In the light of Heidegger's intention, even the word *Presence* is deceptive: better by far is it to say *Presencing*. Art when authentically understood is *aletheia*, or unconcealment, so art should not be treated as a substance with attributes, or a unified manifold impressed on the senses, or a synthesis of matter and form (these three formulations perpetuate the Cartesian fissure). Art is mankind "dwelling"— dwelling in the Presencing which is Being. Dwelling is a "home-coming," since through it mankind recognizes its "ground." Recognition is a commemoration, so true thinking is "commemorative thinking." Mankind's life-style should be a *Gelassenheit*, or a "letting be" of what *is*. Hearing this, any student of mysticism thinks at once of Juliana of Norwich, and of her dictum (popularized by T. S. Eliot): "All shall be well, and / All manner of things shall be well." Or one thinks at once of the *Fiat mihi* motif, Mary's words in the New Testament: "Let it be done unto me according to your word." Undoubtedly, Heidegger speaks in the mystical tradition. One may also notice he has coalesced the search for Being and the quest of Art. This confluence allows us to broach the first *leitmotiv* of Heideggerian esthetics (and I retain the word *esthetics*, understanding by it nothing more than "theory of art").

### LANGUAGE SPEAKS

The literary work, huddled in the midst of a technological age, is frail and elusive. The work is a *sanctum* to be "guarded" and held with a nestling Care. The way each literary text "presences" is unique in its concreteness and particularity. Thus Heidegger says, "The work belongs, as work, uniquely within the realm that is opened up by itself"(H41). But he also says "the art work opens up in its own way the Being of beings"(H39). The implication is that Being is infinite action, with the result that each text presences an activity of Being revealed nowhere else. The literary work is "originative"; that is, it does not *point to* Being (as a sign would); instead, within the text's own unique realm, the literary work *brings forth* Being (as a symbol does). Origin is not to be confused with temporal beginning, causal explanation, or logical determination. These three definitions of origin lure the critic away from the rightful concern, the text, and towards alleged but meretricious sources, such as the artist, spectator, or society. No, the literary work alone "shines," but the light it harbors is Being. Actually, Heidegger is suggesting another of his hermeneutical circles. Being is the origin of the work, in that Being is the primal ground which inaugurates the text, but the work is the origin of Being, in that the text "originates" a new and unique epiphany of Being—an epiphany no other work can ever duplicate.

Another way of putting this is to say that poetic language calls forth Being from out of the Stillness. As a "calling forth," the literary work is an action, a happening, a becoming. The literary "work" is just that: a "working." Art is a work-being, not an object-being, says Heidegger, and the failure to make this distinction has mislead literary consciousness for centuries. Poetic language speaks. Individual man does not. Poetic words are not tools, contrived to transmit information. In the essay "Language," Heidegger avers "language is neither expression nor an activity of man"(H197). In his essay "The Origin of the Work of Art," he says "the artist remains inconsequential as compared with the work, almost like a passageway that destroys itself in the creative process for the work to emerge"(H40). Later in the same essay, he remarks: "It is not the 'N.N. fecit' that is to be made known. Rather, the simple 'factum est' is to be held forth into the Open by the work: namely this, that unconcealedness of what is has happened here, and that as this happening it happens here for the first time; or, that such a work is at all rather than is not" (H65).

That the above contradicts the Geneva School should be quite evident. Even though the Geneva critic distinguishes the author's empirical ego from the text's phenomenological ego, the patterns of experience sublatent in the former "pass over" into the latter. In this sense, the author's "deep self" remains the *fons et origo* of his or her literature. For the Geneva School, the individual human speaks in person—that is, one's own selfhood (understood, of course, as a reciprocal relation of self and outside). For Heidegger, not an individual human, but language itself speaks. At first blush, one might think this akin to the Parisian Structuralist formula. But for the structuralist, language speaks itself—that is, it speaks its own structure, and its own structure alone. For Heidegger, language speaks Being. So we proceed to the second *leitmotiv.*

LANGUAGE SPEAKS BE-ING

Language utters Being, and the various existents (such as *Dasein* and *Seienden*) are prismatic rays, if you will, of this Being which "shines." Language speaks Being, and speaks as well the individual beings which are fractions of Being. Those individual beings which are human, and therefore constitute *Dasein,* are organically related to each other. Language, in speaking *Dasein,* must also tell of the relationships among human existents. For this reason, language founds human history. And history, for its part, is a "single conversation." Heidegger remarks:

> We are a conversation, that always means at the same time: we are a SINGLE conversation. But the unity of a conversation consists in the fact that in the essential word there is always manifest that one and the same thing on which we agree, and on the basis of which we are united and so are essentially ourselves. Conversation and its unity support our existence (B278).

Note, however, that he follows so assertive a statement with a warning:

> Where there is to be a SINGLE conversation, the essential word must be constantly related to the one and the same. Without this relation an argument too is absolutely impossible. But the one and the same can only be manifest in the light of something perpetual and permanent. Yet permanence and perpetuity only appear when what persists and is present begins to shine (B278).

Language is a single conversation only when it bespeaks the "one and the same," the "perpetual and permanent"—that is, Being. Objective language, be it that of the scientist or logician, or that of the hackneyed everyday world, is not authentic utterance at all. Heidegger adds, "Only after 'ravenous time' has been riven into present, past and future, does the possibility arise of agreeing on something permanent" (B279), and only literature can really do this. In "What Are Poets For?" Heidegger describes the semantic function of poetic language:

> Language is the precinct (*templum*), that is, the house of Being. The nature of language does not exhaust itself in signifying, nor is

it merely something that has the character of sign or cipher. It is because language is the house of Being, that we reach what is by constantly going through this house (H132).

The formulation above strikes middle ground between the radical structuralist position and that of the more conventional linguistic schools. For a pure structuralist, written or spoken words (*paroles*) refer only to each other and do so through couplings of sound and sense determined by the grammar and lexic of a people's language (*langue*). The system of language (which is a "bank" of arbitrary correlations between sound and sense) is thus self-enclosed and does not recognize reference to the real world. On the other hand, conventional linguistics has interpreted language as "sign or cipher" (to use Heidegger's words) and has considered language referential: words point to the real world, and according to some linguists, even correspond to the real form of that world. Martin Heidegger denies that poetic language is referential in the ordinary sense, that of pointing towards the outside. But (unlike the Parisian Structuralists) he does not exclude referentiality in a broader sense, that of language referring to a pre-linguistic world. For Heidegger, language refers to Being, but not by pointing at it. Rather, language refers to Being by making it "present" within words. Heidegger takes the "outside" and brings it "inside" the house of language. Thus the import of his words, "It is because language is the house of Being, that we reach what is by constantly going through the house." Being, the "what is," is pre-linguistic, but we reach the "what is" by "going through" the "house," namely, language. Language is not Being, but is the house of Being.

### LANGUAGE SPEAKS BE-ING AS WORLD AND THING

The third *leitmotif* concerns the nature of the "what is." In the nine essays that constitute our source material, Heidegger uses the terms *Earth* and *World* in different senses at different times. Likewise, the words *rift, striving, intimacy, penetration,* and *difference,* and the idea of mutual implication they all denote, are placed sometimes at one place in the ontological scheme, and sometimes at another. I offer here a synthesis which, I believe, is faithful to Heidegger's thought. The Being that is "one and the same" refracts itself into "World" on the one hand, and "Things" on the other. The world is the World of *Dasein,* but *Dasein* is understood as the intersection of four powers (*das Gevierte*) which transcend individual man. Heidegger provides a description of this "Fourfold" (Earth, Sky, Divinities, and Mortals) in the essay, "The Thing." Earth is not earthly things, but the matrix which supports earthly things: "Earth is the building bearer, nourishing with its fruits, tending water and rock, plant and animal" (H178). Sky is not atmospheric things, but the celestial field against which these things are foregrounded: "The sky is the sun's path, the course of the moon, the glitter of the stars, the year's seasons, the light and dusk of day, the gloom and glow of night, the clemency and inclemency of the weather, the drifting clouds and blue depth of the ether" (H178). Divinities are personified supernatural forces (such as Wisdom, Providence, and Love); Divinities "are the beckoning messengers of the godhead" (H178). And finally, "mortals are human beings. They are called mortals because they can die. . . . Death is the shrine of Nothing. . . . As the shrine of Nothing, death harbors within itself the presencing of Being" (H178,179). What is more, the Fourfold powers "mirror" each other and "belong" to each other:

> Earth and sky, divinities and mortals—being at one with one another of their own accord—belong together by way of the simpleness of the united fourfold. Each of the four mirrors in its own way the presence of the others. Each therewith reflects itself in its own way into its own, within the simpleness of the four. This mirroring does not portray a likeness. The mirroring, lightening each of the four, appropriates their own presencing into simple belonging to one another (H179).

Counterbalancing the World of *Dasein* and its Fourfold is the realm of Things as things (*Seienden* again). Things as things are the actual rocks, waters, and plants. Things are sustained by the Fourfold but different from them. Between the World of *Dasein* and Things is the "rift" (*Riss*), also called the "dif-ference." At this juncture Heidegger puts a theory of mutual implication to brilliant employ. He is not speaking of the exchange between individual self and outside (as the Geneva School does), nor is he speaking here of the Heideggerian discourse between critic and text. Rather, he applies the theory to the involution of Things and the World of *Dasein*. He describes their mutual implication as follows:

> For world and things do not subsist alongside one another. They penetrate each other. Thus the two traverse a middle. In it, they are

at one. Thus at one they are intimate. The middle of the two is intimacy—in Latin, *inter*. The corresponding German word is *unter*, the English *inter-*. The intimacy of world and thing is not a fusion (H202).

The dif-ference is neither distinction nor relation. The difference is, at most, dimension for world and thing. But in this case "dimension" also no longer means a precinct already present independently in which this or that comes to settle. The dif-ference is THE dimension, insofar as it measures out, apportions, world and thing, each to its own. Its allotment of them first opens up the separateness and towardness of world and thing. Such an opening up is the way in which the dif-ference here spans the two. The dif-ference, as the middle for world and things, metes out the measure of their presence. In the bidding that calls thing and world, what is really called is: the dif-ference (H203).

What role does literature play in this context? In poetry, says Heidegger, "the poem bids the things to come which, thinging, bear world." And the poem "bids that world to come which, worlding, grants things" (H203). A simple way of putting this is to say that literature concretizes the "dif-ference." And how does the dif-ference obtain? It obtains because at bottom the World of *Dasein* and the realm of Things as things are both orchestrated by Being, and Being is One: "The ground of beings has since ancient times been called Being. The relation of Being which grounds to the beings that are grounded, is identical for man on the one hand, plant and beast on the other" (H101). I said earlier that *das Gevierte* is a fourfold power which functions like an "energy field," and silhouetted against this "field" is "thing as thing." Now let us look a bit more closely at the dialectic of part and whole, of foregrounded thing and backgrounding power. Heidegger chooses as his practical example a jug, a vessel of clay. He makes clear from the beginning that the carefully crafted jug is a work of art, so that what he says about it can apply analogously to all esthetic works. First, he notices that the vessel is a self-sustaining thing. He remarks "the thingly character of the thing does not consist in its being a represented object. . . . The jug remains a vessel whether we represent it in our minds or not" (H167). Second, "the jug's thingness resides in its being *qua* vessel." The jug, in other words, is a "holding." Holding is not really accomplished by the jug's bottom and sides, but "by the jug's void," or inner space. The potter who forms the bottom and sides "does not, strictly speaking, make the jug."

At this point I am compelled to intervene, and to quote from David Steindl-Rast, a specialist in Buddhism:

> You point, in the West, to a vase or an ash tray and ask: 'What is this?' No matter how manifold the answers you receive, they will generally conceive of the thing as a certain material formed in a particular way: glass pressed or blown into a certain shape, clay shaped on a potter's wheel, fired and glazed. Of course, it never occurs to us that someone's bent of mind could be so different that the answer centers with the same directness on the empty space of our vase or dish. Surprise. 'Empty space? Is that all?' 'Well, of course, the emptiness has to be defined by this shape or that. But this is less important. What really matters is the emptiness of the vessel. Isn't this what makes it a vessel?'[15]

No wonder now that Heidegger admires the Eastern mystical tradition! But back to Heidegger's description.

Heidegger goes on to speak further of the vessel's space. He asks, "And yet, is the jug really empty?" The function of the jug's space is "taking and keeping," "giving and outpouring." The space can hold water or wine, and these can be taken as drink or given to the gods as libation. Water and wine are things, but they evoke the Fourfold:

> The spring stays on in the water of the gift. In the spring the rock dwells, and in the rock dwells the dark slumber of the earth, which receives the rain and dew of the sky. In the water of the spring dwells the marriage of sky and earth. It stays in the wine given by the fruit of the vine, the fruit in which the earth's nourishment and the sky's sun are betrothed to one another. In the gift of water, in the gift of wine, sky and earth dwell. But the gift of the outpouring is what makes the jug a jug. In the jugness of the jug, sky and earth dwell (H172).

The water and wine can also be "libation poured out for the immortal gods." Water and wine can evoke mortals and divinities. "In the gift of the outpouring," says Heidegger, "earth and sky, divinities and mortals dwell together ALL AT ONCE." The jug, as work of art, gathers together Things as things on the one hand, and the fourfold powers on the other. The work of art *is* mutual implication. The work of art is "dif-ference."

The Heideggerian dialectic of part and whole finds a place, then, for the individuated thing, which as "part" discovers the "whole" which is Being. The dialectical also finds a place for the individuated art work, which, though just a part, gathers into itself the "whole" of Being (and this "gathering" is a mutual implication of Things and the Fourfold). But, curiously, Heidegger seldom finds a place for the individual human being. It seems to me that literature permits discussion of individuality in two ways: one can discuss the individuality of the author who writes the work and possibly "presences" himself or herself therein, and one can discuss the individuality of a character who may appear in the work but need not be confounded with the writer. Let us consider the second alternative first. Neither in his theoretical passages nor in his practical criticism does Heidegger make mention of individual characters. He mentions "mortals," of course, but as a collective Power. He mentions the World of *Dasein*, but as a corporate space where the Fourfold converge. He describes the World of *Dasein*, calling it the "perpetually altering circuit of decision and production, of action and responsibility" (B276). He describes the World of cultural *Dasein*, calling it "the historical being of the German people" (B268). He even describes the Poet as type, calling him one who "names the gods and names all things in that which they are" (B281). But Heidegger nowhere describes the singular experience of one human character. The closest he comes is in "The Origin of the Work of Art," when he examines the "peasant shoes" in Van Gogh's famous painting. Even here, however, he adverts not to an individual peasant, but to a type—the collective "*world* of the peasant woman."

Now let us consider the first alternative, discussion of the author's individuality. Here we must filter out Heidegger's theoretical statements from his practical exegesis. His theory declares that the poet is "one who has been cast out—out into that BETWEEN, between gods and men" (B288). The poet intercepts the signs of Being, and hearkens to the "voice of the people" (B287). So far Heidegger sounds like a German romantic, trumpeting the priestly role of the vatic seer. But again and again Heidegger insists that the author, once he has completed the literary text, effectively disappears. The author has been a conduit which receives Being, delivers it to the written word, and then self-destructs. History leaves to the "hearers" the task of meditating on the text and "preserving" it, so that discourse between work and society develops. Thus the poet is just a vehicle in the first place, and a nonentity in the second. The practical criticism, though, strikes quite a different note. Here is the jarring discordance in Heidegger, one which we shall soon examine in greater detail. It suffices now to say the practical criticism does not isolate text from author; the criticism views the literary work in terms of the author's individuated *Lebenswelt*. Even biographical facts and such things as private correspondence are diligently consulted. What is more, the whole timbre of the criticism bespeaks a theory of immanence. Heidegger behaves as if Hölderlin, Rilke, and the other sayers are still present and speaking, speaking from out of the text.

I close this reconnaissance of Heidegger's literary theory with two other *puncta*. The first is that Being (identified in the essay "Remembrance of the Poet" with God, or the "Most Joyous") is a mystery, and is *proximate, yet reserved*. Heidegger avers "the essence of proximity seems to consist in bringing near the Near, while keeping it at a distance. Proximity to the source is a mystery" (B259). In this context, one thinks at once of Moses unable to face the brilliancy of Yahweh, and of the many variants of this motif in other myths. Any attempt to "objectify" God (objectification is bound to fail anyway) is a failure to "reserve" Him or keep Him at a distance:

> But now if homecoming means becoming at home in proximity to the source, then must not the return home consist chiefly, and perhaps for a long time, in getting to know this mystery, or even first of all in learning how to get to know it. But we never get to know a mystery by unveiling or analysing it; we only get to know it by carefully guarding the mystery AS mystery (B259).

The good poem embarks on a delicate enterprise which must cradle but not crush the divine message:

> In order therefore that the reserving proximity to the Most Joyous may remain guarded, the poetic word must take care that what sends greeting out of the Joyous (but sends greeting as the Self-Reserving), must now be too precipitate or become lost (B261).

What has just been said of Being applies analogously to all beings: "Each being we encounter and which encounters us keeps to this curious opposition of presence in that it always withholds itself at the same time in a concealedness" (H53). Again, the poetic word must "bring near the Near," but not too near.

The second *punctum* is a disheartening one. It is one thing to name, most carefully, a God who is proximate but reserved. It is quite another thing not to know the name of God at all. Modern man often does not know God's name. Heidegger echoes the lament of Hölderlin, ". . . Holy names are lacking" (B263). Heidegger calls this situation the "Default" (H91) of God. The modern poet lives in a "destitute time." Heidegger sounds strangely like Michel Foucault, who likewise reminisces of past Golden Ages when the Divine was known. Unlike Foucault, however, Heidegger regards the Default of God as a temporary situation, since God is a positive Nothingness (as in Mahayana Buddhism, I might add), and not a negative Nothing (as in Hinayana):

> The default of God and the divinities is absence. But absence is not nothing; rather it is precisely the presence, which must first be appropriated, of the hidden fullness and wealth of what has been and what, thus gathered, is presencing, of the divine in the world of the Greeks, in prophetic Judaism, in the preaching of Jesus. This no-longer is in itself a not-yet of the veiled arrival of its inexhaustible nature (H184).

Here my explication of Heideggerian theory ends, and I proceed to an evaluation of the practical criticism.

In our nine sources, Heidegger interprets the poetry of Hölderlin (in "Remembrance of the Poet," "Hölderlin and the Essence of Poetry," "What Are Poets For?," and "Poetically Man Dwells . . ."), that of Rilke (in "What Are Poets For?"), of Trakl (in "Language"), and C. F. Meyer (in "The Origin of the Work of Art"). The most significant quality of this practical criticism is its neo-realist epistemology. Criticism is a pre-objective dialogue between critic and text: hermeneutics "will lead thinking into a dialogue with poetry, a dialogue that is of the history of Being" (H96). This will be the case even if "scholars of literary history inevitably consider that dialogue to be an unscientific violation of what such scholarship takes to be the facts." Authentic criticism, says Heidegger, is "an exercise in poetic reflection," (H100) so that Being manifests itself in the engagement or mesh of hermeneut and poem.

But what about some practical examples of this engagement? I recommend that the reader consider the following instances. First, there is Heidegger's treatment of the beginning lines in Hölderlin's poem, "To Kindred Ones" (B236). The poem begins, "There amid the Alps it is still bright night and the cloud, / Writing of the Joyous, covers the night within the yawning valley." Exceeding the "facts" provided by the poem taken as object, Heidegger raises the image "cloud" to the status of an allegorical figure: the "cloud" becomes a symbol of the archetypal poet (B247-250). The "Alps" come to represent "proximity to the source," and the "Joyous" stands as the Heideggerian ground which is Being. Hölderlin's text, taken by itself, does not provide these correlations between image and value (though the text permits them). Werner Brock, Heidegger's English translator here, is constrained to recognize the unorthodoxy of correlations such as these. In the introduction, Brock notes that Heidegger, of his own initiative, imputes values to imagery. Brock says that the mutual implication of Heidegger and text is so fluid that it would be "senseless to try to analyze what is Hölderlin's and what Heidegger's in this dual unity. Yet, in a repeated reading one finds sometimes the one, sometimes the other stepping forth" (B178). An associated theme in Heidegger, one that seems at first blush to contradict his theory of hermeneutical "discourse," declares the following: ". . . the most difficult step of every exposition consists in vanishing away together with its explanations in the face of the pure existence of the poem"(B234). Actually, Heidegger is alluding here to what I shall call in Part Two "Heideggerian authenticity." That the latter does not contradict a theory of mutual implication will become clear when the reader meets my discussion of the matter in said part.

As a second example of mutual implication, again in the essay on "To Kindred Ones," the reader may consult Heidegger's gloss of the "High Ones" (B241). According to Heidegger, the "High Ones" constitute a trinity of powers (and without doubt, Heidegger's model here is the Christian Trinity): "At one and the same time it [the Serene, or the Holy Ones] is the clarity (*claritas*) in whose brightness everything clear remains, and the highness (*serenitas*) by whose strength everything high stands firm, and the joyfulness (*hilaritas*) in whose play every liberated thing hovers" (B251). In the poem concerned, Hölderlin nowhere speaks of such a trinity (keep in mind the Latin words in parentheses are Heidegger's own): the trinitarian values are projected upon imagery which seems neutral in the face of so theological a formulation. A third example, also from the same essay, is a very unexpected interpretation of the following lines: "Far on the level of the lake was one joyous undulation / Beneath the sails . . ." (B238). The text speaks only of a burst of wind which sends the sails into billowing movement, but Heidegger glosses the lines as follows: ". . . and beneath the wings of the vessel that carries him off, there appears the Joyous" (B255). The joyous undulation of the sails develops into a full-fledged apparition of the divine Joyous. I think I have made my point. Hermeneutical discourse causes the critic to make an active contribution to the meaning of the text.

Though Heidegger's practical criticism clearly employs a

theory of mutual implication, and is to this extent phenomenological, a fatal problem is at hand. The second litmus test for
phenomenological criticism, you will recall, demands the "seeing"
of essence concretely and in experience. And in the case of
Heidegger's practical criticism, the test proves negative. Heidegger
for the most part speaks not of symbolism (wherein meaning is
concrete and nuanced), but of allegory (wherein meaning is abstract
and constant). Since Heidegger ignores verbal texture, his discourse
with the text is not concrete discourse. On the contrary, his practice
is thematic in the bad sense. One would think that notions such as
the Fourfold and Thingness (so attractive in Heidegger's theoretical
work), would produce a new and original kind of archetypal
criticism. Unfortunately, Heidegger's critical practice at its worst is
merely allegorical, and at its best is archetypal in a very conventional way (see his exegesis of Trakl). In short, Heidegger's practice
does not even make a contribution to the archetypal criticism which
has long been a mainstay of the literary establishment, both
Continental and Anglo-American.

Heidegger misses another opportunity, too. He does not demonstrate *in concreto* what is one of the most fertile of his theories, the
"workly being" of the literary work. He dismisses formal considerations, though surely form must play a prominent role in "workly
being." He likewise shunts beauty aside, granting only (and
begrudgingly) that "Beauty is one way in which truth occurs. . . ."
In his literary theory, Heidegger had insisted on the radical absence
of the author from the completed literary work. But in practice,
Heidegger consistently adduces the author's biography, notebooks,
and private correspondence to illuminate the text. For example, he
quotes a letter of Rilke to determine the meaning of the term *the
Open* in the eighth Duino Elegy (H107, 108). He does the same to
establish the meanings of the terms *being* and *the other draft* in
relation to another poem by Rilke, this one untitled (H124). A few
pages later, he does the same again to gloss the meaning of Rilke's
term *Worldly* (H128). And he maintains this practice as fixed policy
throughout his exegesis. Though his theory had repudiated the
expressive function of language, Heidegger leaves no doubt that
biographical facts are essential for an understanding of Hölderlin's
"Remembrance of the Poet," for example, (B243) and, more importantly, that the poetry of Hölderlin, Rilke, and the others must
be identified with their respective biographical voices. Hence, when
paraphrasing a poem, Heidegger consistently says "Rilke speaks

(H128)," or "Hölderlin spoke (B282)" and not "the poem says" or
"Being speaks."

A comparison of Heideggerian hermeneutics and the Geneva
School now assumes pertinence. An appraisal of their respective
critical practice reveals that both approaches treat an author's
collective work cross-sectionally: Heidegger on the one hand and the
Geneva critics on the other both pursue images and ideas laterally,
arranging an author's world-view in dialectical fashion, and usually
without regard for the integrity of single poems as such. Besides
the difference between the Geneva School's objective stance and
Heidegger's pre-objective one, another difference is that Heideggerian hermeneutics is ultimately metapersonal. Even though
Heideggerian practice (as opposed to the theory) dwells in the
enverbalized *Lebenswelt* of the author, the latter's inner space is the
intersection of transcendental forces (the Fourfold, Things, and
finally Being). If we wish to locate Heidegger within traditional
conventions, we must conclude his practice is "philosophical
criticism." Thus he is very selective, much more so than the Geneva
School, because he must limit himself to poetry which accommodates Being as his theory understands it. One wonders what
Heidegger would or could do when explicating an absurdist author,
for instance. A comparison of Heideggerian literary theory and
Genevan theory shows an even wider breach than exists between the
two critical practices. In theory, Heidegger denies the enverbalized
presence of the author. For the Geneva School, the poet still *uses*
language; in Heidegger, language is not used, but *speaks* of its own
accord. Heideggerian theory is metapersonal. Is it also "ideological," as I have defined the term? In my opinion, no—simply because
I believe Heidegger's theoretical insight into Being (as opposed to
his practicing insight) is a specimen of concrete thinking, and is
valid. In other words, I concur that the Fourfold and the realm of
Things are not products of speculation, but are concretely intuited
essences. Heidegger, of course, insists on this, and says his
comprehension of essences is not conceptual, but "opens itself up"
through and only through poetic naming.

In this context it is worth noting that Heideggerian Being is not
limited to the present and the actual: "Nor is Being in any way
opposed to being-no-longer and being-not-yet . . . possibility
belongs to Being just as much as do actuality and necessity" (H183).
The fact remains, however, that Heideggerian Being is absolute, and
cannot accommodate a "possible world" where Reason dominates

(as in Diderot) or the Absurd is articulated (as in Beckett). Since it is personal rather than metapersonal, the Geneva School is basically relativist; Heideggerian hermeneutics, in contradistinction, is absolutist. Since the Western world of the twentieth century is pluralist, even promiscuously so, it seems to me that the Geneva School is ultimately more useful to Western society than Heideggerian hermeneutics. To sum up, I believe Heidegger's philosophy is true, but I realize full well that most people don't agree with this Truth—so I am compelled to conclude Geneva criticism is more serviceable.

A final consideration involves the impact of Heideggerian thought on the Anglo-American literary world. The most important influence, already well in progress, is not on literary criticism but on aesthetics (monopolized in America by philosophers rather than professors of literature), and on linguistics (which in America is also a separate discipline, effectively isolated from literature). Empirical science, arch-enemy of hermeneutics, has already had Anglo-American aesthetics and linguistics in tow for decades. American aestheticians have not faced up to the simple is-ness of the poem, but have treated the latter as just another sign, pointing variously at the author, the world, and the reader. The aestheticians and linguists have indulged in all sorts of "correspondence theory," and have not recognized literature as "commemorative." Anglo-American literary critics, on the other hand, have followed good instincts. American "New Criticism" in particular has appreciated and even sacralized the uniqueness and the concrete nature of the literary work. And American "New Criticism," like Heideggerian theory, has excluded the empirical author from the text. W. K. Wimsatt's analogy of the literary work and sacramental activity is very much to the point: the poem, like a sacrament, is a symbol which "presences" what it symbolizes. This is as good a formula as any in Heidegger, and says much the same thing he does. Unfortunately, Anglo-American critics in general are atheoretical, and it is in the area of supportive theory that Heidegger can make his best contribution here. The intuitions of recent American criticism have been valid, but Heidegger proffers an articulated theory which can sustain them. What can Heidegger offer that is really new to American criticism? One contribution can be to theory of the symbol. Anglo-American critics recognize the literary work as symbol, but as symbol of what? What does the literary work "presence"? "Felt life" is not a sufficient answer. If the Anglo-American critic could accept Heidegger's

ontology, quite an advance would be made. But let me leave the last
word to Heidegger himself:

> The poetic character of thinking is still veiled over.
> Where it shows itself, it is for a long time like the utopism of a
>     half-poetic intellect.
> But poetry that thinks is in truth the topology of Being.
> This topology tells Being the whereabouts of its actual
>     presence (H12).

# chapter 4

# *Phenomenology Confronts Parisian Structuralism*

The phenomenological philosopher Paul Ricoeur tells us in his *Le Conflit des interprétations* that "structural linguistics proceeds from a decision of epistemological character, that of holding itself to the interior of the enclosure of the universe of signs; in virtue of this decision, the system has no outside; it is an autonomous entity of internal dependencies. But this is a methodological decision which does violence to the linguistic experience."[1] For this and other reasons, structuralism "loses the sense of its limits."[2] It seems fitting to broach our present topic with a discussion of phenomenological versus structuralist definitions of language. I advise the reader that phenomenology in this chapter is identified most often with that of the Geneva School and that of French philosophers compatible with the school. Since Parisian Structuralism is a French movement, the confrontation for the most part has been with French phenomenologists rather than Heideggerians. We start, then, with Paul Ricoeur and his definition of the verbal sign.

Ricoeur accepts Ferdinand de Saussure's original distinctions: *langage* is composed of *langue* (the institution of language, the ensemble of linguistic habits which permit a subject to understand and be understood) and *parole* (particular and individual acts of linguistic expression). But he accuses the structuralists of wrongly subordinating *parole* to *langue:* "The phonological level, the lexical level, the syntactic level . . . these levels constitute the dead part of language."[3] Furthermore, structuralism "loses the sense of its limits" because it treats *parole* solely in terms of *langue. Parole* for the structuralists is only a particular combination of elements drawn from the *combinatoire.* For Ricoeur, on the other hand, *parole* is a "mediating act" which necessarily involves reference. Let us survey in serial order how Ricoeur builds his case. At the outset he posits that the problem of language is ultimately the problem of meaning. He goes on to say it is on the level of the sentence that we first have meaning:

> We might suppose that the problem of meaning belongs to the lexical level of our language, but this is not so inasmuch as we cannot say that a word in the dictionary has a meaning, not only because it has several meanings . . . but also because in fact the word is not yet a meaning . . . it is merely a value, and a differential value. Only in relation to the sentence, in position within a sentence, does a word itself have a meaning.

This meaning is not so much generated as it is evoked:

> In the sentence we experience language not as an object, not as a closed system, but as a mediation. . . . We recapture here the essential function of language, which consists of saying something about something. In the sentence and through the sentence language escapes [transcends] itself toward what it says. It goes beyond itself and disappears and dissolves into its intentional referent.

For this reason, even the distinction between signifier and signified depends on reference:

> . . . sign loses its significance as a sign if it loses its external transcendent relation . . . we could not define a sign as the difference between the significant [signifier] and the significate [signified] if there were not the reference. It is the reference which differentiates, so to speak, the sign in its own unity.

Finally, Ricoeur addresses what presents itself as an immediate objection to his formula. Simply put, some sign-networks have a sense ("object of thought") but no referent (real object in the world): "For example, if I speak of the heavenly body which is farthest from the earth, for a physicist there is no such body, or at least I cannot determine such a body." Ricoeur answers that, even in a case such as this, the thrust of the language-act pushes beyond the sense, toward the reality. Indeed, he says the sense-without-reference situation is only the extreme form of all sign situations. Sign can never be perfectly fulfilled, since knowing is "by nature perspectival, incomplete." Perfect fulfillment of sign by referent is an ideal toward which the language-act moves. What is important to the phenomenological position here, however, is precisely that the language act is movement toward referent.

What about the role of subjectivity in the language-act? The Geneva School links language not only to the objective referent in the world but also to the subjectivity which is speaking. The phenomenologist Serge Doubrovsky explains it most succinctly: "Whenever something is said, someone must be saying it."[4] Or, if we use Ricoeur's formulation, "the display of a world and the positioning of an ego, are symmetrical and reciprocal."[5] Though Ricoeur, pressured by the opposition of the structuralists, has a more technical definition of the subject-object relation than did the generation of phenomenologists preceding him, the basic formula of Merleau-Ponty still applies: for the phenomenologist, meaning (in and through language) arises from the action, or more precisely the interaction, between self and world. Meaning is densest and richest in literary discourse. This is so because literary language can best embody non-conceptual as well as conceptual intentionality. Intentionality is by its very nature unique to the *Lebenswelt* of the individual speaker, since each person's self-world relations are unique. It is through the intentionality unique to any given author, and present in the language of that author, that he is present in his literary work. In fact, language does not only embody intentionality; language is an extension of the author's intentional field. Language becomes a vital theater of exchange through which the author interacts with world.

That all this clashes with the pronouncements of the Parisian Structuralist, Roland Barthes, is at once apparent. Whereas for Ricoeur the sign consists of signifier, signified, and referent, the sign for Barthes is composed of signifier and signified alone. Nor is there any chance that Barthes's signified includes reference to the real. When Barthes takes up a discussion of the "degree of 'reality' " of the signified, he says the signified "can be defined only within the signifying process, in a quasi-tautological way"[6] He concludes that "in this way we are back again to a purely functional definition. . . ." Remember that, in Ricoeur, discourse is the vital movement of elements of language toward the world. In Barthes, discourse is not substantial fulfillment, but rather an instrumental, and one senses, a purely ancillary kind of exercise. The speech act is made up of selection (the combining of words) and actualization (the "psycho-physical mechanisms" whereby the combinations are exteriorized). In the case of literary language, Barthes restricts the focus still more. Not only is there no operating referent; even the signified is diminished in importance. In an often-quoted passage, he tells us "it is the attention given to the organization of signifiers which founds a true critique of signification, much more than the discovery of the signified, and of the relation which unites it to its signifier."[7] Debilitated, too, is the relevance of the author's subjectivity, since the literary work has become autonomous. Literary criticism becomes the deciphering of a "coherent system of signs," and "the purpose is not at all to discover 'truths,' but only 'validities.'"[8]

In 1966 a symposium which concerned itself with theories of literary criticism met at the Centre culturel international de Cerisy-la-Salle. Heated disagreement between phenomenologist and structuralist often dominated the discussion. Serge Doubrovsky maintained that structuralism, by scissoring off subject and world both, artificially isolates the literary work.[9] He pointed specifically to a persistent theme of Parisian Structuralism, that language can no longer represent, that its primordial contact with world has been lost, so that now it can reveal only absence. Doubrovsky argued, in effect, that the structuralists had been cooked in their own stew. They had without justification negated the origins of meaning, namely, self and world, and then, with curious blindness, lamented the very loss of meaning they had occasioned. Gérard Genette answered that structuralism does not isolate language from experience. On the contrary, it postulates that "language and experience are one and the same." This exchange between Doubrovsky and Genette is typical of the semantic jockeying that is all too frequent during critical "dialogues." The two discussants share the term *experience* but understand its workings in very disparate ways. By experience Genette does not mean intentionality. He sees experience, rather, as grounded in autonomous language: experience rises out of the closed system of signs which is the literary work. Indeed, in an earlier passage he tells us that "one of the functions of language, and of literature as language, is to destroy its speaker and to designate him as absent." The mutual misunderstandings between structuralists and phenomenologists abound. Philip Lewis, in an informative article, has already given examples of the distortions of structuralism which characterize phenomenological polemic.[10] (For example, the claim that structuralism is a species of sterile formalism, whereas it really studies the "form of content," not form excised from content.) I shall examine at this point the other side of the coin—distortion which emanates from the structuralist camp and misreads the legitimate phenomenological position. The specimen I have chosen is a strategic one involving issues important to structuralism and the Geneva School alike. The structuralist author is Tzvetan Todorov, in literary theory perhaps the most influential member of Parisian Structuralism's "second generation." His work is outstanding, and I shall have recourse to it throughout this presentation. I think he misinterprets phenomenological theory in one very crucial area however, and thus provides my example.

In the chapter "Comment Lire" of his book *Poétique de la prose*,[11] Todorov proposes two "modalities" whereby the structuralist can "take the literary text as object." One is poetics (*poétique*), which has for its purpose a description of the properties of literary discourse. From the functions of individual works, the theorist infers a general theory of literary processes. The second modality is that of critical reading (*lecture*), which aims to discover the functions unique to a given work. One of the approaches from which "critical reading" differs is interpretation (*interprétation*). Interpretation "refers here to all substitutions of another text in place of the present text, to all procedures which try to discover across the apparent textual tissue, a second more authentic text." Todorov tells us that the conscious or unconscious intention of the author constitutes the systemic structure of this second text. The actual text becomes merely "symptomatic." The allusion to the Geneva School here (as well as some forms of psychoanalytic criticism) is easily recognized. As we have seen in detail, the Geneva critic reads "surface configurations" as symptomatic of "latent experiential patterns." However, these patterns are not "outside-of-text" (*hors-texte*), as Todorov suggests, but rather are immanent in appearances (with Husserl's *Abschattungen* providing the closest analogy).

When Todorov reports that critical reading accomplishes "a certain upheaval of the apparent order of the text" and that "apparent order is not the only order," he is siding with the phenomenologists against the phenomenalists, who make essence equivalent to appearance. Todorov compares critical reading and translation, since both "rest equally on the possibility of finding an equivalent to a part of the text." He tells us that critical reading begins "by the discovery of resemblances" (among the various elements involved). He is actually describing a typical structuralist activity, what Barthes calls the manufacture of a "simulacrum" (*simulacre*). In Barthes's words:

> The end of all structuring activity . . . is to reconstitute an "object,"
> in such a fashion as to manifest in this reconstitution the rules of
> function (the "functions") of this object. The structure is thus

made into a simulacrum of the object, but a simulacrum which is
directed, interested, since the imitating object makes something
appear which remained invisible, or if one prefers, unintelligible
in the natural object.[12]

Todorov rightly distinguishes critical reading and translation in
this respect: that "in translation one orders the text . . . towards an
outside-of-text," whereas in critical reading one is directed towards
an "in-text" (*in-texte*). But if a structuralist reading is "in-text,"
certainly a Genevan reading is "in-text" also. If a structuralist
exposes the immanent but latent functions of a literary work, the
Geneva critic uncovers the immanent but latent intentionality. For
both, the surface level is symptomatic.

The outstanding difference between the two approaches does
not concern degree of immanence but the nature of that immanence.
As indicated previously, the Geneva critic sees the verbal sign as
movement towards outside reality. To the extent, then, that a sign is
"fulfilled" by its referent, the world "comes to stand" in language.
As Merleau-Ponty explains, literary language can best "retrieve the
world." Thus occurs what Serge Doubrovsky, after Sartre, calls the
*présentification* or *matérialisation* of the world in literature. But
intentionality has as its other pole the subjectivity of the author,
so selfhood also "comes to stand" in the work. The literary work
has immanent within itself a dynamic interaction of self and
world.

Nevertheless, at this point a problem intervenes. Ricoeur has
identified intentional referent with real entities in the world. And he
has said that "sense" is at most a half-way house, as it were, so that
language always pushes beyond "sense" towards a reality. But real
entities, at least according to Ricoeur's ontology, seem necessarily
outside of language (since language transcends itself towards them,
or "goes to meet them"). How then can he maintain that the world
is absorbed into language, so that world "comes to stand" in words?
My own solution to this conundrum is, first, to identify "movement
toward reality" with the act (energized by the reader) whereby
language projects an intentional object. And I would argue that the
intentional object (even if it is what Ingarden calls a "purely
intentional object") possesses enough of reality so that it can be
called real. Thus language does, in a very true sense, move towards a
real referent. Second, I recall that the intentional object is indeed
projected by language, so that in a true sense the object (taken as
real) also "comes to stand" in words. The two notions are not

contradictory: they merely look at the phenomenon of language from different angles. On the other hand, the structuralist, when speaking of patterns immanent but latent in the literary work, eliminates reality completely. These patterns are what are technically called "transformation systems." Such a critic contrasts the notion of structure with definitions which are either "ideal," "classificatory," or "extreme."[13] These latter three definitions, each because of its own defects, cannot account, the structuralist tells us, for all the elements in the object under study; nor, conversely, does the object under study match all the specifications of the proposed structure. The structuralist notion of "deep" structure has for its ultimate model algebraic "laws of transformation."[14] Laws of transformation, by their very nature, include all the elements which make up the object and render these elements susceptible to mutual comparison. The Geneva critic, who sees literature as consciousness-in-language, classifies literary elements according to psychological modes and contents of consciousness. The structuralist, instead of drawing upon psychological criteria, borrows directly from linguistics and mathematics.

As exemplified in our prior discussion of Ricoeur, Barthes, and their definition of the verbal sign, structuralism and phenomenology have conflicted with one another, and dramatically so. As also demonstrated, the situation has been complicated by the mutual misreadings which have characterized the polemic. Yet for some time Barthes has been calling for a "peaceful coexistence of critical languages."[15] He suggests that the many criticisms can cooperate in one grand enterprise, so literature will be better elucidated than ever before. It is my own thesis that the work of structuralist and phenomenologist can be complementary, and furthermore, that at times the two approaches can actually overlap. For the remainder of this part, I propose to survey indications which point to this complementarity, and even to occasional coincidence. Ricoeur has long argued for this complementarity, of course, though he accomplishes it by reducing structuralism to a somewhat diminutive role: his version of its "proper" role makes of it little more than a prologomenon to the really important task, the phenomenological one. As for the other side of the coin, structuralism's practical moves towards compatibility, one is obliged to turn once more to Tzvetan Todorov. Though I have shown how Todorov's treatment of intrinsicality does the Geneva School an injustice, he remains in my opinion the most responsible of the structuralists. With great finesse and tenacity he has worked at attenuating the more flamboyant theoretical statements of Jakobson, Barthes, and Lévi-Strauss. Let us look briefly at some of the adjustments he has made in the literary theory of the "first generation" of structuralists.

For Roman Jakobson, poetry projects the "principle of equivalence from the axis of selection into the axis of combination,"[16] but Todorov's method of *"superposition intratextuelle . . . shall have for its end the establishment not only of classes of equivalence, but of all describable relations."*[17] Todorov distinguishes his "critical reading" from "description," by which he means the linguistic criticism associated with Jakobson, on two counts: first, linguistic criticism posits in advance all categories of literary discourse, so that only the "combinations" are different; his "critical reading," on the contrary, allows the individual literary work to "transform" *langue* and modify the *combinatoire* from which future individual works will draw; second, linguistic criticism assumes that poetic structure can be extrapolated automatically from linguistic structure; "critical reading" permits poetic structure much more autonomy. As for Roland Barthes and his radical denial of an author's subjective presence in the literary work, the difference with Todorov also seems clear. Barthes, of course, has long since abandoned the phenomenological approach of his *Sur Racine* (1963) and its Genevan appreciation of the *"monde racinien."* The Barthes of *S/Z* (1970) is an absolute structuralist indeed. But Todorov continues to posit a *"personalité poétique"*[18] which has at least some affinities with subjectivity as the Geneva School understands it. More importantly, in his practical criticism Todorov continues to record signs of the author's subjectivity. He can speak of the typical *"L'héroine d'Akhmatova,"* or of the typical *"récit jamesien."* Indeed, in his essay on "Les Fântomes de Henry James,"[19] he says we must stop looking for the "ghost" provided by the regular genre of the fantastic and look for the unique design "which unites the work of James." What can only be the subjectivity of Henry James, contacted in the literature, "prefers perception to action, the relation with an object to the object itself, circular temporality to linear time, repetition to difference."

The propensity of Lévi-Strauss towards the discovery of structure in literally everything has been roundly criticized. It is said he refuses to admit that some phenomena fail to structure. And, akin to this, it is said he avoids contact with meaning as such, and therefore with the substance of poetry, the texture of which is dense with the earthy stuff of reality. Todorov's answer is a compromise of sorts. He readily grants "there is without doubt an untheorizable part of literature,"[20] and that a function of literature is the "subversion" of scientific languages. He tells us he favors the first of three possible alternatives: one can proceed with analysis, all the while realizing that one is to an extent impoverishing the work; or one can write another poem (said to be a false solution, since the second poem will in turn need commentary); or one can simply remain silent. All this can be misunderstood to mean that one has a choice of searching for structure or not commenting on the work at all. That Todorov does not really mean to confront us with so limited an option is clear from another passage of *Poétique de la prose*, where he tells us "literary 'critical reading' will not be able then to model itself in the image of the 'critical reading' of myths, about which Lévi-Strauss says, '. . . all syntagmatic chains must be held as if deprived of meaning.' "[21] Todorov goes on to say that the level of meaning is just as important as the formal level.

Another difference between Lévi-Strauss and Todorov concerns the importance of the temporal unfolding (*déroulement*) in a given text. This topic permits us to begin a contrast (on a limited scale) of structuralism and Heideggerian phenomenology. Todorov reminds us that the role of sequence in a literary work has "no, or almost no importance" for Lévi-Strauss; or, in Lévi-Strauss's own words, " 'the order of chronological succession is reabsorbed into an atemporal, matrix-like structure.'"[22] Todorov's appreciation of temporal "unfolding" makes him somewhat more compatible with the phenomenological tradition, and especially with the Heideggerian branch of phenomenology, which gives such a priority to *Entfaltung* (the specialized hermeneutical term for temporal unfolding). This is not to deny, however, that Todorov's "critical reading" and Heideggerian interpretation encounter the literary work in divergent ways. Todorov aims at objectivity, and remains very intentionally an outside observer of the work. The Heideggerian, as we have seen, claims to transcend the subject-object dichotomy, considering himself or herself operative within an ontological frame which includes both self and the work to be interpreted. This is so because he or she defines a human being (*Dasein*) as a "being whose existence consists in the comprehension of being" (and here comprehension aims at meaning and truth, not "validity").[23] In that the Heideggerian does not objectively distantiate himself from the text, he or she is not scientific, but, as Ricoeur says, "existentialist and philosophical." This enterprise uses a "hermeneutical circle of understanding and believing which disqualifies it as science, and qualifies it as meditative thought."[24] Because critic and work ultimately belong to the same ontological ensemble, the Heideggerian critic can move dialectically from the experience of the work to personal experience and back again. In his treatise, "Poétique,"[25] Todorov takes up another area of conflict between structuralism and hermeneutics: the possible relations between criticism and literary history. Lévi-Strauss, the Heideggerians protest, synchronizes change. By spatializing diachrony, he tends to convert even it into synchronic form. Hermeneutical critics claim they work from *within* history, so they can experience the "force" of change and relive time. And they can live the dialectic whereby tradition "transmits and sediments interpretation," and interpretation "supports and renews tradition."[26] Todorov, it seems, moves in a direction which strikes middle-ground between Lévi-Strauss and Heideggerian phenomenology. He abrogates the old Russian Formalist repudiation of literary history, and looks for a way "to approach the true subject of history, which is evolution."[27] His purpose is to investigate the evolution of literary discourse and the ongoing literary tradition which is the matrix of individual literary works. He concurs with Juri Lotman, who "has well shown that the meaning of a text is always more than the text itself."

Paul Ricoeur, cautiously approaching middle ground from the other direction, has also made his adjustments. He hopes to conduct hermeneutics "across the [structuralist] discipline of objectivity," with its "concepts of synchrony and diachrony," so that hermeneutical phenomenology can arrive at a "mature intelligence."[28] As already indicated, Ricoeur has for some time regarded structuralism and phenomenology as distinct but complementary disciplines. He usually assigns structuralism the scientific (and subordinate) task of analyzing "semiology" (the laws which characterize *langue*) and phenomenology the philosophical task of interpreting semantic (which can only arise in and through *parole*). But in several passages he says something more: that the practices of the two disciplines cannot even survive in their pure states. Thus he tells us "there is no recovery of meaning . . . without a minimum comprehension of structures," and conversely, "the structural intelligence never proceeds without a degree of hermeneutical intelligence."[29] In the chapter "Structure et herméneutique" of *Le Conflit des interprétations,* he provides the following example of the latter case: Lévi-Strauss, in *La Pensée sauvage,* discusses at one point the homology between rules of marriage and alimentary prohibitions. His apprehension of their metaphoric relation precedes and renders possible the apprehension of their formal relation. The formal relation is effected by a kind of structuralist "transforming." Ricoeur quotes Lévi-Strauss's admission that the transformation is achieved at a great price: the "'semantic impoverishment'" of the relation. Thus Ricoeur makes his point: the substantive awareness precedes the structural one, and the latter is dependent on the former.

A further step towards rapprochement has been taken by Jean Piaget, the renowned structural psychologist. In his book, *Structuralism,*[30] he relates dialectic (a procedure identified with phenomenology) to the overall history and operation of structuralist disciplines. He argues that "the dialectical attitude seems essential to the full working out of structures." Conflict between analytic reason and dialectic has occurred only because Lévi-Strauss's version of structuralism "has been relatively static and ahistorical." This has led him "to underestimate the importance of dialectical processes." The "work of construction for which the dialectical attitude calls" is not merely a matter of "throwing out bridges over the abyss of a human ignorance" (as Lévi-Strauss maintains). Rather, "It is often construction itself which begets the negations along with the affirmations, and the syntheses (*dépassements*) whereby they are rendered coherent as well." In the realm of structure this dialectic "matches a recurrent historical process well described by G. Bachelard" (a thinker associated, of course, with the phenomenological tradition). Piaget goes on to elaborate:

> . . . given a certain structure, one tries, by systematic negation of one after another attribute to construct its complementary structures, in order later to subsume the original together with its complements in a more complex total structure. . . . Dialectic is both complementary to and inseparable from analytic, even formalizing, reason. . . . Dialectic over and over again substitutes "spirals" for the linear or "tree" models with which we start, and these famous spirals or non-vicious circles are very much like the genetic circles or interactions characteristic of growth.

It seems safe to surmise that further exploitation of Piaget's line of inquiry will expose even more coincidence between dialectic and specific structuralist operations. The "binary opposition" and modes of "mediation" which earmarked form for the first generation of structuralists, and the "laws of transformation" which now do the same for the second, both seem explicable (at least potentially) in dialectical terms.

This chapter, and with it Part One, come to a conclusion with some remarks on practical criticism, for certainly both structuralist and Geneva critic intend their approaches, at least ultimately, for the illumination of the literary work. A century from now, when today's literary approaches will have ceded, in Roland Barthes's words, to a "new [critical] language," so that structuralism's "task will be terminated,"[31] the structuralist movement will probably be remembered for one great contribution to the praxis of criticism. Whereas the Geneva School sees language as the expression of self and world, structuralism recognizes and examines the converse of this: that self and world are shaped by the structure of language. It seems to me that these two intuitions, radically inadequate when treated disjunctively, best operate in conjunction with each other. Tzvetan Todorov, most synthetic of the structuralist theorists, has also led the way towards synthesis in practical criticism. A good example of this is his article "The discovery of language: *Les Liaisons dangereuses and Adolphe.*"[32] Todorov finds that Laclos's epistolary novel is controlled from the start by the artificial conventions which attach to the "'letter' as a social phenomenon." The genre of the letter, as a kind of social language, creates its own meaning, "and this connotation is in addition, or even in opposition, to the literal message of each letter." The letter as genre connotes "news, or more precisely, the possibility of a change in the preceding situation." The letter means "that one is on intimate terms with the person with whom one corresponds." And thirdly, it means "authenticity. . . . As opposed to the spoken word, the letter asserts a sure proof." In both Laclos and Constant, the reader must cross what are fictional barriers to the actual text: the publisher's foreword and editor's preface in *Les Liaisons dangereuses;* and the preface to the second edition, preface to the third edition, and editor's foreword, in *Adolphe.* These forms, too, speak a social language which antedates and controls what the two authors wish to say. In short, these forms of language, the signifiers, create their own signifieds.

Still, the writers in question are not wholly trapped by the semiological systems with which they deal. Literature, Todorov reminds us, "is, by definition, a conscious *use* of language, as opposed to that unconscious, careless use of it in practical discourse . . ."

(emphasis added). Many signifiers, with their projected signifieds, are already "given" before either Laclos or Constant begins to write, but both authors can manipulate the semiological frames involved. This creative manipulation can mark their literary works off from those of other writers, so Todorov can say these two share "an essentially similar world vision." There is "something in common in the way they portray love, something which would oppose them to, say, l'Abbé Provost." The creative act is even more individuating than this, however, for the imaginative literary worlds constructed by Laclos and Constant also differ from each other in many respects. For example, Todorov can draw the conclusion that "in Constant's world, then, a word is not one action among others (as it is with Laclos); it is the reversal of all languages, a reversal which is more powerful than action itself." What are we to infer from all this? Only that Todorov's overall essay discloses a kind of non-vicious (or dialectical!) circle at work in literature: language controls the writer, but the writer also controls language.

What can we expect of the phenomenological critics? That in the long run they will affirm and integrate into their own approach the basic intuitions of structuralism. Jean Starobinski seems most likely to adopt this attitude: Georges Poulet already distinguishes some of Starobinski's recent work from "identificatory and contemplative criticism,"[33] that is, the pure Genevan tradition. It is my prediction that structuralism and phenomenology will come to see themselves as contiguous spans on Piaget's historical spiral. The two approaches will experience the "interactions characteristic of growth," and the whole critical enterprise will profit from the result.

# part 2

# Phenomenology and Literary Theory

# chapter 1

# The Problem of Validity: Hirsch and Husserl

In his essay "Objective Interpretation," Hirsch endeavors to separate meaning (which he equates with the author's verbal meaning) from significance, which is the relation of the unchanging author's meaning to some other factor, such as the critic's own *Weltanschauung* or subjective circumstances (significance is therefore changeable).[1] Hirsch begins his argument with a borrowing from Frege, who he says distinguishes between *Sinn* (the sense) and *Bedeutung* (which Hirsch understands here as the *designatum*). Different *Sinne* (for example, the name *Scott* and the name *author of Waverly*) can obviously refer to one and the same *Bedeutung* (here, the person Sir Walter Scott). Hirsch goes on to say that while Frege only considered cases where different *Sinne* have identical *Bedeutungen*, it is also true to say that the same *Sinne* may, in the course of time, have different *Bedeutungen*. Hirsch, following Frege, also ties together here the notion of *Bedeutung* and truth value. For example, the sentence "There is a unicorn in the garden" may have the same sense in realistic discourse and fictional discourse, but in the former the statement would be false and in the latter it could be true. Hirsch then equates "meaning" exclusively with *Sinn*, saying that unless this were the case, we would have nothing constant to label true or false.

Further along, trying to use Husserl as support for his general argument, Hirsch draws upon Husserl's *Logische Untersuchungen*. In Hirsch's explication of Husserl's notion of intentionality he says correctly that Husserl distinguished between the intentional act and the object intended: "Different intentional acts (on different occasions) intend an identical intentional object," but says incorrectly that "The general term for all intentional objects is meaning. Verbal meaning is simply a special kind of intentional object, and like any other one, it remains self-identical over against the many different acts which intend it."[2] And again, "Verbal meaning, being an intentional object, is unchanging. . . . The meaning is determined once and for all by the character of the speaker's intention."[3] The conclusion is that the interpreter must take as his task the discovery of this unchanging meaning, and he is not to validate senses which are not the author's sense.

My own response to all this is that while Hirsch's general thesis may be valid, his argument is at several points inconsistent, and that he misunderstands Husserl. First of all, in the Frege section, the fusion of referent and truth-value is very ill-advised. Apropos the "unicorn in the garden" example, the *Bedeutungen* are not different in fictional and realistic discourse. The *Bedeutungen* are unicorn and garden in both kinds of discourse—only their ontological status is different (ideal in the first instance and real in the second). When Hirsch draws upon Husserl, a strange thing happens. The author's sense becomes the *Bedeutung* (or referent or intentional object) of the reader's act. But, as will be proved below, Husserl says repeatedly that meaning never comes from the side of the intentional object and is never an intentional object. Rather, meaning *(Sinn)* is always an intentional act, be it the act of the author in naming a referent *(Bedeutung)*, or the act of the reader in duplicating the author's sense through the medium of an intentional object (which here would be the verbal sign, or text). To put it in another way, the meaning of the referent (author's sense) is the perceiver's sense (which should, for Hirsch, coincide with the author's sense). Or again, just as the meaning of a cat *(Bedeutung)* is the perceiver's sense (which correlates to the cat), so too is the meaning of the author's sense (here functioning as *Bedeutung*) the perceiver's sense, which correlates with the author's sense. The conversion of author's sense into a referent (in terms of the reader) also makes the earlier part (the Frege section) of Hirsch's argument inconsistent. To be consistent, Hirsch should have equated meaning with *Bedeutung* or intentional object from the start, and understood the array of different *Sinne* for one and the same referent as different senses in which the *Bedeutung* (or meaning) could be taken. To save his argument, he would then of course have to specify that the only legitimate sense is the one the author intended (otherwise, this phase of his case would support his opponents, the Heideggerians).

The essay "Objective Interpretation" was written considerably before Hirsch's book *Validity in Interpretation*, but the essay reappears therein as the first appendix. In the body of the book (page 38), however, Hirsch again says meaning is an intentional object. Somewhat later, in the same chapter, he says in the essay "Objective Interpretation" he had failed to make a necessary distinction between the referring-meaning and the subject matter.[4] Hirsch claims furthermore that Husserl also failed to make the distinction. Though Hirsch doesn't further pinpoint the relevant section of his appendix, I assume he is referring to his treatment of Husserlian intentional object in that essay, and that now Hirsch wishes to call the intentional object the subject matter, and the intentional act the referring-meaning. If my understanding of Hirsch's revision is correct, then the change doesn't correct Husserl's conception, but rather, more accurately reflects it. In short, Husserl from the start made what Hirsch calls the matter-meaning distinction (though his terminology is different), and only later did Hirsch discover the distinction.

In chapter four Hirsch is also close to Husserl's conception. Here the interpreter confronts the intentional object which is the text, but meaning is not in the object, but in the interpretative act.[5] On the basis of the verbal components of the text, plus all other relevant information about the author and his tradition, Hirsch's interpreter actively reconstructs as best he can the meaning of the author. Thus Hirsch (perhaps without knowing it) seems to come around to the authentic Husserlian formula. Hirsch goes on to say that "if the implication of verbal meaning were invariably determined by the 'objective' character of what it refers to, then nobody could ever communicate a conceptual mistake." I hope that Hirsch doesn't lay this unfortunate consequence at the door of Husserl, for it doesn't really represent Husserl's thought. The Husserl of the *Logische Untersuchungen* would simply say that some intentional acts misconstrue objects. Inasmuch as Husserl's phenomenology of meaning "founds" all later phenomenologies of meaning (even those which disagree fundamentally with his version), I shall at this point present a relatively full-dress account of the role of meaning in the *Logische Untersuchungen*. At the same time, Hirsch's early misinterpretation of Husserl will become much clearer.

For the Husserl of *Logische Untersuchungen*, intentionality refers simultaneously to the object intended and the act intending (that is, directed toward) it. Consciousness as such is defined then as "intentional experience." Husserl distinguishes among sense-data (which are immanent in the mind), the intentional act, and the intentional object. The sense-data provide the sensations for the intentional act, but are neither the act (which is a purely relational attitude toward the object) nor the object. Thus Husserl says:

> . . . Immanent contents, which belong to the real make-up [*reellen Bestande*] of the intentional experiences, are not intentional: they constitute the act, provide necessary *points d'appui* which render possible an intention, but are not themselves intended, not the objects presented in the act. I do not see color-sensations but colored things, I do not hear tone-sensations but the singer's song, etc.[6]

The intentional act organizes a successive stream of sensations, and refers them to the same object:

> I see a thing, e.g., this box, but I do not see my sensations. I always see one and the same box, however it may be turned or tilted. I have always the same 'content of consciousness'—if I care to call the perceived object a content of consciousness. But each turn yields a new 'content of consciousness,' if I call experienced contents 'contents of consciousness,' in a much more appropriate use of words. Very different contents are therefore experienced, though the same object is perceived.[7]

As for the intentional object, it transcends the intentional act or acts:

> In each act an object is presented as determined in this or that manner, and as such it may be the target of varying intentions, judgmental, emotional, desiderative, etc. . . . Many new presentations may arise, all claiming, in virtue of an objective unity of knowledge, to be presenting the same object. In all of them the object which we intend is the same, but in each our intention differs, each means the object in a different way.[8]

This formulation sounds quite relativistic, in that meaning seems to depend exclusively on intention rather than the object. Actually, Husserl's theory is much more complicated, and in the section on verbal expression we now approach, tends to confirm Hirsch (though not in the way Hirsch thinks).

In a large part of the chapter entitled "Meaning and Expression" (which is Hirsch's precise source), verbal meaning receives Husserl's explicit attention. He begins by saying that sign and expression are not synonyms: "Every sign is a sign for something, but not every sign has 'meaning,' a 'sense' that the sign 'expresses.' "[9] Note that by meaning Husserl means "sense," that is, an idea represented by a sign. The "intimating function" of verbal expression he defines as follows: verbal expression (which is a kind of intentional act) manifests "the 'thoughts' of the speaker, that is, of his sense-giving inner experiences, as well as of the other inner experiences which are part of his communicative intention." Husserl defines verbal expression thus:

> . . . The articulate sound-complex, the written sign, etc., first becomes a spoken word or communicative bit of speech, when a speaker produces it with the intention of 'expressing himself about something' through its means; he must endow it with a sense in certain acts of mind, a sense he desires to share with his auditors. Such sharing becomes a possibility if the auditor also understands the speaker's intention. He does this inasmuch as he takes the speaker to be a person, who is not merely uttering sounds but speaking to him, who is accompanying those sounds with certain sense-giving acts, which the sounds reveal to the hearer, or whose sense they seek to communicate to him. What first makes mental commerce possible, and turns connected speech into discourse, lies in the correlation among corresponding physical and mental experiences of communicating persons which is effected by the physical side of speech.[10]

To summarize, an expressive act (that is, a meaning-act) places a sign to communicate a sense (for example, the word *cat* relates to the idea *cat*). The sense (meaning) in turn is related to an object (for example, the relation of the idea *cat* to its object *a cat*). Notice that Husserl's assumption throughout is that the hearer should strive to reenact the intending sense of the speaker (thus he supports Hirsch's central thesis). However, Husserl takes care to distinguish between meaning and intentional object: "The necessity of distinguishing between meaning (content) and object becomes clear when a comparison of examples shows us that several expressions may have the same meaning but different objects and again that they may have different meanings but the same object."[11] And later, Husserl says: "In meaning, a relation to an object is constituted. To use an expression significantly, and to refer expressively to an object (to form a presentation of it), are one and the same. . . . Meanings are often spoken of as signifying the objects meant, a usage that can scarcely be maintained consistently, as it springs from a confusion with the genuine concept of meaning."[12]

We now turn to the problem of intersubjectivity in Husserl, and how he accounts for it. How can people communicate with each other? Husserl distinguishes first between the "act-character" (or "act-quality") operative in intentionality, and the "content" (which he later calls "matter" to avoid confusion) also operative therein. Thus he posits a "distinction between the general act-character, which stamps an act as merely presentative, judgmental, emotional, desiderative, etc., and its 'content,' which stamps it as presenting *this,* as judging *that,* etc."[13] Matter is that "side" of every act which determines what aspect of the object is intended: "The matter, therefore, must be that element in an act which first gives it reference to an object, and reference so wholly definite that it not merely fixes the object meant in a general way, but also the precise way in which it is meant. The matter . . . is that peculiar side of an act's phenomenological content that not only determines *that* it grasps the object but also AS WHAT it grasps it. . . ."[14]

The "intentional essence" is the unity formed by an intentionality's act-quality and its matter. At this point Husserl introduces a second term, the "semantic essence" of an act: "To the extent that we deal with acts, functioning in expressions in sense-giving fashion, or capable of so functioning, . . . we shall speak more specifically of the *semantic essence* of the act. The ideational abstraction of this essence yields a 'meaning' in our ideal sense."[15] An earlier passage (in *Logische Untersuchungen* I) can be used to further gloss this: "The ideality of the relationship between expression and meaning is at once plain in regard to both its sides, inasmuch as, when we ask for the meaning of an expression, e.g., 'quadratic remainder,' we are naturally not referring to the sound-pattern uttered here and now, the vanishing noise that can never recur identically: we mean the expression *in specie.*"[16] Communication, then, occurs when two or more people, through the mediation of an expression, share the same "semantic essence." Thus Husserl's theory of communication depends on an idealism, though it must be stressed that in the *Logische Untersuchungen* all Husserl claims is that universals have enough identity of their own so that assertions can be made about them. They are not necessarily the eternal and constant Ideas of Plato.

The question most relevant to our enterprise is simply this: if a text can be taken in several senses, is the only legitimate sense (and therefore the only meaning) the author's sense? Actually, despite Hirsch's claims, Husserl does not address himself directly to this question in the *Logische Untersuchungen,* but his general position in its regard can be inferred. It is clear Husserl takes for granted a speaker's sense can be shareable, and that the auditor should try to duplicate it (through a correlate sense in his own mind, mediated by way of the speaker's expression). The closest Husserl comes to a discussion of expression which offers several senses simultaneously is in his treatment of equivocation. In sections 12 and 15, Husserl distinguishes between general or class names (such as the number two or redness) which have one sense but many values, and equivocal names (such as the German word *Hund,* which can mean a truck used in mining or a dog) which have two (or more) senses. In section 26, he distinguishes between "essentially subjective and occasional expressions" (those which use words such as *I, here, above,* and so forth) from "objective expressions" (such as the word *elephant*).[17] An essentially occasional expression "belongs to a conceptually unified group of possible meanings, in whose case it is essential to orient actual meaning to the occasion, the speaker, and the situation." Husserl gives the following example:

> The word 'I' names a different person from case to case, and does so by way of an ever altering meaning. *What its meaning is at the moment can be gleaned only from the living utterance and the intuitive circumstance which surround it. If we read the word without knowing who wrote it, it is perhaps not meaningless, but is at least estranged from normal sense* . . . we know it to be a word, and a word with which whoever is speaking designates himself. But the conceptual meaning thus evoked is not what the word 'I' means, otherwise we could simply substitute for it the phrase 'whatever speaker is designating himself.' Such a substitution would lead to expressions, not only unusual, but also divergent in sense, if, e.g., instead of saying 'I am pleased' I said 'Whatever speaker is now designating himself is pleased.' It is the universal semantic function of the word 'I' to designate whoever is speaking, but the notion through which we express this function is not the notion immediately constitutive of its meaning.[18] (Emphasis added.)

What concerns us here specifically is the italicized passage. The sense of the occasional expression should be controlled by living context, in the case of the word *I* by knowledge of who wrote the pronoun (if the writer was referring to himself or herself). Husserl's implication here seems then to favor Hirsch's position, though the application to a literary text as such is still exceedingly difficult to draw.

As opposed to an occasional expression, Husserl says, an

objective expression pins down (or can pin down) its meaning by its manifest auditory pattern, and can be understood without necessarily directing one's attention to the person writing it, or to the circumstances of the utterance. However, some objective expressions may be equivocal (like the word *Hund* above), and it is in regard to these that Husserl again makes a statement somewhat relevant to our needs:

> An objective expression may be in varying ways equivocal: it may stand in the stated relation to several meanings [senses] *so that it depends on the psychological context (on the chance drift of the hearer's thoughts, on the tenor of the talk already in progress, and the tendencies it arouses, etc.)* which of these meanings it arouses and means. *It may be that a glance at the speaker and his situation may help this.* (Emphasis added.)

In the italicized passage above, the notion of context reappears. Except for the phrase "the chance drift of the hearer's thoughts" (which suggests the "sense" is determined by the auditor; this would be a quasi-relativist position, though it is important to remember Husserl is explaining what *can* happen, not what is necessarily valid), the assumption seems to be that the auditor should strive for agreement with the speaker's sense. To sum up, how can Husserl be useful to Hirsch's position? In the case of a text which makes several senses possible, the perceiver enacts the relevant sense, and he decides this relevance in terms of adequation to the author's intended sense.

At this point I would like to proceed to Husserl's *Ideen,* since the new formulation of intentionality found therein lays the groundwork for our subsequent discussion of Heidegger. Incidentally, it also happens to be more useful for Hirsch than the *Logische Untersuchungen,* and he would have been better advised to have drawn from the *Ideen.* The *Ideen,* of course, already belongs to the later-phase Husserl, who describes a transcendental subjectivity, a "sense-giving consciousness, which . . . is absolute and not dependent in its turn on sense bestowed on it from another source."[19] Reality and world become "titles for certain valid unities of meaning, namely unities of meaning related to certain organizations of pure absolute consciousness which dispense meaning and show forth its validity in certain essentially fixed, specific ways." In the *Logische Untersuchungen,* the intentional act conferred "sense" on the "presentation" of an object in consciousness (and specifically on the "matter" of that presentation). In the *Ideen,* transcendental subjectivity (which transcends empirical egos) "constitutes" intentionality, and intentionality divides into two structures which are distinct yet unified: the noetic (or intending act) and the noematic (or intended elements). The noematic structure corresponds to the world outside: ". . . whatever the world and reality may be or be called must be represented within the limits of real and possible consciousness by corresponding meanings and positions. . . ."[20] But what is really so new in the *Ideen* is that not only the noetic structure, but the noematic structure as well, carries meaning. Husserl indicates that his earlier work (such as the *Logische Untersuchungen*) focused too exclusively on, and gave an unjustified priority to, the intending act, but that the "one-sidedness of the noetic orientation . . . is easily overcome by a proper regard to the noematic parallels."[21] In the *Ideen,* the concept of parallelism is all-important: the manifold layers of the thetic (positional) act (which belongs to noesis) is mirrored very precisely in equivalent layers of noematic structure. A significant change in nomenclature also takes place. The word *Sinn* now represents "Sense or Meaning *simpliciter,"* that is, "in its more embracing breadth of application."[22] The word *Bedeutung* becomes more specialized, and represents "logical meaning" or "expression."[23]

Though the noetic act still bestows a meaning,[24] a corresponding meaning also belongs to the essence of the "noematic object in its modal setting."[25] Indeed, it is through noematic meanings that an intentional experience is related to an object. Noematic *Sinn* is not present *in concreto,* but does inform the noema: "Meaning *(Sinn)* as we have determined it is *not a concrete essence* in the constitution of the noema as a whole, but a kind of abstract *form* that dwells in it."[26] In other words, what bears the name "ideal content" in the *Logische Untersuchungen* here carries the name *Sinn.* To further complicate matters, when "obscure consciousness" and "lucid consciousness" synthesize themselves, the "full nucleus" of meaning appears:

> But there is nothing to hinder the determining content whereby the obscurely grasped object is indicated from being absolutely identical with that of the clearly grasped object. The descriptions would coincide, and a synthetic consciousness of unity could so envelop the twofold consciousness that it might really be one and the same object that was indicated. We shall accordingly reckon the concrete fullness of the noematic constituent in question as the *full nucleus, the meaning in the mode of its full realization.*[27]

Husserl goes on to deal with perception as such, using the concentrated optic of eidetic intuition. He insists that we "extract by force of vision from out the 'perceived object as such' the meaning of object, the thing significance (*Dingsinn*). . . ."[28] An important feature of the *Logische Untersuchungen* is preserved, however, though it is translated into the new conceptual framework of the *Ideen* (and is important for our later treatment of Heidegger). At the end of section 130, Husserl distinguishes between "the way in which we are aware" (equals act-character or act-quality of the *Logische Untersuchungen*) and the "objectivity" which belongs to the noema. Also, one may recall that in the *Logische Untersuchungen*, the intentional object was not just intended, but intended in a special way by each act. In the *Ideen*, the noematic structure at various times can represent one and the same object under different aspects (that is, with different "determining contents,"[29] also called "variations"[30] of the full noematic nucleus, and different "modes of appearing"[31]). However, in the *Ideen* it is not the noetic act alone which determines what aspect is intended; as indicated above, the noema offers a corresponding aspect of the object itself.[32] That all this would have been useful to Hirsch in a general way should now be clear. Hirsch wishes to maintain that "the general term for all intentional objects is meaning"; he would have been well advised to indicate the *Ideen*, where a kind of meaning inhabits the intentional object itself. I have uncovered the notions of validity stated by Hirsch and implied by Husserl, and I have treated Husserl's definition of intentionality. In the forthcoming chapters, comparisons with Ingarden, Dufrenne, and Heidegger will be effected.

# chapter 2

# Roman Ingarden

My exposition of Roman Ingarden will give a thorough account of his most important book on the theory of literature, *Das literarische Kunstwerk.*[1] Extensive accounts of Husserl are available in English; as far as I know, none do the same job in English for Ingarden. Ingarden's very finessed definition of intentionality, and specifically of intentionality's relation to the literary work, will emerge quite naturally from the "unfolding" of his work chapter by chapter. Regarding my more specialized task, the locus of valid meaning in literature, I will deal with Ingarden's treatments of the subject as I meet them. As for the determinants of the "correct" sense when language offers the possibility of several, Ingarden seldom if ever confronts this problem (that of "correctness" per se), but his general position seems evident.

In his preface, Ingarden sets forth his purpose: a description of the basic structure and mode of existence of the literary work of art. Part one concerns itself with preliminary questions, such as the inadequacy of contemporary definitions of the literary work and the elimination of factors extraneous to the literary work. Ingarden's destructive critique of physicalist and psychologistic definitions provides the basis for René Wellek's critique of the same in *Theory of Literature,* and since Wellek's discussion is well-known, I shall pass over most of Ingarden's account here. Ingarden refuses to describe literary structure as either ideal or real; furthermore, he rejects the need of a compulsory choice between these two ontic modes. If the literary structure were to belong to the former class of objects, it could not originate at a point in time, exist for a duration of time, possibly change during that duration, and maybe even cease to exist. If it were to belong to the latter class, it could not be composed of determinately ordered sentences (since sentences

involve specific ideal senses related to a pool of ideal concepts).
Psychologism, which claims that the literary work is identical with
the psychic experiences of author or reader, is also rejected, and on
the usual grounds. As for the author's experience, it is manifestly
inaccessible. As for the reader's, it is non-reiterative, so one would
have to concede what is for Ingarden unacceptable: that each
experience is a new literary work. Since Ingarden intends to focus on
the essential nature of the literary work, a nature that assumes full
stature only when the work as such is already "finished," he excludes
for the most part the formative stages of the work. He announces he
will not concern himself with the author's creative processes, except
insofar as they relate to the essence of the literary work. He will refer
to the author's acts of consciousness when necessary, but not in
psychologistic fashion. Nor will these acts of consciousness be
confused with the literary work itself. Ingarden laments "the
perennial confusion of two fields of investigation: that of the
ontology of the literary work and that of the psychology of artistic or
literary creativity." Much of the value in *Das literarische Kunstwerk*
will depend on the agility with which Ingarden acknowledges the
relation between author and work, yet preserves the distinction
between the two. A paragraph in which he declares the author's
"psychic states" are extraneous to the work is worth quoting in full:

> First of all, the author, with all his vicissitudes, experiences, and
> psychic states, remains completely outside the literary work. In
> particular, however, the experiences of the author during the
> creation of the work do not constitute any part of the created work.
> It may happen—and one should not dispute this—that there are
> various close relations between the work and the psychic life and
> individuality of the author. The genesis of the literary work in
> particular may be conditioned by the author's determinate ex-
> periences, and it may be that the whole structure of the work and
> its individual qualities are functionally dependent on the psychic
> qualities of the author, his talent, and the type of his "world of
> ideas" and his feelings, and that the work thus carries the more or
> less pronounced traces of his total personality and in his way
> "expresses" it. But all these facts in no way change the primary and
> yet frequently unappreciated fact that the author and his work
> constitute two heterogeneous objects, which, already on the basis
> of their radical heterogeneity, must be fully differentiated. Only the
> establishment of this fact will allow us to expose correctly the
> manifold relations and dependencies existing between them (22).

The above statement is only programmatic, of course, and the technicalities which validate it appear late in the book. The perception of the literary work by the reader is also excluded from discussion (with the exception of "concretizing acts," as we shall see), and these perceptions, along with concretizations themselves, are distinguished from the ontic status of the work.

Part two, entitled "The Structure of the Literary Work," describes a structure consisting of four heterogeneous yet interdependent strata: (1) word sound and higher phonetic formations, (2) meaning units, (3) manifold schematized aspects and aspect continua, and (4) represented objectivities. A fifth valence, that of "ideas" or "metaphysical qualities," is a characteristic of great works of art, but is not essential for the literary work per se. Of the four strata, the second is "central," since it requires the other three, yet determines them so that they have their ontic bases in it. Each stratum has an esthetic value of its own, and also contributes to the "polyphonic harmony" and therefore the organic esthetic value of the structure as a whole.

*Das literarische Kunstwerk* examines the four strata in succession, and thus begins with the stratum of phonetic formations. Since phonic material (intonation, quality of timbre, strength of voice, and so forth) is individually new with each articulation, Ingarden excises it from the literary work, and carefully distinguishes it from word sound (which is unchangeable and intersubjective). Word sound is a "typical phonic form" (*Gestalt*) which is transmitted by way of phonic material, but transcends it. Word sound is neither a real or ideal ontically autonomous object, but is "anchored in reality." The word sound, in turn, "carries" a meaning, though the perceiver passes through it immediately to the object it determines. Poetic speech is characterized by "living" words (as opposed to clichés). Living words not only express an intended meaning, but also "manifest" the experiences of the speaker. Borrowing the concept of manifestation from Husserl, Ingarden says that living words evoke in the perceiver not a "bare rational act" whereby he "knows" the speaker's experiences, but a substantive act whereby he feels the experiences in all their concreteness. Living words even express an intended meaning differently, however. In another borrowing from Husserl, Ingarden says that rich expression gives an object "intuitive fullness." The more independent linguistic formation is not the word but the sentence, so *Das literarische Kunstwerk* proceeds to a discussion of phonetic formations of a higher order.

After some passages on rhythm as a "typical Gestalt quality,"

Ingarden explains the essential service whereby the first stratum founds the second. The demonstration is straightforward enough: meaning units are necessarily bound to word sounds, and are determined by them. In a lengthy aside, Ingarden describes the function performed by the phonetic stratum for the perceiving psychic subject. It is important for us to note that Ingarden accepts the earlier Husserlian notion of meaning-bestowal, and does not convert meaning into an object:

> . . . When a determinate word sound is apprehended by a psychic subject, the apprehension leads directly to the execution of an intentional act in which the content of a determinate meaning is intended. Here, this meaning is not given as an object (of thought) but is rather set into a function; and, for its part, this setting-into-function brings about the fact that the corresponding objectivity which belongs to the word meaning or to the meaning of the sentence is intended, and thereby the subsequent strata of the literary work are revealed (60).

*Das literarische Kunstwerk* gives the most spacious treatment to the second stratum, that of meaning units, and this stratum will have important repercussions upon our later inferences concerning "correct" meaning according to the Ingardenian scheme. Meaning in general Ingarden defines as "everything bound to a word sound, which in conjunction with the sound forms a word" (63). He distinguishes between nominal word meanings (such as *table, redness, black*), and functioning concepts (such as *and, is, or*), and later, between these and verbal meanings.

For our purposes, it suffices to review his intense treatment of nominal meanings, which include names and meanings that belong to names. In nominal word meanings five factors can be distinguished: (1) the intentional directional factor, (2) the material content, (3) the formal content, (4) the moment of existential characterization, and sometimes also, (5) the moment of existential position. A sixth group of elements, called apophantic-syntactic, occurs only when a name appears as a part of a higher unit of meaning (such as a sentence), and will be treated later. The first factor is the moment wherein word simply refers to this and no other object, or in other cases, to this kind of object. The second is the moment wherein word determines the qualitative conditions of the object, such as material features. It is necessary to remember that at this point Ingarden is practicing the phenomenological *epoché*, so that the autonomous existence of the object, and the nature of that existence, is bracketed out. In a manner which parallels Husserl's own treatment of aspects, we are told that the intentional object presents, with respect to its qualitative constitution, those aspects, and only those, which are attributed to it in the material content of the meaning. The intentional directional factor, for its part, indicates precisely the object that is determined by the material content, and throughout remains dependent in its direction on the content.

The third factor involved in nominal word meaning executes a "forming" function with respect to the object; that is, it treats what is determined by the material content as a formally determined entity, such as a "thing," a "property of something," a "process," a "state," and so on. Through the factor of existential characterization, there appears yet another moment in nominal word meaning: the intentional object is intended as either real, or ideal, or whatever. For example, in the meaning of the expression "the capital of Poland," the city involved is not intended simply as a "city," but also as something which, according to its mode of existence, is real. Likewise, the object of the meaning "the equilateral triangle," in the mathematical sense, is intended as ideal. Here Ingarden also discusses fictional objects, and adumbrates what he will say later about the ontic status of these specialized objects. The name "Hamlet," for example (in the sense of the Shakespearian character), intends an object that never really existed nor will exist, but one which, if it were to exist, would belong among that class of objects to which the existential mode of "reality" applies. Finally, some nominal word meanings also intend an existential position. The expression "the capital of Poland," for instance, can be intended not only as something real according to its ontic mode, but also as something factually existing *somewhere*. And the expression "Hamlet" intends its object not in factual space-time reality, but in the fictional reality created by the sense contents of Shakespeare's play.

In section 16 of this same long chapter, Ingarden undertakes a discussion of the "actual and potential stock of word meaning" (84). In this section Ingarden's explanation becomes very entangled. Indeed, he follows Husserl in this! So what follows is my interpretation of what he is saying. I have rearranged the sequence of his arguments somewhat, but also at times paraphrase and quote directly. Ingarden begins by asserting that "the same word, indeed with identically the same meaning, can be used in different situations in different ways, so that despite the identity of the meaning, a

distinct change can be ascertained in it" (85). One can say, for
example, that the word *square* means (and here Ingarden understands the verb *to mean* as *to intend material content*) an "equilateral rectangular parallelogram," or "an equilateral rectangular
parallelogram with sides of any length," or "an equilateral rectangular quadrangle with two pairs of parallel sides of any length."
Certainly the word *square* has these meanings (that is, these material
contents). One may further notice, however, that these three meanings are different from each other and even somehow different from
the meaning of *square*. Apropos the latter, the three expressions of
material content are each of them compound units of meaning,
whereas this cannot be said in the same way about the expression
*square* itself. How are all these meanings different, and how the
same? And do we really mean by the word *square* the compound
meanings of the above three expressions?

In what is undoubtedly a reference to Frege and others,
Ingarden indicates an apparent solution: the expressions are
different meanings (roughly analogous to what Hirsch calls
different "senses"), but are in a way equivalent, since they refer to
one and the same object (Hirsch's *Bedeutung*). Ingarden rejects this
solution out of hand, however. He grants that the expressions can
share the same intentional direction factor, and the same intentional
object, but asserts these do not suffice for equivalence of meaning.
Nor does recourse to a possible identity of "formal objects" succeed.
If by "formal object" (what was called above the factor of formal
content) one understands that which exclusively possesses those
qualitative properties explicitly assigned to it in the material
content of the meaning, then the formal objects of each expression
must also be different. While the formal object of the expression
*square* is constituted exclusively of squareness as the qualitative
element of its nature, the formal object of the expression *equilateral
rectangular parallelogram*, for example, is constituted by an entirely
different qualitative element, namely, "parallelogramness."

Ingarden then broaches his own solution (87). He says that
the situation is really one in which several meanings belong to
the same ideal concept of the same object. For example, it is part
of the concept of a square that it be constituted by squareness
as the qualitative moment of its constitutive nature, but that it contain in its nature (using the same example as above) the doubly
dependent element of "parallelogramness." Likewise the essence of
"squareness" is a derived essence that is equivalent to the deter-

minately ordered manifold of essences: "parallelogramness," "rec-
tangularity," "equilateralness," etc. The meaning of the expression
*square* contains in its material content actually only part of what is
contained in the concept (or "idea") of "the square"; and the
meaning of the expression *equilateral rectangular parallelogram*
contains actually a different part of the content of the same concept,
one which, moreover, allows the object of the concept to be
constituted by a manifold of essences that is equivalent to
squareness. Each ideal concept has a number of word meanings for
the same object. That aspect of the ideal concept that is actualized in
each case creates the actual stock of the meaning. And above all, this
actualization creates the material and formal content of the
meaning. On the other hand, that which is still contained in the
given concept and ensues directly from the actualized stock
constitutes the potential stock of the given meaning. By converting
the potential stock of a nominal word meaning into an actual stock,
the full meaning is indeed modified, but the modification is based
only on an enrichment of the actual contents of its material content.
A modification of its formal content may also accompany it.

If I interrupt this exposition for a moment, I can identify more
precisely what Ingarden's formulation achieves. First, it posits a
realm of ideal concepts which correspond to objects. These ideal
concepts transcend meanings, so that only the concepts, and not the
meanings, are ideal. Here Ingarden's definition differs from that in
the *Logische Untersuchungen,* where meanings themselves are
ideal. Ingarden avoids this snare for several reasons. For one, he
believes it would necessitate the ontic ideality of the literary work.
And second, Ingarden's theory describes meanings as partial
actualizations of the manifold aspects available in the ideal concept.
Thus, meanings are equivalent to the same concept, but not to each
other. If I now proceed with my exposition, I find Ingarden next
copes with explicit and implicit expression, and the problem of
implication as such. Here I quote in full:

> If this conversion of a potential stock into an actual one occurs in
> such a way that each of the newly actualized elements of, first of all,
> the material content finds its *own* "expression", i.e., is "clothed" in
> a corresponding word or manifold of words, then the newly
> actualized stock appears "explicitly" in the meaning of the given
> expression. Otherwise we arrive at a compound nominal expres-
> sion. The change of the potential stock into the actual can also be
> conducted in such a way that the meaning that still contains the

potential stock and the meaning that already contains it (or at least a part of it) in actual form, are both bound to *the same* word sound (or to the same manifold of word sounds) [e.g., the word *square*]. In this case the newly actualized part of the actual stock does not find any particular expression of its own. This stock is contained "implicitly" in the corresponding word meaning (88).

Ingarden proceeds to raise the thorny hermeneutical problem: ". . . there arises the difficulty of how one can convince oneself, on the basis of the text alone, that the text and, in particular, the nominal word meanings entering into it contain an implicit potential stock." In short, how can one know whether one (or more) meanings which belong to a word's potential stock are actually operative in the text? Ingarden suggests what he considers a useful procedure. First, of course, one should consult (independently from the text) the whole scale of meanings a given word has in a given *langue*. Then one should narrow down this range of meanings by analyzing the word's immediate and global function within the verbal context of the work; tracking down recurrences of the same word in various parts of the work is an important technique here. This whole process effects a further distinction between potential meanings which are merely possible ("empty potentialities"), and potential meanings which are not yet actualized but approach actualization in that they are "suggested" ("ready potentiality").

Ingarden closes section 16 with a consideration of more hermeneutical complications, though his treatment is tantalizingly incomplete. He explains that the actual stock of a meaning can be the actualization of not one but two or more concepts which the reader may not yet have distinguished. The potential stock of this meaning, of which he is almost totally unconscious, may thus contain content elements whose total manifold has no single ideal concept corresponding to it. As the reader works through the text and continues that ongoing process whereby potential stock is actualized, he or she should eventually detect the bifurcation of concepts. Words whose meanings actualize two or more concepts account for much of the ambiguity in literature. At this point, Ingarden declines to evaluate ambiguity in esthetic terms, though he will later. In any case, recognition of real ambiguity, or resolution of apparent ambiguity, is to be decided exclusively by verbal context. Ingarden's next section makes the important point that isolated word meanings are modified when they interact with other words in a sentence. The original meanings of individual words do not disappear fully but do lose their mutual rigid delimitations. Individual words become functional parts of a larger unit of meaning, that of the sentence as a whole. This transformation of roles even causes differences in what were a word's original material content and formal content. Nevertheless, Ingarden's general theory of intentionality and meaning, as presented in the previous section on nominal word meanings, remains intact, so I pass over this section and proceed to Ingarden's next topic, the role of subjective operations in the formation of meaning units.

Here Ingarden begins by resuming his attack on Husserl's unmitigated idealism, arguing again that if meanings were themselves "ideal species," they would be necessarily timeless, and absolutely unchangeable. That one and the same meaning can undergo modification Ingarden notes he has already proven in the preceding sections, where he demonstrated how meaning can take on various modes of actuality or potentiality, of explicitness or implicitness; and where he also demonstrated that one and the same meaning undergoes transformation when it combines with other meanings to form a sentence. He then goes on to make what seems to be a self-defeating concession, a surprising surrender to psychologism: he grants that determinate conscious operations (which are subjective psychic events) assign a sentence's mode of existence and the determinants of its content and form. But then he saves his case by making a distinction that recalls Husserl: the sentence may be heteronomous, that is, dependent on conscious operations, but it nevertheless transcends these operations. The sentence *qua* sentence is a self-enclosed unit not to be identified with concrete consciousness, and only the constituent facts located in this unit found the unique ontic mode of the sentence itself.

The role, however, of subjective operation in "assigning" meaning units leads to a discussion of meaning-bestowal, and then the meaning-duplication effected by the perceiver. Ingarden focuses here on nominal word meaning. As we have already seen, an essential aspect of the word is that it possesses a meaning, a meaning by which it intentionally designates an object and determines it *materialiter et formaliter*. If the word sound carries a meaning, however, this is so only because a meaning has been bestowed on it. This bestowal can be accomplished only by means of a subjective act of consciousness. (Again Ingarden's reliance on the Husserlian formulation is apparent, though with an important difference: in Husserl, the subject confers an ideal sense on the word, whereas in

Ingarden the subject confers a meaning which is not ideal, but which "belongs to" an ideal.) The subjective act of consciousness initiates what is a concatenation of processes. The intentional thinking contained in the subject's meaning-bestowing act determines the intentional designation which as a result belongs to the word. To put it another way, the intentionality of the word (its directedness toward an object) is bestowed by the corresponding intentionality of the speaker; but this "corresponding intentionality of the speaker" is one entity, and the "intentionality of the word" is another. Nevertheless, because the intentional designation of a word is dependent on a bestowing act external to it, the intentional designation lacks ontic autonomy. The word's intentional designation is "created"; it is something that did not exist before. In comparison with the existence of the real, the ideal, and the purely conscious, the word's intentional designation is analogous only to "illusion." And all this proves in yet another way that meanings cannot be ideal: ideal entities are beyond the reach of a spontaneous conscious subject who can "create" them and change them at will.

Finally, Ingarden describes the subjective operations of the perceiver of meaning units. While the speaker performs a "primal, truly sentence-forming operation," the perceiver, through contact with the intentional designations built into the resultant sentence, performs a "duplicating or reactualizing operation." Though Ingarden assumes that this duplicating operation corresponds to the primal one of the speaker (thus he calls it "duplicating"), one must recall that the primal operation, once performed, is lost forever, and that (in the case of recorded language) only the intentional designation of the word remains. Thus in the case of ambiguous meaning (where, for example, the object intended is in doubt), the intentionality of the speaker is unavailable for consultation. Apropos the ontic mode of meaning units, Ingarden has thus far established that it is a heteronomous but distinct mode, and that it is neither ideal, nor "psychic," nor real.

The next section concerns general characteristics of the sentence, which is an "objectivity" in its own right. A sentence itself is a "functional-intentional unit of meaning"—"functional" because it specifies which syntactic roles the word meanings within it are to perform, "intentional" because it *represents* a "state of affairs." At this point Ingarden treats elements really belonging to the third stratum, that of represented objects, but for strategic reasons he interpolates a partial treatment here. Just as individual words correlate to intended objects, whole sentences correlate to intended "states of affairs." Both intended objects and intended states of affairs are called intentional correlates (of words and sentences respectively, though for the remainder of our discussion I'll focus exclusively on sentence correlates). States of affairs find their ontic base in the sentence. Sentence correlates are always "purely intentional correlates"; that is, they are intended by a meaning-unit's intentionality and transcend this intentionality, but are not to be confused with an existing correlate in the world (be it real or ideal). Indeed, many sentences do not have existing correlates in the world, but are still sentences; and Ingarden's definition must be broad enough to accommodate them.

"Judgmental" sentences, that is, sentences with existing correlates, are just a species, then, belonging to a larger genus. In the judgmental sentence the subjective sentence-forming operation is effected on the basis of an intuitively apprehended existing state of affairs. The resultant sentence requires an "intentional moment" which both transcends the purely intentional correlate and finds its mark in the existing reality. To quote Ingarden, "the purely intentional correlate of the sentence is thereby intentionally transported into reality in a characteristic manner and is not only identified with a really existing state of affairs but is also recognized as *really existing along with it*" (110, emphasis added). To simplify matters, then, yet remain true to Ingarden, I think it most helpful to say that in a judgmental sentence the purely intentional correlate abides "alongside" the existing state of affairs, but is technically distinct from it. In the case of a non-judgmental sentence, there is simply no existing state of affairs at all, but the purely intentional correlate stands firm and on its own.

After a discussion of "nominal" and "verbal" intentionality (so that the declarative sentence becomes a synthesis of these two types) and a few other matters, Ingarden goes on to distinguish between "originally purely intentional" objects and "derived purely intentional" objects (here the term *object* is expanded to include states of affairs). The former is the purely intentional object placed at the very moment of intention by the speaker or writer; obviously, it draws its existence and essence directly from his concrete acts of consciousness (though it transcends these acts!). The latter is the purely intentional object generated by the listener or reader, and it owes its existence and essence to language formations and in particular to units of meaning of different orders which contain a

"borrowed" intentionality (118). Ingarden grants, however, that
since these language formations refer back to the original intentionality of the author's acts of consciousness, even the derived purely
intentional objects have their "ultimate" source of existence in these
acts.

Ingarden next examines "instances of purely intentional
objectivities," and then coins a memorable phrase: he declares the
purely intentional objectivity an "ontic nothing" (122). Since an
intentional objectivity can be constituted only by the author, or by
the perceiver (in what Ingarden has already called the "duplicating
or reactualizing operation"), it is created and heteronomous. The
purely intentional object, too, like the meaning units in which it has
its ontic base, is an "illusion." In section 21, Ingarden telescopes his
optic, bringing it to bear on the derived purely intentional correlates
of meaning units. As already indicated, meaning units have an
intentionality "borrowed" from the author's acts of consciousness.
The meaning units project purely intentional correlates whose ontic
relativity refers back directly to the borrowed intentionality now
immanent in the meaning units, and only indirectly to the author's
intending acts of consciousness. Whereas primary purely intentional correlates are accessible only to the conscious subject creating
them, derived purely intentional objects are *intersubjective,* since
they are based in meaning units that are themselves intersubjective.
Because derived purely intentional objects are detached from the
author's acts of consciousness, they lack the imaginational fullness,
the intuitive contents, that only subjective acts can provide (127). To
rephrase it, as soon as the purely intentional object loses its direct
contact with experience (the author's, in the first instance), and finds
its immediate ontic support in the borrowed intentionality of
meaning units, it also loses its imaginational intuitiveness, and its
manifold feeling and value characteristics. It becomes schematic
content which can be returned to "fullness" only by the intending
subjective conscious acts of the perceiver (of the language). Thus
Ingarden introduces his important notion of schematic aspects,
which will receive elaborate treatment as the aspect stratum, and
allow him to show how literature both "changes" and "stays the
same."

In section 22, Ingarden lists several differences between the
purely intentional correlates of simple word-meanings on the one
hand and sentences on the other. He then lists differences between
purely intentional correlates which coordinate to ontically auton-

omous states of affairs in the world, and purely intentional correlates which do not so coordinate (the latter would be the same as Husserl's "mere intentions"). Since literary works usually belong to this second kind, his remarks are very relevant. For instance, in the case of an intentional correlate which adequates to an existing state of affairs, the correlate must mirror this affair (142). On formal-ontological grounds, an objectively existing ontically autonomous state of affairs cannot contain material elements which are mutually contradictory. Neither, then, can the intentional correlate that mirrors it. Thus a "realistic" description of a real tree in the world cannot describe that tree as half elephant and half ostrich. However, a purely intentional correlate which does not correspond to an existing objectivity can contain mutually contradictory elements. Thus an imaginative piece of literature can legitimately project any kind of intentional correlate, including a self-contradictory one.

Another interesting distinction is that between the nature of an autonomous really existing entity in the world and the purely intentional correlate of a sentence. The former, since it really exists, is completely and unequivocally determined. As already indicated, the latter can never be completely determined, but only schematic. And if a sentence is ambiguous in its meaning content, this ambiguity is reflected in the accompanying purely intentional correlate, which then shows forth an "OPALESCENT MULTIPLICITY" (143). The ambiguity of a sentence can be based either on the ambiguity of individual words appearing in it, or on an ambiguity in sentence construction. One can read such a sentence in various ways and so arrive in each case at a different, and thus already unambiguous, sentence (the reader would be actualizing a series of different intentional correlates). But even then, says Ingarden, the reader would be in a quandary, because in the really ambiguous sentence nothing empowers us to favor any one of these readings.[2]

No, an arbitrary reduction from ambiguity to the certainty of one reading, or even a set of discrete readings, is not the solution. The ambiguous sentence is not to be identified with the manifold of unambiguous sentences obtained through "interpretation." In fact, it is precisely characteristic of truly ambiguous sentences that they allow a number of interpretations without firmly excluding or favoring any of them. But because all possible interpretations are allowed and equally justified, the purely intentional content of the correlate is also "opalescently" multiform and conceals conflicting elements within itself.

Ingarden is here attacking those theorists who mistakenly treat purely intentional correlates which have no objective counterparts as if they were intentional correlates with counterparts. Thus these theorists reject the possibility of a single ambiguous correlate with contradictory elements (because a real object in the world cannot so exist), and maintain an ambiguous sentence must have a number of correlates, each of them not self-contradictory. The individual correlates would then constitute a discrete manifold, each member of which would belong to a different reading of the sentence (and therefore, actually to a different sentence). In this way these theorists come to the assertion that an ambiguous sentence has no purely intentional correlate of its own but must first be made unambiguous in order to have one. But this view, says Ingarden, overlooks, or attempts to remove, exactly what has to be clarified, namely, the ambiguity itself. And the basic flaw of this view is to impose the law of non-contradiction operative in the real world, and in correlates which represent it, upon the world of those purely intentional correlates which don't have real existing adequations.

Ingarden insists *every* sentence, be it absurd or not, has its own single intentional correlate. A self-contradictory sentence has a single self-contradictory correlate. Finally, there is a special kind of literary work whose "basic character and peculiar charm" reside precisely in the ambiguities contained. These ambiguities are "calculated for the full enjoyment of the esthetic characters based on 'iridescence' and 'opalescence.'" Such literary works would lose their charm if one were to "improve" them by removing ambiguity.

The remaining sections in chapter five answer a string of other questions concerning the stratum of meaning units. I touch on just a few of these here. For one, just as individual word-meanings are modified when combined in a sentence, so too are sentence-meanings transformed when combined in sentence complexes, with the result that a "new whole" crystallizes (153). The "whole" determines and constitutes the roles of individual sentences, in that it provides the global *telos* whereby individual sentences assume contributive purposes; but on the other hand, the individual sentences determine and found the "whole," in that they must be read "first," and read in precise sequence (146). Though he doesn't use the term, Ingarden is actually paraphrasing here what was a contemporary definition of the "hermeneutical circle." We shall encounter more examples of this circle in Heidegger.

A second matter Ingarden addresses is the "quasi-judgmental" character of declarative sentences in a literary work. You will recall that a declarative sentence whose purely intentional object coordinates to an ontically autonomous entity is called a judgmental sentence. In contrast with this, Ingarden calls a sentence whose purely intentional object is not adequate to such an entity a pure affirmative sentence. In most literary works (with the outstanding exception of biographical, and some historical, novels), judgmental sentences do not appear, but nevertheless their purely intentional objects are "transposed" into the real world. The reader invests them with an "ontic setting" that is real, knowing full well, however, that this reality is a pretense. The purely intentional states of affairs or objects are "only *regarded* as really existing, without, figuratively speaking, being saturated with the character of reality" (emphasis added). Thus the declarative sentence of a literary work is a "quasi-judgment," and in an analogous manner, the interrogative sentence is a quasi-question and the imperative a quasi-command.

Just as individual nominal words intend individual objects and sentences intend "states of affairs," sentence complexes (also called "higher order" sentence formations) intend the realm of "represented objects," and the whole stratum of meaning units (of a given work) intends a "represented world." This holistic "represented world," like its constituent parts, is an ontically heteronomous intentional objectivity. Again Ingarden stresses that in terms of constitution, the stratum of sentences enjoys the central role in the literary work, since this stratum projects states of affairs which in turn constitute the whole array of represented objects. States of affairs perform several representing functions (which Ingarden reviews in detail) and can be divided into three groups (among others): states of essence (for example, "Gold is heavy"); states of thus-appearance ("In winter my room is dreary"); and states of occurrence ("My dog is running away quickly"). A special section is devoted to the representation of temporality, and conclusions reached here are used to pinpoint differences between the dramatic and melodramatic forms of literary works. Having thus completed a description of the second stratum's role in constituting the other strata, Ingarden ends chapter six with an outline of the esthetic values which inhere in the second stratum *in se,* and then proceeds to his next massive wave of argumentation: part seven, the stratum of represented objects. (Though earlier he had indicated "represented objectivities" constitute the fourth stratum, at this point he treats them as the third.)

After the introduction to this seventh part, Ingarden again approaches the issue of ontic status. The conclusion is that the represented objects of the literary work possess an "external habitus" of reality; they are simulations which have the character of reality, but are not in any absolute sense real. Next Ingarden scrutinizes space and time as they are represented in literature. His main purpose is to detach "represented" spatiality and temporality from "psychologizing" definitions which place them among the subjective psychic events of a conscious subject. First of all, "imagined objects" are to be distinguished from "imaginational objects." The former transcend the act of imagination, but are this act's intentionally directed target. The latter are not necessarily directed by an intending act, but rather have their own qualitative determinations and their own order (that is, they can be unintended and free-floating). So-called imaginational space is situated squarely in the data of imaginational objects. As opposed to imagined objects, imaginational objects are immanent in imaginational experience, and consequently are psychic and subjective. However, if the imaginational object is performing a function of representation, it behaves as a *proxy* for the imagined intentional object. The derived intentional objects projected by meaning units are in nowise to be identified with imaginational objects; and *ipso facto,* space represented by states of affairs is in nowise to be identified with "imaginational" space.

"Represented" space (that is, space in the literary work) is not abstract and geometric or homogeneous and physical. Instead, it is the kind of space that corresponds to perceptually given space and thus is orientational. The center of orientation for represented space is the represented world of the work, but the location of this center within various represented worlds can vary: in some works, the center is the ego of a represented narrator, whose presence is constant; in others, the center moves progressively from character to character. At this point Ingarden introduces his proof for the distinction between represented and imaginational space. When readers apprehend represented space, they fictitiously transpose themselves into the literary work's center of orientation, and to a certain extent forget their own centers. If literary space were imaginational, the perception of it would be internal to the readers, and their own orientational centers would necessarily become the centers of the literary space. But this is manifestly not so, as shown above; thus, represented space is not imaginational (or private psychic) space.

Hereupon, Ingarden turns to represented time, the temporality characteristic of literary works. Temporality can be homogeneous, "empty" physicomathematically determined world time; concrete, intuitively apprehendable inter-subjective time, in which we all live collectively; and strictly subjective time. Represented time is an analogue, and only an analogue, of concrete intersubjective or subjective time. Like intersubjective and subjective time, represented time is "colored" by the nature of particular occurrences associated with it. Thus, a moment of terror seems infinitely longer than, say, a moment of routine activity. The coloration of represented *tempi,* however, is provided by the literary work's "world," whereas that of personal *tempi* is determined by subjective or intersubjective occurrences (such as the real-life events of author or reader). There are still other differences. In "real" time, be it subjective or intersubjective, the present moment has a decided ontic advantage over the past and future. The "now-moment" is an actuality, what the scholastics used to call an *in actu esse;* and past and future moments are by definition *tempi* which have already undergone or will in some future moment undergo the passage from potency to act. In represented time, present, past, and future are delineated only by the *order* of represented events, and not by the fact that present, past, and future all pass through a distinct phase of genuine *in actu esse.* Other differences are that real time is continuous, and represented time appears in isolated segments; and that real time can never actually retrieve the past, while represented time can—it can make a past moment seem as vivid as a present one. Represented time can also undergo modification precluded by the nature of real time. For example, spans of time in the literary work can be just referred to or named, or they can be represented in a more concrete fullness. And finally, in the literary work past moments can be rendered as "past" or, with a change in style and tone, they can be rendered as if "present."

In the section which follows, Ingarden takes up the special case of "literary" historical works, that is, works which pertain to people and events that exist or have existed,[3] but which are to be distinguished from "scholarly" historical works. In the latter, states of affairs combine to form represented objects (or, more precisely, just as each sentence projects a state of affairs, sentences combined together project represented objects). The represented objects, which are purely intentional objectivities, coordinate to real historical objects in the world. Phenomenologically speaking, the purely intentional objectivities become transparent, so that the reader's intending act seems to "strike directly what is real." In the literary historical work, on the contrary, the represented (*dargestellten*) objects "take the place" of the real historical object in the world. This function, whereby the represented objects perform as proxies for real objects, Ingarden calls *Repräsentation* (rendered in the English translation as the capitalized word *Representation*). *Repräsentation* causes the represented objects to simulate the real objects to which they correspond, so that the latter are in part concealed from the reader, and the reader mistakes (at least experientially) the represented objects for the real objects. Of course, if the reader's understanding of the literary historical work is in accordance with its intrinsic essence, despite the tendency of *Repräsentation* to replace the real object with represented object, the complete concealment of the real object never occurs. Nevertheless, it is clear that scholarly historical works and literary historical works pertain to real objects in radically divergent ways.

Ingarden concludes his tract on this stratum with a key concept, namely, the "spots of indeterminacy" which characterize represented objectivities. Ontically autonomous objects in the world differ from represented objects in several ways. First, the former are unequivocally and thoroughly determined. That is to say, a real object cannot have any "spots" which are simultaneously (and in the same respect) A and non-A. Furthermore, the determinations of a real object constitute a primary concrete unity. Secondly, Ingarden qualifies the latter phrase with a passage useful for our later analysis of Heidegger: "Only when they [determinations of a real object] are distinguished from any others by a perceiving subject and are apprehended in themselves are they intentionally fetched forth from their primary state of fusion, and only then do they constitute an infinite, i.e., inexhaustible manifold." No matter how many determinations of a given object are apprehended up to a given moment, there are *always* other determinations still to be apprehended. Consequently, in primary cognition we can never know how a given real object is determined in every respect.

Thirdly, a real object is absolutely individual. For example, the essence *color* is itself a general, eidetic essence, but in the individual real object, color appears only as an individuation (that is, the quiddity of a determination is a concretization of an essence). In terms of content, the represented objectivities of a literary work do not possess the above three characteristics. For instance, in a simple nominal expression of a work, an expression such as *table* or *man*, the appertaining intentional object is actually projected with respect to its material makeup only in one moment of its constitutive nature. While the intentional object is formally intended as a concrete unit containing an infinite number of fused material determinations, at most only some of these material determinations are actually intended by the expression involved. Thus, as Ingarden will later show, the reader must materially "fill up" these spots of indeterminacy, so that the formal intention of the expression can be fulfilled. The same argument applies to the lack of absolute individuation in represented objects. The formal content of a nominal word meaning intends an individual determination, but the word's limited material content cannot fulfill this need. Again, only the reader can supply the necessary material individuation. So, from all the above, one may conclude that represented objectivities are only *schematic* formations with spots of indeterminacy of various kinds.

The status of schematic formation raises another question for Ingarden, however, and since this question concerns ambiguity again, I turn to it with some diligence. Among spots of determination there are those which can be "filled up" (or "concretized") purely on the basis of textual supplementation, and those which cannot be so easily treated. In the case of the former kind, the represented states of affairs designate a strictly circumscribed manifold of possible completions for the indeterminate sectors. The reader must choose only from those "completions" operative within the perimeters set by the text. For example, if the text reads (and let us assume the setting is contemporary America), "The man appeared at the door in sailor's blue trousers," the reader can concretize the blue trousers as azure-blue trousers, or cobalt-blue trousers, or navy-blue trousers, or any other blue-colored trousers. Since the text just says "blue," all of these concretizations are justified. The fact that in the real world navy uniforms are navy-blue in color, and even the fact (if it were the case) that the text in an earlier section called the trousers navy-blue, do not coerce the reader to concretize the "sailor's blue trousers" of the sentence in question as navy-blue. In Ingarden's words, "The literary work does not necessarily have to be 'consistent' or to be contained within the bounds of what is possible in the actually known world" (253). He then reminds us of his distinction between purely intentional correlates corresponding to ontically autonomous entities, and purely intentional correlates which do not so correspond (and non-historical literary works belong to this second type). There is, in short, no requirement that the non-historical literary work preclude improbable, or contradictory, or impossible states of affairs. In fact, a valid "esthetic impression" can be effected by a literary work which projects "a grotesque dance of impossibilities."

Ingarden does attach a qualification, however, though he says he doesn't have space to explain it in detail: "To what extent such an 'impossible' world can be exhibited and what esthetic value qualities and values it affords, are questions that introduce entirely *new* points of view, which without doubt require strictly regulated bounds for the allowable completions of the spots of indeterminacy." I take him to mean that if a reader wishes the concretizations to contribute to an organic (that is, consistent) reading or to match the real world as faithfully as possible (and all these for esthetic reasons), he or she can limit the choices accordingly. Thus, voluntarily adopting these tighter norms, the reader can impose a discipline which in our example would coerce the concretization of "sailor's blue trousers" as navy-blue trousers. But Ingarden's point is that the nature of the non-historical literary work does not require this. The above discussion applies *a fortiori* to the second kind of indeterminacy situation, wherein the text controls supplementation even less. Thus, if the sentence read "The man appeared at the door in sailor's trousers," the imagined color of the trousers would be fully dependent on the reader's (or in a stage play, the director's) discretion, and the trousers could be concretized as red, yellow, blue, or whatever.

Chapter eight, entitled "The Stratum of Schematized Aspects," studies schematic "aspects" first in relation to real objectivities, and then in relation to represented objects as such. That a study of aspects dependent on the real world can help in an understanding of literary aspects he demonstrates in the following way. In most extant literary works, represented objectivities are "of the nature of real objects," that is, the literary works are written in the "realistic" mode. I add a clarification here that Ingarden omits but is necessary to avoid confusion. The realistic mode is not at all to be confused with literary historical works, whose purely intentional objects coordinate to *actual* autonomous objects (as one may recall, Ingarden earlier made the point that a relatively small number of literary works are "historical"). The purely intentional objects projected by realistic literary works do not adequate to actual autonomous objects, but stand on their own; however, the purely intentional objects are realistically possible and their possibility is measured in terms of correspondence to the real world. Perhaps the matter is best explained by way of example. A historical novel may project a "house" which adequates to George Washington's actual house (though, as already shown, this adequation is partly concealed through the technique of *Repräsentation*); a realistic novel projects a house which adequates to no actual house, but which is "of the nature of a real house."

An examination of "aspects" dependent on the real world helps towards an understanding of literary "aspects" (at least in realistic literature) simply because realistic literature must be "attuned to the characteristic features of primary perceptual reality of real objects." In other words, realistic literature must be modeled after the way perceptual reality functions in the real world. Ingarden thus proceeds to a study of the perceptual modes of appearance of real things. He proposes a case in which a perceiver encounters an ontically autonomous red sphere, present in space before him (256,257). The first distinction to be made is between aspects and object. The sphere has its own existence, independent of the perception or non-perception of a viewer. In contrast, the aspects of the sphere remain in their existence and essence in continuous reference to the perceiving subject. If he were to shut his eyes, the aspects would be reduced to nonexistence. Aspects are not a psychic occurrence in the mind nor are they to be found in the space occupied by the sphere. Aspects are not psychic, but are nevertheless essentially dependent on the behavior of the subject.

Ingarden next proceeds to a description of the relation between aspect and object. Though these two are distinct, there is a "strict affiliation" between the perceptually given properties of a thing and the aspects of a thing. The given properties of a thing regulate the aspects in which the properties appear. And conversely, the aspects reveal the determinate properties of the thing. At this point Ingarden makes his second distinction. The concrete aspects of a thing are in constant transition. In his words, "There are, in fact, *no* two concrete aspects of the same thing, perceived from the same side, experienced *successively* by one and the same conscious subject, which would be *completely similar in every respect*. Both their fully concrete contents and the manner in which they are experienced must always differ in varying degree." Nonetheless, the appearance of the thing retains one and the same identity, and this identity is effected by the schematic aspects of the thing. Concrete aspects and schematic aspects are to be carefully distinguished, and the latter are a "skeleton" which permits the appearance of a thing to retain its self-identity. And Ingarden closes the section with a programmatic statement that remains somewhat enigmatic: "The question of the further filling-out of these schemata in given individual instances in part no longer depends on the object itself and on the selection of its properties but rather on various factors of a subjective nature that change from case to case."

The stage is now set for section 42, which deals precisely with schematized aspects in a literary work. As already indicated, schematic aspects play a role in all appearances of things. They play a special role, however, in the structure of the literary work, where they constitute an important stratum. The stratum is not generated by the experience of a psychic individual, but has its potential existence in the represented objects projected by meaning units. This potential, with predetermined limits, is actualized differently by each reader. In other words, the reader converts schematized aspects within predetermined limits into actualized aspects. That these actualized aspects differ with each reader becomes obvious from one of Ingarden's examples. Romain Rolland, in his novel *L'Ame enchantée*, represents various Parisian streets. Readers who have their own experiential knowledge of Paris actualize the relevant schematic aspects according to their personal and prior knowledge of the streets in question. In so doing, over and above the determinations controlled by the text, they actualize the streets according to concrete matter derived from former experiences of the city. Readers unacquainted with Paris obey the relevant aspects only in so far as they are schematized and predetermined. Their further actualizations of the schematized aspects are dependent on fantasy alone. It follows that the actualizations effected by the two groups of readers above would be different (at least in those sectors which are not predetermined).

Though Ingarden is very obscure on this point, I might add here that "spots of indeterminacy" are not the same as the gaps which characterize an aspect which is just schematic and not yet actualized. Spots of indeterminacy are fissures, if you will, in the determinate topography of a represented object. As fissures, they are part of that topography or part of the represented object (though they await concretization by the reader). The gaps in schematized aspects are not part of a represented object's topography, but part of the topography identified with aspects as such. And here I can resume an exposition of Ingarden, because his next thesis is precisely that literary aspects are not part of the represented object. Just as in real perception aspects are to be distinguished from the perceiving subject on the one hand and the object perceived on the other, so too in literary perception schematized aspects are to be respectively distinguished from the perceiver and the represented objectivity. Schematized aspects are not the represented objectivity, but "belong" to it by way of "coordination." This coordination arises "on the basis of a strict predetermination, between *possible* schematized aspects and corresponding represented objectivities."

Apropos this coordination, factors situated beyond represented objects are necessary for aspect actualization. Some of these factors can be *evoked* by various properties of the literary work, and others inhere in the experiencing psychic individual. In the case of factors evoked by the literary work, the language of that work is so constructed that it evokes factors which in turn "prepare" an actualization. Another way of explaining this is to say that some factors influence a schematic aspect, so that it is "held in readiness." The schematic aspect is "held in readiness" for a certain special actualization, and the reader is obliged to generate the unique actualization for which the schematic aspect is held ready. Exhibiting, and in particular exhibiting the thus-appearance of an object, brings with it this holding in readiness. Without elaboration, Ingarden avers that good figurative language and adept sound configuration (onomatopoeia, rhythm, and so forth) evoke the factors which hold schematic aspects in readiness. While not essential to a literary work, this "preparedness" characterizes esthetically successful works, since without it literature becomes "dead" and abstract. Ingarden winds down chapter eight with a short sketch of "internal aspects." Just as aspects of inanimate things reveal the properties of said things, internal aspects reveal psychic states. If relevant internal aspects are not held in readiness, the human characters of a novel or poem become "lifeless, 'paper' figures."

Chapter nine, entitled "The Role of the Stratum of Schematized Aspects in a Literary Work," brings yet more specificity to the basic theses (relevant to schematic aspects) laid out in the preceding section. I mention here only what are in my opinion the more important services performed by chapter nine: further clarification of the privileged esthetic status enjoyed by schematic aspects "held in readiness"; practical exemplification (sorely needed) of "prepared" schematic aspects; and discussion of the decorative function of aspects. Schematic aspects "held in readiness" are to be preferred over schematic aspects which do not so tightly bind the reader, and the reason for this preference seems clear: in Ingarden's words, if the reader is not sufficiently bound by the work, "it would be entirely a matter of chance as to what aspects were in fact actualized" (277).

The key assumption seems to be that the author should "build into" the literary work an esthetic wholeness, and that aspects "held in readiness" advance the cause of this wholeness. When actualization is left to "chance," such a wholeness can easily break down (unless the reader himself is esthetically gifted, and can engineer esthetically appropriate actualizations). At this point, it seems to me Ingarden is also implying a value-judgment concerning a kind of ambiguity. Ingarden has already stressed the esthetic value of meaning-units which are intended as ambiguous by the author, especially if the ambiguities are ordered by the author towards an overall aesthetic harmony. It seems reasonable to assume that schematic aspects (which can also be ambiguous) can be aesthetic precisely because of their ambiguity, as long as this ambiguity is predetermined by the author, and "built into" the "preparedness" of the aspects. That is, a schematic aspect can be purposely designed in such a way that two or more variant actualizations of it can occur, though these are all predetermined by the "held in readiness" of the aspect in question. Altogether different from this case is the one in which the aspects are ambiguous because they lack sufficient "preparedness." The disparate actualizations which result from "unpreparedness," abandoned to chance as they are, receive Ingarden's disapproval. He does not deny that unprepared aspects are sufficient to constitute a necessary stratum (in other words, with the other three strata they are enough to make a "literary work"), but he considers their presence proof of aesthetic mediocrity.

Among the examples of "prepared" schematic aspects cited by Ingarden are acoustical ones (278). For instance, through "two words identical in meaning but different in word sound *different* aspects can be held in readiness"; or in another case, "by virtue of its word sound, a word may hold in readiness a *different* aspect than the one predetermined by its meaning"; or in still another case, "an aspect held in readiness by a word sound may *exceed* the objective 'something' that is determined by the meaning." Even from these few examples, it seems clear to me that Ingarden is attempting to account for what are more ordinarily called "connotations," especially connotations controlled by non-conceptual elements of language. But it is crucial to remember here that Ingarden, conforming to the emphases allocated by Husserl himself, regards intentionality as a conceptual act. Thus purely intentional objects can only be intended conceptually, and there is no room within the intentional process for the intending of non-conceptual elements. Heidegger, and Merleau-Ponty after him, will later postulate non-conceptual intentions (and corresponding intentional objects), so that what Ingarden calls "schematic aspects" are absorbed into represented objects themselves. For Ingarden, there can be no talk of "emotive" meaning, but only of conceptual meaning; non-conceptual elements, such as "intuitive appearance," must be relegated to another process, namely that of "aspects" (and these are not part of the meaning as such, but are just "strictly affiliated" to the meaning).

Finally, chapter nine deals with the decorative properties of aspects, for the aspect stratum, like the others, not only contributes to the literary work as a whole but also possesses aesthetic qualities in its own right. To make his point, Ingarden makes use of a quite apposite analogy. The artistically gifted photographer chooses from among the possible aspects of a given object those which, "comparatively speaking, best bring out the similarity of the picture to the given object." However, the gifted photographer goes on to do more: he or she organizes color, line effects, and light so that they form a decorative whole which is pleasing *in se*. Ingarden argues that the talented writer also executes this decorative task, by the distribution of aspects in a way which is aesthetically gratifying.

Chapter ten offers Ingarden's very fecund treatment of "metaphysical qualities," and bears the title, "The Role of Represented Objectivities in a Literary Work of Art and the So-Called Idea of a Work." Ingarden begins with what seems to be a conundrum: all other strata of the literary work have as their primary purpose the representation of objects (that is, they actively construct represented objectivities); but the stratum of represented objects, for its part, seems not to constitute anything else, but simply to "be." Yet literary scholars have not been satisfied with such a proposition. They have sensed there is "something" which is directly dependent on the object stratum, and to which the object itself is accessory. Fallaciously they have assumed the "something" is a mood, or possibly ethical instruction, or even the "expression" of the author's experiences or ideas. Ingarden is soon to propose that the "something" is "metaphysical quality," but before so doing, he describes what metaphysical qualities (essences) are. In section 48, he first gives examples of metaphysical essences, citing "the sublime, the tragic, the dreadful, the shocking, the inexplicable, the demonic, the holy, the sorrowful," and several others. He then avers these essences are not properties of objects, nor features of psychic states, but are "usually revealed, in complex and often very disparate situations or events, as an atmosphere which, hovering over the men and the things contained in these situations, penetrates and illumines everything in its light." Most importantly, metaphysical qualities do not allow purely rational determination. Instead, they are "seen" in a quasi-ecstatic way and are "what makes life worth living."

Ingarden next examines the role of metaphysical qualities in the literary work (section 49), saying that the most significant function of the object stratum is the exhibiting and manifesting of these qualities. Precisely because the object stratum is ontically heteronomous, however, and only feigns a *habitus* of reality, metaphysical qualities cannot be realized in represented objectivities. The qualities can only be revealed therein and "simulate their own realization." In fact, metaphysical qualities as revealed in literature assume the ontic status of represented objectivities and become, like these objectivities, purely intentional. In a passage somewhat reminiscent of Kant, Ingarden claims that the peculiar ontic status metaphysical qualities possess when in literature actually works to the reader's advantage. Whereas metaphysical qualities realized in the real world often cause turmoil, the same qualities revealed in literature can be contemplated with relative calm. At this juncture I might add for purposes of clarification that metaphysical qualities are not a stratum of the literary work: if they were, an ideal level would become part of the work (since metaphysical qualities are ideal), and this consequence Ingarden has been at pains to avoid.[4] Metaphysical qualities are therefore not essential to literary structure, though their revelation is an earmark of great literature.

In section 52, Ingarden engages the problem of "truth" and "idea" in literature. Recall that already in sections 25 and 25a he had distinguished between judgmental sentences, which coordinate to ontically autonomous entities, and pure affirmative sentences (characteristic of all literary works except some historico-biographical novels), which do not have autonomous adequations.

Now dilating this notion somewhat more, Ingarden declares that "reality" is a "determinate relationship between a true judicative proposition and an objectively existing state of affairs selected by its meaning content." If such a relationship prevails, the judicative sentence carries a "relative quasi-feature," which is expressed by the word "true." Obviously, no such relationship normally exists in the case of the literary work, so literature cannot be in the strict sense "true." Recall, however, that in those same sections, Ingarden had argued most literature, being "realistic" in mode, produced a kind of "quasi-judgmental" sentence. Now Ingarden amplifies this notion too, suggesting that "truth" can mean "objective consistency." If a literary work establishes represented objects which are "of the nature of reality" (or of any other holistic network of entities), a consistency must be maintained in the work's further determination of these objects, so the whole object stratum is constituted as ontically identical.

To put it more simply, entities in the real domain (and in the ideal domain, too!) follow consistent laws; a novel which simulates the real (or ideal) world must imitate these laws throughout, and thus be "objectively consistent." And this objective consistency is a kind of literary "truth."

Before proceeding to the question of an "idea" in the literary work, Ingarden adds almost *en passant* a second sense of "truth" or "untruth" in literature. Whether a work is objectively consistent or not, it may manifest a "metaphysical quality." Here the "truth" is the metaphysical quality itself, or its revelation in the literary text. Then Ingarden penetrates the notion of literary "idea," dismissing on aforesaid grounds any identification of "idea" and "true propositions" (and he intends to reject in particular the *Geistesgeschichte* school). The concept of metaphysical quality reenters, however, and Ingarden is willing to acknowledge the word *idea* in literature if by it is meant the mysterious non-rational "sense" that metaphysical quality entails. According to this definition, the "idea" of a work is founded on "the *essential connection*, brought to intuitive self-givenness, that exists between a determinate represented life-situation, taken as a culminating phase of a development preceding it, and a metaphysical quality that manifests itself in that life-situation and draws its unique coloration from its content" (304).

Though Ingarden's main activity throughout has been vertical cross section of the literary work, in chapter eleven he attempts a longitudinal section. Entitled "The Order of Sequence in a Literary Work," chapter eleven discusses whether literary structure is temporally extended, or if its sequential nature is of another sort. Here as elsewhere, the distinction between literary work and its concretizations is quite practicable. Yes, Ingarden asserts, the reader's apprehension of a literary work is a temporally extended process, and the concretization produced thereby is likewise extended. But the literary work itself is not a temporal sequence. If it were, one and the same literary work would achieve different temporal extensions according to the variant lengths of given readings! The actual case is that a work "exists *simultaneously* in *all* of its parts," and "none of these parts is 'earlier' or 'later' in a temporal sense." Nevertheless, the literary work does quite obviously present a sequential order of some kind: "determinate states of affairs must be 'already' projected so that others may be constructed upon them" (309). If one were to reverse the sequential order of sentences in a work, the meaning would become nonsensical, or at least undergo radical change. There is, in other words, a *"one-sidedness of conditioning* in the constitution" of literary sequence, and Ingarden draws upon Husserl's concept of "founding" to explain it. Every phase of literary structure (except the first) has its foundation in moments of an "earlier" phase; every phase also has some elements requiring no foundation in other phases; and every phase (except the last) founds moments of a "subsequent" phase.

Part three, flying under the banner "Supplementation and Conclusions," begins with studies of "borderline cases" such as the stage play, the film, pantomime, and other scientific work (I pass over these sections, since they are tangential). Part three then confronts those factors which were excluded from the body of Ingarden's book, simply because they are not part and parcel of the literary work itself, but only associated with it. Heretofore, says Ingarden, he has treated subjective operations only where the literary work itself indicated them. Now he will restore literature to its contacts with reader and culture, in order to discover what situations and problems result. Though a literary work contains "spots of indeterminacy" and "schematized aspects" (and these await fulfillment "from the outside," as it were), the reader does not normally advert to these. How then does the literary work appear during reading, and what is the "immediate correlate" of this reading? Earlier chapters have already suggested the answer: concretizations are the immediate correlate constituted during the reading, and concretizations form the mode of appearance of the work. They are "the concrete form in which the work itself is apprehended." In part three, Ingarden intends to describe concretizations further, and indicate their relationships with both the literary work and the reader's subjective experience. He undertakes the latter task first, examining in section 62 the concretizations of a literary work in relation to the experiences of apprehension. He distinguishes three kinds of apprehension: (1) cognitive acts, such as perceptual ones, (which apprehend word signs and sounds, and phonetic formations of a higher order), (2) meaning-apprehending acts (based on cognitive actions), and (3) acts of imaginative beholding (which regard represented objectivities and situations). Over and above these, experiences of aesthetic enjoyment are aroused and emotions evoked. Because of the complexity of literary structure, the reader's attention is forever shifting; the literary work "is never *fully* grasped in *all* its strata and components but always only partially."

Ingarden's controversial thesis, however, is that concretizations, though dependent on these variable acts of apprehension both existentially and materially, are to be strictly distinguished from them. Concretizations, unlike acts of apprehension, are neither psychic nor experiential. To argue that the concretizations are psychic because they depend on psychic acts is to commit a logical fallacy: to so argue "would be the same as saying that two objects, A and B, that are mutually dependent in their existence must *eo ipso* always be of the same kind or be related as part to whole!" Concretizations indeed have an ontic base in subjective acts, but they have a second ontic base in the literary work itself, and with respect to acts of apprehension, concretizations are just as transcendent as the literary work itself is. While Ingarden disclaims here a comprehensive theory coordinating conscious experience and ontically heteronomous objectivities, (he earlier refers the reader to his *The Cognition of the Literary Work* for such a treatment), he does provide some indications. I take them to mean that psychic components are only known through an attentive gaze into experience itself (a process Ingarden calls, after Geiger, "*inner perception*"). But when reading a literary work, the reader focuses attention not on his or her own inner psychic life, but on the literary work. Thus concretizations *ipso facto* cannot be psychic components. Ingarden concludes on a polemical note: "Only a theorizing literary critic could hit upon the bizarre idea of looking for the literary work 'in the mind' of the reader."

Section 63 illuminates the other distinction that renders

Ingarden's formulation unique, the distinction between literary work and its concretizations. In that Heideggerians reject this distinction, Ingarden's treatment is especially relevant for our overall enterprise. The section begins with the claim that a reader apprehends a literary work "only in the form of one of its concretizations." In a footnote Ingarden answers what is the immediate objection: how can the reader contrast the actual work with a concretization if the work is apprehendable from the start only in the form of a concretization? His answer is that a concretization "is not a cloak that impedes access to the work itself. The individual differences between concretizations already enable us to establish what belongs to the work itself and what pertains to the accidentally conditioned concretizations" (336, 337). And this response really suggests two answers, one phenomenological and the other analytic. First, in the very phenomenology of the esthetic experience, the reader "sees" the difference between the personal contribution to that experience and the contribution rendered by the work itself. And second, the reader can isolate the "literary work itself" through an analytic procedure, comparing many experiences of the work and identifying the work itself as that part of the multiple experiences which remains constant. Both phenomenological and analytic attention to the line between work and concretization is very calculated however, and Ingarden makes the point that a reader normally does not make such a discrimination. Ingarden, of course, as an aesthetician doing an aesthetician's necessary work, must make it, and he proceeds to list seriatim several differences between literature proper and the concretizing activity.

The first difference, naturally enough, is a phonic one: in the literary work itself, word sounds appear only as typical Gestalt qualities; in the concretization, the Gestalt qualities achieve concrete expression. In fact, a "good" declamation can even add esthetic values to the work-as-concretized. Next, on the morphemic level, a concretization "fills" spots of indeterminacy, and even changes at times the relation between a word meaning and its meaning contents (that is, the contents a word represents). For example, readers from different regions of a country may interpret a word according to what are varying dialectical meanings. Even if these variations produce "no significant deviation," they can determine objectivities "more closely or differently than these are predetermined by the work itself." One can quite legitimately ask at this point, "no significant deviation" from what? Ingarden's assumption here is that the reader's "duplicating or reactualizing operation" should correspond to the "primal operation" of the author, and that this correspondence is mediated by the "intentionality of the word" (which should correlate to the intentionality of the author). Some distortion is distributed throughout this nexus of processes, and occurs primarily because the "intentionality of the word" is schematic. But when correspondence between author's intention and reader's actualization breaks down "significantly," there emerges what must be called "a new work, one that is only more or less related to the original." It seems, furthermore, that "significant deviation" is for Ingarden purely a matter of degree. Ingarden introduces here a third distinction between work and concretization, one that flows from what has just been said, and from his earlier treatment of literary intentionality. In sum, the intentionality of a literary work is "loaned" or derived, but a concretization has an intentionality which is actual and concrete: the concretizing process restores "fullness" to intention, a fullness qualitatively tantamount to that it had in the author's primal intentionality.

A fourth distinction, one which Ingarden calls the "most radical difference" of all, appears in the aspect stratum, where schematic aspects are raised to the level of imaginational concreteness. Even when the aspects are "held in readiness," part of their concretization inevitably escapes the control of the text. These uncontrolled elements are so dependent on the individuality of the reader and the moment of his reading that no two concretizations can be entirely alike. All of this we have already heard from Ingarden before, but he adds here two criteria for discriminating between "same work" and "new work" (340). When can a given concretization be considered a concretization of the same literary work the author produced, and when is a concretization so different that it is an expression of a new work? Ingarden answers first that "the identity of the work presented in various concretizations can be maintained only if the objectivities represented in it permit in their thus-appearance various styles of modes of appearance. . . ." In other words, if the predetermined aspects of the work are not contradicted, and if, over and above these, the aspects leave open (or undetermined) a whole range of further concretizations, the reader may legitimately effect these in any way he wants, and still claim to be "rounding out" the original work. Second, Ingarden insists that if the original work is to be preserved, the reader's execution of thus-appearances must leave intact the original metaphysical qualities predetermined by the text: the identity of the work can be maintained only if "the change in the style of appearance does not effect the manifestation of metaphysical qualities predetermined in the work itself."

Then, in a passage that concurs with the position of E. D. Hirsch, though it of course pre-dates Hirsch's by several decades, Ingarden says that falsifying concretization can obscure a literary work for centuries at a time. Ingarden says a work "can be expressed for centuries in such a masked, falsifying concretization until finally someone is found who understands it correctly, who sees it adequately, and who in one way or another shows its true form to others." And he continues, again anticipating Hirsch, "Herein lies the great role of literary criticism (or literary history). . . . Through it the true form of the work can again be expressed." The literary historian, then, has as his specific charge the placement of a literary work in its original authorial and cultural context, so that its linguistic determinations and predeterminations can be properly understood, and thus concretized "correctly." Ingarden closes the section with two last distinctions between work and concretization: just as concretizing activity fulfills the first two strata, it brings a kind of *plenum* to the object stratum as well, so that only in concretization proper do represented objectivities achieve truly explicit appearance; and likewise, only in concretization does the sequential order of a literary work convert into phenomenal concrete time as such.

Section 64 copes with the "life" of a literary work and its concretizations, and it is from this section that Wellek apparently borrowed the notion of literary "life" which appears in *Theory of Literature* (though Wellek mutates Ingarden's original concept substantially). The term *life* in general (and without necessary application to a literary work's life) can mean, first, "the *totality* of events happening to a living being from its beginning to its death," and, second, "the 'process' of becoming of these events." If one takes the word *life* in its second sense, one may infer that every being which is alive retains its individuality for a span of time. If one takes the word in its first sense, one may also infer that every living being continually changes during its life-span (while still retaining its own identity). Ingarden now narrows his focus to the "life" of a literary work. He grants that literature does not "live" in the strict sense, because it is passive rather than active; and also because it need not change (despite changes in its concretizations). Literature does have a "life" in two figurative senses, however: it lives "while *it is expressed in a manifold of concretizations,"* and it lives "while it undergoes changes as a result of ever new concretizations." In terms of the first sense above, Ingarden apparently intends to make two points. First, concretizations imaginatively flesh out the literary work, so that the work has a "life" it could not have when isolated from concretizing acts. Though distinct from its concretizations, the literary work takes on life when in relation to concretizations. And second, concretizations themselves vary, operate within a tradition, and influence each other (all through the medium of individual readers). Though the given literary work can remain constant, its many individuated concretizations constitute a tradition which is forever changing. This "history" of concretizations is after all a "totality of events happening to a living [in the figurative sense] being," namely the literary work. The tradition of concretizations, then, quite apart from the literary work itself, has a "life."

In terms of the second sense defined above, (that is, literature's life "while it undergoes changes as a result of ever new concretizations"), Ingarden wishes to advance a different proposition. Not only is the literary work *vivified* by its relation to concretizations; it can also be changed under the influence of the concretizing process. Ingarden has already said the literary work can remain constant despite concretization. The other side of the coin is that it can also change. (Whether the original work becomes a new work thereby or not depends on the degree of deviation.) I have shown in a previous section how a word projecting one meaning in the original work can be interpreted elsewhere according to a different meaning, and this because of dialectical variation. Ingarden adds at this point a second example: the author may have intended a particular meaning for a given word, and the "derived intentionality of the word" in the text would then theoretically correspond to the author's intention; but the reader may actualize a different part of the potential stock of meanings belonging to that word. The reader's "duplicating intention" would not be "duplicating" the true "intentionality of the word." Both of the above actions, caused respectively by dialectical variation and faulty actualization, effect a real change in the object stratum and not just in the concretization proper. On the other hand, these changes, at least when isolated and occasional, are not by any means "significant deviations" which repress the original work and establish a new one. The literary work retains its own identity despite them. Thus Ingarden is able to conclude that one and the same literary work can mutate, and a history of these mutations constitutes a kind of "life."

In chapter fourteen, "The Ontic Position of a Literary Work," Ingarden performs a reprise of his previous statements on ontic status and then secures his theory with some substantive additions. He distinguishes between "the basis of the *coming into being* of the literary work," and "the ontic basis of its *existence*" once it has been formed. The former process, as indicated earlier, rests squarely on the subjective operations of the author while forming the work. The author bestows meaning through selective actualizations of the meaning-stocks belonging to given ideal concepts. The work, of course, transcends these subjective intentional acts of the author. As for the ideal concepts themselves, they constitute the ontic base of the completed and existing work, and the ideal concepts too transcend the work. Represented objects, and the meaning units which project them, are heteronomous and purely intentional; to use Ingarden's earlier term, they are "ontic nothings." In section 67, Ingarden adds a third ontic base, one which supports (along with ideal concepts) the *existence* of the literary work. This third base is the array of word-signs, be they oral (as in a dramatic performance) or written (as in printed matter). The intersubjective availability of the literary work, then, is guaranteed by two intersubjective factors: ideal concepts and their meaning stocks, and word sounds as such (as long as these word sounds correlate to their appropriate word-signs in an intersubjective manner).

The last chapter[5] of *Das literarische Kunstwerk* answers a final objection. Is it possible that the "polyphonic harmony of esthetic value qualities" is the real work of art, so that the four strata only "found" the work, but do not belong to it? Ingarden's answer is of course in the negative, and he answers by way of a brief phenomenology—a phenomenology of the reader's attentive gaze on the literary work. The phenomenology reveals that a reader's attention views all four of the strata and fixes with special concentration on the stratum of represented objects. The reader's gaze cannot and does not view a polyphony which transcends the strata; rather, the polyphony is a network of relationships among the strata, and is inseparable from them. But if the polyphony is not itself the "aesthetic object," what is? Ingarden is unwilling to grant the status of aesthetic object to the isolated literary work, since a work needs contact with a reader if its potential qualities are to be fulfilled. Ingarden settles for the following formulation: "the literary work of art constitutes an *esthetic* object *only when it is expressed in a concretization."* The concretization is not the aesthetic object, mind you, but the literary work is, as long as it is expressed in a concretization. *Das literarische Kunstwerk* ends, appropriately, on a poetic note. "The literary work," we are told, "is a true wonder. . . . It is a 'nothing' and yet a wonderful world in itself—even though it comes into being and exists only by our grace." Roman Ingarden has produced an impressive if labyrinthine theory of literature. I hope my exposition has helped the reader through the maze. What is more, Ingarden has said much pertaining to the question of valid meaning in literature. Again, I ask the reader to remember these formulations, and to await my analysis in the last chapter.

# chapter 3

# Mikel Dufrenne

Mikel Dufrenne's *The Phenomenology of Aesthetic Experience* (hereupon called *The Phenomenology*) deals with all the arts.[1] In order to stay within the allotted subject-matter of my book, I shall concentrate only on those sections of *The Phenomenology* which concern literature as well as the other arts. Dufrenne's title is a misnomer of sorts, since only parts one and three are phenomenological. Part four is in large part Kantian, and Ingarden has publicly taken Dufrenne to task for this (there is also considerable dependence on Hegel). I shall devote most space to *The Phenomenology*'s first part, since in my opinion it contributes most, strictly speaking, to a phenomenology of literature. Throughout, I shall compare Dufrenne's theories to those of Ingarden. Dufrenne's introduction charts the cartography of his overall enterprise. By aesthetic experience Dufrenne means not that of the author, but that of the perceiver. The aesthetic object then becomes the correlate of this perceiver's experience, just as the experience in turn is the correlate of the aesthetic object. This reciprocity of definition is circular, but in the legitimate Heideggerian sense of the *Zirkel im Verstehen*. And Dufrenne argues that aesthetic object as coefficient of the perceiver's experience receives a securer definition than it would as coefficient of the author's; the latter correlation comports a dangerous fallacy: that the author's creative energy is transferred to the aesthetic object without detrition or loss. Dufrenne consigns his definition of phenomenology to a footnote (strange?), and I quote it *in toto* because of its contrast with the Husserlian school:

> It will be seen that we are not striving to follow Husserl to the letter. We understand phenomenology in the sense in which Sartre and Merleau-Ponty have acclimated this term in France: a description which aims at an essence, itself defined as a meaning

immanent in the phenomenon and given with it. The essence is
something to be discovered, but by way of an unveiling, not a leap
from the known to the unknown. Phenomenology applies
primarily to the human, because consciousness is consciousness of
self; in this, we have the model of the phenomenon: appearing as
the appearing of meaning to itself.

At this point, Dufrenne follows Ingarden in two respects. First,
he denounces psychologism and distinguishes between intending
act and object intended. The aesthetic object is not reducible to acts
of either the perceiver or the author. Second, he distinguishes
aesthetic object from the "work of art." Aesthetic object and work of
art are "noemata having the same content but differing in that the
noesis is different." The aesthetic object is the art object aesthetically
perceived, and the work of art pure and simple is the same object
non-aesthetically perceived (or, presumably, not perceived at all).
Then, in a covert attack on Ingarden, Dufrenne denies that the work
of art is real and the aesthetic object ideal, "as if the former existed as
a thing in the world and the latter as a representation or
signification in consciousness." In a later section devoted to *Das
literarische Kunstwerk,* Dufrenne will equate Ingarden's notion of
purely intentional being with idealism (despite Ingarden's arguments to the contrary in that same book), and he will deny the
uniqueness of that status Ingarden calls heteronomy. Heteronomy,
Dufrenne declares, is not unique to the aesthetic object, but
characterizes all objects: "Every object, including natural objects
and works of art considered as things given in the cultural world, is
an object for consciousness" (lxv). Dufrenne, though he must grant
that the aesthetic object needs perception, will soon stress the
priority of the perceived over the perceiving; thus, he here wishes to
deny that the aesthetic object is more dependent on conscious acts
than other objects are.

Dufrenne announces that *The Phenomenology of Aesthetic
Experience* is divided into four parts. Part one, "Phenomenology of
the Aesthetic Object," describes the art object as aesthetically
perceived. Part two, "Analysis of the Work of Art," analyzes the art
object not as perceived, but as "reflected upon." The purpose here is
to expose the "objective structure" of the work. We cease to perceive
the object in order to study it as "an occasion for perceiving." Part
three, "Phenomenology of Aesthetic Perception," describes aesthetic
perception as the correlate of the aesthetic object. And finally, part
four, "Critique of Aesthetic Experience," examines in *vue globale*

the mutual implication of art object and perceiver. *The Phenomenology*, then, (as Dufrenne readily admits), displays not only
phenomenological inquiry, but analysis and metaphysical speculation as well.

Part one begins with an ontological question, and moves to an
epistemological one. Is the art work real or unreal? And where is the
locus of the art work's meaning? Dufrenne's first conclusion is that
in relation to the art work, "I do not posit the real as real, because
there is also the unreal which the real designates; I do not posit the
unreal as unreal, because there is also the real which promotes and
supports the unreal." Though Dufrenne is speaking of all man-
made aesthetic objects, we can readily apply his notion to the
literary aesthetic object. Phonic material is réal, but the represented
objects projected by the meaning units it founds are unreal: the
aesthetically perceived literary work suggests both real and unreal,
because each ontological status "refers to the other which denies it."
The aesthetic object *in se* is neither real nor unreal, however, since
each status is "disqualified through neutralization," and is thus not
grasped in itself.

Dufrenne goes on to propose the central thesis of his whole
book (and the influence of Merleau-Ponty is obvious): "Therefore,
what is irreplaceable, the very substance of the work, is the sensuous
or perceptible element [*le sensible*] which is communicated only in
its presence. . . ." "Meaning or sense [*sens*]" is immanent in the
sensuous and is both multiple and single. Meaning is multiple
because each color motif or musical phrase or rhythm sequence has
a unity of its own; yet meaning is single because the aforesaid lesser
unities constitute one larger unity. And what about the represented
object? It is "unreal with respect to the real, everyday world around
me, but, insofar as it is the life of the poem, the meaning which gives
unity to the words, it is not unreal. Yet it becomes again unreal with
respect to a higher form of meaning, which unifies the previous
meanings." Dufrenne is here taking fearsome dialectical turns, but
his ultimate devalorization of the represented object is inevitable.
Whereas Ingarden considers represented objects the most important
level of the work (and this because he, like Husserl, is cognitively
oriented), Dufrenne considers the perceived most important. Thus
Dufrenne declares that the "higher unity" characterizing the
aesthetic object transcends the intelligible and is "expressive" in
nature. This expressive unity is the organic coalescence of sensuous
elements. Another name for this unity is the "idea" of the work, as

long as we understand by "idea" a concrete idea that is enmeshed in sensuosity. Perception, not rational cognition, "delivers" the sensual to the witness. Contemplation has priority over reflection. Dufrenne here takes the opportunity to discredit idealism. As we've already seen, the "realism" of the aesthetic object is relative to the frame of reference (and, as happens so often in Dufrenne, is at the same time quite paradoxical). Its possible idealism, however, suffers a worse fate: Dufrenne flatly rejects any such theory. He argues that the "idea" of the work cannot be an objective ideal, because expressive unity is identified with the sensuous, and the sensuous, alas, is eminently mutable. Nor can the aesthetic object be ideal in the subjective sense, since the coordinates of the object's structure precede perception and are "pregiven" in the art work.

Chapter two, "The Work and Its Performance," depends heavily on Ingarden's concept of concretization, though Dufrenne's term for the latter is "performance," and his notion of performance underplays imagination in favor of perceptual enactment. Like Ingarden, Dufrenne draws upon Husserl's "qualities of manifestation," but even in this instance the manifestative qualities are carried quite exclusively by the sensuous (for example, by intonation in the case of literature). This stress on the sensuous naturally tends to prefer poetry (which is rich in rhyme, rhythm, alliteration, and so on) over prose forms, though later Dufrenne tries to salvage genres such as the novel through a bit of casuistry: he notes that even silent reading is accompanied by a kind of internal articulation based in the autonomous nervous system. The next sequence in Dufrenne's argument resumes close association with Ingarden. Dufrenne insists on performative fidelity to the art work, even if the hermeneutical process is circular: "When we abandon the aesthetic attitude in order to appraise the interpretation of a work, we judge the interpretation in terms of the work—but only because we know the work from its interpretation" (23). He goes on to add (significantly) that "nevertheless, we do have to grant a *truth* of the work which is independent of its performance or anterior to it." This last proposition will ultimately commit Dufrenne to the battlelines arrayed against the "New Hermeneutic."

To resume our exposition, however, we must here note that Dufrenne, like Ingarden, grants that performances can distort an art work. A given tradition of performances "sometimes guides, if not alters, our judgment by imposing too exclusive an image of the aesthetic object." All this is not meant to deny the positive role of performance, of course. The art work does not manifest truths until it is performed. The touchstones of successful performance, though, are the anterior "demands" of the work. And these demands are "inexhaustible," simply because they arise from the work's inexhaustible "depth" (a concept Dufrenne is to define later). Again following *Das literarische Kunstwerk* very closely, Dufrenne describes "a life of the work through history," so a given work "waxes or wanes, is enriched or impoverished, according to the warmth of our devotion to it, and the meaning we discover in it" (25). He then attacks the New Hermeneutic frontally, arguing that "If everything were caught up in the swirl of history, there would be no history at all." That is, unless there are constants, there can be no history. Things must in a way stay the same, if we are to notice that in other ways they change. If I might add a practical example, we cannot speak of French history unless we retain the constant which is the French people. Or, we cannot speak of changes in the performance of *Hamlet* unless we retain a bedrock constant which is *Hamlet*. Various interpretations of a work then become realizations of the various anterior demands of that work, and since these demands arise from the work's "inexhaustible depth," many diverse interpretations can be valid. To be valid, however, they must actualize a demand that is really there in the work; they must, in Dufrenne's words, "remain pliant and deferential" before the art object, so its "objectivity" is confirmed.

Chapter three, "The Work and Its Public," deals with what the art work demands of its perceiver, and what the perceiver expects of the art work. In regard to the perceiver's contribution to aesthetic experience, Dufrenne poses what is to become an increasingly important motif in his thought: "the sensuous is an act common to the sensing being and to what is sensed." In the case of literature, for example, the sensuous does not arise until the abstract existence of written sign is transformed into concrete existence by means of the reader's articulation. The sensuous, in other words, results from the complicity of the work's signs and the reader's voice. I might add parenthetically that the above implies the intending act accounts for the sensuous as much as the intended object does; such a formulation is much sounder, from a phenomenological point of view, than what Dufrenne suggests in some other passages, namely, that the sensuous is an intentional object exclusively.

Dufrenne proceeds to focus on literature, distinguishing as Sartre does between prose and poetry. In prose, language is largely instrumental, so the reader's attention "passes through" the words at once, and comes to rest in the projected conceptual meaning. A hasty conclusion at this point, says Dufrenne, might be that the novel is not quite an art, because the sensuous is short-changed in it. However, in collusion with Sartre, he grants that the language of the novel does more than signify concepts; its language represents by "imaging" and thus achieves a certain density and personality. The function of "imaging" is enough to vindicate the novel as an art, but poetry (since it is phonically sensuous) much outranks the novel (which is imaginative but non-sensuous).

It is to poetry that Dufrenne turns next, though here he significantly alters the Sartrean position. With Sartre, he agrees that the poetic word is a thing rather than a mere sign. But where Sartre considers the poetic word an image-thing, Dufrenne considers it a sound-thing. Characteristically, Dufrenne is again shifting the aesthetic locus from imagined object to perceived object. If the reader is a witness to the perceived object, he or she is also a performer of it, and *vice versa*. Thus Dufrenne introduces another phenomenological formulation, one that claims to transcend the Cartesian dichotomy of subject and object.[2] The reader is not a subject outside of an object which is the work. Instead, the reader is both performer and witness. He or she is both inside and outside the work, so that the Cartesian formulation isn't really serviceable. The reader is inside the work in that he or she psychologically projects the self into its world, and allows it to govern performance. Yet the reader is outside the work, for by remaining at the same time a witness, one does not actively generate meaning of one's own. The art work, then, demands that the perceiver be performer and witness. What in turn does the art work do for the perceiver? Dufrenne suggests two functions of art: it forms "taste," and it forms a "public." Taste, in this conception, is not a return to subjectivity and to personal preferences. Rather, taste is a transcending of subjectivity, a movement toward the art work and an openness to it. The perceiver with taste is one "who allows the truth to unveil itself and is content to pronounce his sanction." In a passage reminiscent of Kant (whose influence will become dominant later in *The Phenomenology*), Dufrenne argues that the art work mediates the role of the particular in subjectivity, and eventually converts it into the universal. The art work also forms a "public," and this public embodies the universality which taste has shaped in the solitary perceiver. Each perceiver of an art work wants to share that work with others, and compare his experience of it with theirs. Furthermore, the sustained homage rendered to a work by a public or tradition is "the best assurance" of the work's value. Dufrenne next advances a more controversial postulate—that the art work "is detached from its spatiotemporal context," and exists "in universal space and time, aś though instituting a space and time of its own." Such a postulate is in clear defiance of the New Hermeneutic, which stresses the radical historicity of the art work.

Dufrenne next takes up the instance of plural and divergent interpretations, apparently with the intention of better explicating the role of a work's "public." Although earlier he located meaning in the aesthetic object, he here seems to say the opposite. Witness the following passages: "The aesthetic object is enriched in the measure that the work finds a vaster public and a more multifarious meaning"; and "the public continues to create the work by adding to its meaning." I have not made it my policy to point out such apparent discrepancies in Dufrenne, since my purpose is to explicate each of his chapters in terms of his global intention. However, any reader of *The Phenomenology* is advised to read its text much as one reads scripture: individual passages cannot be interpreted in isolation, but must be balanced (in the name of consistency) against other passages and against his more programmatic statements. In the case of the two passages cited above, Dufrenne's real intention is clarified by a closer reading of context and a recollection of the following statements (which appear several pages before): " . . . the meaning of the work and even its density vary according to what different spectators find in it. But it is in the work that they find this meaning, not in themselves as something to transfer onto the work" (59); and again, "The identity of the work is not altered, since its content appears and is refracted differently in different consciousnesses. All these views only display or exfoliate its possibilities, minting the capital which it conceals" (60). Dufrenne's intention, then, is to develop Heidegger's notion of "possibilities" in literature: various meanings as potentialities are firmly embedded in the art work, but these meanings are realized only when discovered and articulated. Since the meanings of the work are definitive and fixed (the technical word would be *determinate*), yet inexhaustible. nonetheless, a plurality of interpretations is indispensable for adequate understanding of the work in question. Unfortunately, neither here nor elsewhere in *The Phenomenology* does Dufrenne analyze the special case of contradictory interpretations, an issue so vital for my own purpose.

In Chapter four, "The Aesthetic Object Amid Other Objects," Dufrenne first distinguishes aesthetic objects from living beings (such as humans or animals), from natural objects (such as stones and soil), and from objects of use (which are instrumentalized by man).[3] In the face of those theorists who blithely characterize the art work as a "human object," Dufrenne goes on to accent the contribution of nature to art. The art work "converts from nature whatever lends itself to being aestheticized," and in a unique way disseminates the appearance and essence of nature. In fact, one can say "that the aesthetic object is nature in that it expresses nature, not by imitating it but by submitting to it." The aesthetic object, both "useless" and sensuous, has the exteriority of a Sartrean in-itself (or *être-en-soi*).

Dufrenne's description here is particularly suited to sculpture and painting, but I think one can apply it to literature as well. All one need do is draw upon the Baroque, and upon several of the modern traditions (such as Cubist poetry and the like). These traditions undercut language as sign (even as emotive sign), and instead, as I mentioned earlier, create a language which is a sound-thing. Sometimes this sound-thing stands alone in the world, so that it is added to the world as just another object (though with the special difference that it is aesthetic). And at other times the sound-thing is a sensuous *equivalent of,* though most emphatically *not a sign of,* other objects in the world. Whether as just another thing, or as a sensuous equivalent, poetic language is just "there." Language as sound-thing can thus qualify as *être-en-soi*. Dufrenne next introduces a Heideggerian concept—that art reveals "nature," and by nature is meant in this case that mysterious "being" which is immanent in appearances, yet normally concealed by them. I am sure that in this context Dufrenne would treat literature only as sound-thing, and see the sound-thing as a sensuous equivalent of "being" (so that language reveals by way of equivalence). In other words, Dufrenne would see the "form" of the sensuous as equivalent to the form of being. It is pertinent to note, however, that Heidegger defines the revelative function of language in much broader terms: he includes the significative level of language, so that what Ingarden calls "represented objects" (projected, you will recall, by meaning-units) *also* reveal being.

The aesthetic object, as we have already seen, shares with *être-en-soi* the characteristic of substantive intransigence. But the aesthetic object is also a profoundly human object; it is to this extent an *être-pour-soi,* and one of the reasons for the object's humanity is

the "presence" of the artist within the art. The relationship between
work and author can be examined in two ways. The critic can study
the author's biography, or even the "existential project" (as Sartre
does), and *explain* the work in terms of this information. Or one can
experience the aesthetic object alone, and find the artist revealed
therein. At this juncture Dufrenne develops ideas identified with
Marcel Raymond, Albert Béguin, and what has come to be known as
the Geneva School; and adds the notions of artistic gesture and
stylistic expression associated with Merleau-Ponty. The aesthetic
object reveals the artist as he or she really is, and not as causes
"explain" the artist. Dufrenne even utilizes a Husserlian concept
that has been put to use before: artistic language may designate an
object, but it also "exhibits" the artist. In particular, the aesthetic
object reveals the artist through style: style is gestural, and exhibits
its maker much as a bodily gesture does. Dufrenne puts the matter
appositely when he says that style "defines a [sensuous] form capable
of attesting to the personality which created it, a form which is a
meaning and which, at this level of our analysis, means its creator."

I call the reader's attention, however, to the qualifying phrase
Dufrenne has taken great care to insert. He has specified "at this
level of analysis" because he will in his final chapters transcend the
subjectivity of the individual artist. In so doing, he will preserve the
basic insights of the Geneva School, but raise their logarithm, as it
were, so they are operative in a Heideggerian matrix. In passages
that seem a bit proleptic, Dufrenne is already suggesting his later
tactics. Thus, one is told that in the presence of primitive formulaic
artifacts, "we feel that the artist has been the prey of his art and that
the motions he performs betray a necessity to which he has
completely subjugated, if not sacrificed, himself" (104); and that "a
humanity in search of itself stammers through him." In a later
passage Dufrenne equates style and a vital relation of man to the
world, but he defines the artist "as the one through whom this
relation exists, not because he brings it into being but because he
lives it." And still later, in a passage which treats collective styles
(and especially those that dissolve individual personality in
convention), he says that "type then points to a spiritual reality . . .
which is still singular, even though not inscribed in the unfolding
of a subjective consciousness." Dufrenne is implying yet another
paradox: the individual artist, in acting out the gesture of creation,
is in a deeper sense being acted upon (or, more precisely, acted
*through*). He is "possessed" by the human tradition, and perhaps by

Heidegger's mysterious "being." He speaks, yet his voice is both his and not his. Dufrenne has us on tenterhooks now, but he turns to another subject.

The next chapter concerns the aesthetic object and signifying object, which are said to oppose each other in their manner of being. The signifying object points to the outside and labels that outside in a conceptual way. The aesthetic object possesses a truth internal to it, and this truth is concrete and formal (that is, stylistic). Dufrenne's definition of the aesthetic object thus devalues not only verisimilitude, which measures the work in terms of an external reality, but also representation, which focuses attention on "represented objects" (regardless of their verisimilitude). The form of the sensuous can signify in only one important sense: the form can signify the "expressiveness" immanent within it. Dufrenne next turns to the language arts *per se*, and here he is forced by the nature of language to restore a verisimilitudinous function, though he attempts to do so in terms of expressive style (129). Following Merleau-Ponty's lead, he says that the aesthetic word can indeed signify objects, but not by way of conceptualization. The concrete "essence" of the object is duplicated in the poetic word's expressivity (which is in turn present via sensuous form), so that the word contains within itself the object's real (that is, affective) meaning.

I insert at this point two comments. First, the success of a word's expression is again measured in terms of the outside—that is, in terms of how well it duplicates an external object's essence. And second, meaning is in the external object (though it is duplicated in the poetic word). When Dufrenne says a word "must be understood and interpreted as a sign of something else which is its meaning," he is at loggerheads with Ingarden, for whom meaning is always an intending act. In a short recapitulation, Dufrenne reminds us he has shown how aesthetic language both exhibits the author and expresses the object (132). These two functions of language furnish the grounds for intersubjectivity, since both are accessible to the perceiver through the language. But what if expressive behavior is ambiguous? Dufrenne poses the question but does little to answer it. He simply says that in some cases meaning is "undefinable" (because it is non-conceptual?), and in others the perceiver "may not be truly attentive." In either case, "It is not that the meaning is concealed but that we ourselves are blind." Nowhere are we advised that the perceiver can legitimately furnish a meaning for the expression. The meaning is pre-given, and is apparently determined by the author of the expressive behavior. Chapter four of *The Phenomenology* closes with a carefully orchestrated conclusion. The aesthetic object carries a core of expressivity within it (and, Dufrenne might have added, it renders the author "present"); thus, it is like a "for-itself." Yet, as we've also seen, the aesthetic object has the intransigence of an "in-itself," and absorbs nature into its own "world." The aesthetic object is therefore "a for-itself of the in-itself," or better yet, it is a "quasi-subject."

Chapter five engages the topic of the aesthetic object and the world. The aesthetic work is autonomous, but foregrounded against the world of everyday objects. The temporal arts, such as music and literature, gain autonomy more easily than the spatial media. All aesthetic objects are also embedded in history, with the result that their "nontemporal truth" (which seems to be the "truth of the work" spoken of earlier) is phenomenalized. It is precisely the form of the aesthetic·object which is the nontemporal truth, and the form "is the singular and sensuous essence of the object and bestows on the object something of the eternity proper to essence." In a footnote Dufrenne qualifies this "metaphorical" statement, saying instead that "the essence as real is timeless and not eternal." Moreover, the "eidetic must appeal to the empirical" because only in history is the essence revealed, and constituted in being revealed. He sums up by averring that "through its form, the aesthetic object is nontemporal; but because its form is the form of a body [a body of sounds, in the case of literature], it is consecrated to the world and to time." I fail to see how this formulation avoids idealism. Earlier, Dufrenne argued that the "idea" of the aesthetic work cannot be an objective ideal, because the idea is identified with the sensuous, and the sensuous is subject to change. But when Dufrenne now says that the aesthetic object is nontemporal because of its form, yet temporal because the form is that of a body, he is driving a wedge between form and body. If form were equivalent to body, form would be exclusively temporal. Instead, Dufrenne implies that form transcends body, but needs body (that is, the sensuous) for its appearance. And such is a Platonic formulation. Indeed, Dufrenne comes closer to idealism here than Ingarden does.

Dufrenne's next question concerns the so-called world of the aesthetic object. That the art object's world is not the real world he takes for granted; but is the art object's world that of its represented objects? Though Dufrenne does not mention *Das literarische Kunstwerk* in this context, one may recall that Ingarden places the pivot of aesthetic world in what he calls represented objectivities. Ingeniously, Dufrenne exploits Ingarden's very notion of "indeterminate spots" (the lacunae in the represented level) to renounce the "worldliness" of represented objects. To be a world, insists Dufrenne, an entity must be self-sufficient and determinate. An alleged "represented world" imitates the real world, and thus is insufficient by itself (even literature of the fantastic is imitative, he says, since it forms identifiable objects by borrowing from the real). And an alleged "represented world," no matter how dense with information, still remains necessarily indeterminate in some respects.

No, one must look elsewhere for a justification of the aesthetic object's worldliness, and, predictably, Dufrenne looks again to the notion of expressivity. The world of the art object is an "expressed world," that is, a sensuous form which renders present the author's affective "being-in-the-world." The author's "being-in-the-world" is immanent in the art work through style and gives the art work an indispensable unity. If one recalls that earlier Dufrenne defined sensuous meaning as determinate yet (in practice) inexhaustible, one can see how, at least on one count, the expressed world indeed qualifies as a "world." Unlike represented objectivities, the expressed world *is* determinate. But does the expressed world qualify on the second count? Is it self-sufficient? Dufrenne answers yes and I answer no. If, on the represented level, even the most fantastic represented objects borrow from the real (as Dufrenne correctly notes), so too does sensuous "being-in-the-world." The author as author can duplicate (in the heart of the work) his own affective *Weltanschauung* only by referring the duplication to his own affectivity; and likewise, the perceiver can recognize the duplication only by referring it to analogous experiences that he, the perceiver, has felt in his own life.

Dufrenne proceeds to finesse the viability of the representational level by saying that represented objects can be unified, but only when the expressive world informs them; he then broaches the next pressing issue: is the "world" of the aesthetic object subjective or objective? Is it the case that only the objective world is real? The aesthetic object is a network of signs, even if its signs are of a special kind which carry immanent within them their own signifieds. How can a mere network of signs be real? And how can the aesthetic object, linked as it is to a concrete subject, qualify as real? Against this broadside of arguments, Dufrenne shores up the ontological reality of the art work, using a coalition of Kant and Heidegger to do so (191). Dufrenne is quite opaque throughout this upcoming section, but I shall try to clarify his argument. With Heidegger (as the reader will recognize), Dufrenne says that a "world" can never be purely "objective": on the contrary, the "outside" world is implicated in the subject's inner world, and vice versa. There is an "irreducible reciprocal causality" operative here, so that "world" in the broader sense is just as subjective as it is objective. In fact, even use of the word "subjective" is deceiving, since the inner world, for the person living it, is "real, pressing, and irreducible." The so-called subjective world "derives its value from the fact that it is deeply rooted in the human experience of the world which is the common world of coexistence." World in the meaningful sense is the ontological field of coexisting subject and object; these two coexistents constitute the world and are also constituted by it.

In adumbration of a theme which will appear later in *The Phenomenology*, Dufrenne now introduces "feeling" as a pre-objective mode which enables the subject to be *at one with* the object. World in the meaningful sense is thus preobjective. The debt to Heidegger's notion of *Verstehen* (which I shall discuss in the next chapter) is obvious. Dufrenne also allows himself a Kantian turn, however, telling us "the world of the subject is not a subjectified world but a world in which and on which the subject harmonizes with other subjects." Somewhat like Kant's subjective universal, "feeling" renders world "common to all subjects," and "rejects the claims of the solipsistic *cogito*" (192). It becomes evident, though, that Dufrenne must accomplish a transition to the unique subject who is the individual author. He does so in the following passage: "The fundamental project which constitutes the subject as transcendence and discloses the world can be made determinate in singular projects, each of which discloses a peculiar world. In this case, the world is the singular world of a subject who loses nothing of his quality as subject when his project is the concrete project of a singular being in the world" (196).

Here Dufrenne veers away from Heidegger, whose interest in *Dasein* is pitched towards a general ontology, and towards Sartre, whose interest is in individual existential projects. If we can speak of the "world" of a subject (and we've seen that this world of a subject is not "subjective"), can we speak of the "world" of an aesthetic object? Yes, answers Dufrenne, because the art work was shown earlier to be a "quasi-subject," and the immanence of the work's phenomenal author thus guarantees its humanity. Is the aesthetic object real? Yes, because its expressivity is real (though its represented objects are not). The reasoning here is that represented objects are not the things they signify, and thus are unreal, but that the expressivity of the author is real and is truly present in the aesthetic object. At the mention of this, I must demur again. The expressivity of the author isn't in the aesthetic object; it is in the real author, and its sensuous translation, or equivalent, is in the object. In this respect, despite Dufrenne's protestations, sensuous form is much like an imaginative symbol. Sensuous form can be the equivalent of its author's feeling, and imaginative symbol can be the tangible equivalent of what the symbol signifies. In both cases, equivalence is not to be confused with "pointing at," which is the function of a sign. But neither should it be claimed that the signified is immanent in the signifier. The real rose is not in the metaphor that symbolizes the rose.

Dufrenne winds down chapter five with one last significant assertion: "We suspect that this world [the world of the aesthetic object] cannot reveal itself except to a subject who would be not only the witness of its epiphany but also capable of associating himself with the movement of the subjectivity which produced it . . ." (197). Here, for the first time, Dufrenne overtly states that the subjectivity of the aesthetic perceiver should duplicate the author's project, and this through the mediation of the work's world; he thus identifies with that species of *Einfühlung* we have already seen in Ingarden. Thus, Hirsch acquires another ally. Convinced he has shown the aesthetic object is real, Dufrenne proceeds to the last issue posed in his phenomenology of the aesthetic object: if the aesthetic object is real, what precisely is the nature of its being?

Chapter six of *The Phenomenology* is devoted to this last question of part one, and the treatment is of special interest because the chapter critiques, among others, Sartre and Ingarden. Below, I plan to present Dufrenne's critique of Sartre without comment (since Sartre has not been in my purview), but the critique of Ingarden will be evaluated in detail. Sartre tries to settle the debate between realism and psychologism by urging what he considers a third option: that the aesthetic object is "imaginary" (and unreal). According to Sartre, the work of art as perceived is an *analogon* which solicits the perceiver to imagine the unreal. Whereas in Dufrenne the work of art as perceived is itself the aesthetic object, in Sartre the imagined object plays this role, and the perceived object is nothing more than a catalyst. Dufrenne sorties, "If the Seventh

Symphony is what I imagine when I hear and not *what* I hear, what prevents me from making it responsible for the outlandish reveries which it may awaken in me?" Despite its equivocations, says Dufrenne, Sartre's esthetic never succeeds in guaranteeing the perceived object's control over the imagination. As a result, the aesthetic object dissolves into the private fantasies of a myriad of perceivers. Furthermore, why consider the aesthetic object unreal? Unreality can be predicated here in only one case: if one wants to call incompleteness an unreality, for admittedly the total object always transcends individual perceptions of it.

Dufrenne next critiques Ingarden, permitting one the very welcome opportunity to compare the two (206). At the start, Dufrenne represents Ingarden quite accurately: "Ingarden speaks of 'the purely intentional being' of the aesthetic object," and advances a "conception of language that distinguishes the sign, the thing signified, and the apprehension of the signification." Since Dufrenne wants to read Ingarden as an idealist, he says that the latter's notion of "purely intentional being . . . makes the being depend on significations which are ideal objects." Actually, Ingarden carefully distinguishes between meanings (which operate in the concretized work) and the ideal concepts to which the meanings belong (but which are not part of the work). Dufrenne is correct in this sense, however—that in *Das literarische Kunstwerk* the concretized work has a pool of ideal concepts as its ontic base (along with a second ontic base, namely the array of word signs).

When Dufrenne turns to theory of language in Ingarden, the attack begins in earnest. Whereas Ingarden distinguishes among sign, signified, and apprehension of signification, Dufrenne embeds the signified in the sign: " . . . In the literary arts, the words which these [written or oral] signs deliver to us, far from being reduced to the function of signifying and to being obliterated by their signification, are perceived as things and end by bestowing on their signification this same quality of the perceptible" (210). Dufrenne goes on to argue that the sensuousness (that is, sonorous recitation) of words, and the affectivity which sensuousness embodies, constitute the crucial meaning in literature, and he further argues that this meaning is the intentional object of the perceiver. Since sensuousness is manifestly real, he can then maintain that the aesthetic object is real; and that Ingarden is wrong in imputing "purely intentional being" to said object. Dufrenne has not really disproven Ingarden here: he has just begun from a different premise, namely, that meaning is sensuousity. It is worth recalling, however, that earlier Dufrenne said the aesthetically sensuous must be organized by "sensuous form," and again such a proposition makes Dufrenne more of a Platonist than Ingarden himself is. One may remember also that Ingarden (like Husserl, and like the vast majority of practicing literary critics), sees represented objectivities as the most important dimension of the literary work. For Ingarden and the early Husserl alike, the word sign or sound is a signal correlated to a meaning; in the perceiver's act of meaning-bestowal,[4] the meaning is enacted as part of the intending act, with the result that the represented objectivity is intended as intentional object. Dufrenne could interject here that this formula casuistically displaces meaning, and that the *functioning* meaning is the signal (which, even according to Ingarden, is the intentional object of a "cognitive act"). And he could further add that the signal is real. Ingarden would be able to parry quite effectively, however. First, the word sound cannot be the meaning because words different from one another, and drawn from several languages, can mean the same thing. And second, even word sounds as such are not real; only their phonic material is real.

To resume the thread of my exposition, however, I must deduce what Ingarden deduces: since the literary work is an intentional object projected by meaning units, and since this intentional object is an unreal entity (though it may correspond to a real entity), the literary work is necessarily unreal. Even Dufrenne in part grants this, when in the section on Sartre he asserts: "It can be said that the meaning is an unreality—it is even a banality, if one means by this only that the subject of the work is not situated in the real world. . . ." Well, it is this "banality," and only this "banality" that Ingarden means. The real problem in Dufrenne's attack on Ingarden is that the two men are for the most part discussing different issues, yet Dufrenne behaves as if he and his "adversary" are truly flailing away at each other. The controversy is complicated because Dufrenne doesn't give *Das literarische Kunstwerk* due credit in several sectors. For example, the Frenchman suggests Ingarden does not appreciate the sensuous.

To discredit this charge, one need only recall Ingarden's deft treatment of rhythm and of rhyme and his heavy stress on "prepared" schematic aspects of an "acoustical" nature. Even the charge that "Ingarden does not specify the status of the imaginary" (207) is unjustified. As is clear, Dufrenne himself suppresses the imagination in favor of perception. Such a gambit is perhaps permissible in the case of the plastic arts, but precious few literary theorists would be willing to grant Dufrenne his point in terms of literature. Ingarden, instead, gives full play to "living words" and to rich expressions which give an object "intuitive fullness." Living words evoke not a "bare rational act," but a concrete act which intends imaginative fullness. The intending act of the perceiver, in one of its five constitutive moments, intends "material content," and elsewhere *Das literarische Kunstwerk* calls the intended object the "imagined object." Admittedly, in Ingarden imaginative fullness is supplied from the side of the perceiver, who in part obeys "prepared aspects" and in part simply fills schematic gaps. This mechanism makes the end result (namely, the aesthetic object) no less the imaginative, however. It seems to me that Ingarden's imagined literary object is indeed more meaningful than the mere acoustics of Dufrenne's version.

Dufrenne next charges that Ingarden is guilty of two equivocations and that in both cases, "Ingarden is unfaithful to Husserl." The first equivocation involves the notion of a purely intentional correlate (or object) of meaning units. As one may recall, even when there exists a "real correlate in the world," Ingarden maintains that the meaning-units project a "purely intentional correlate" which stands alongside the real correlate. Dufrenne compares this formulation with that of Husserl, which he expresses as follows: "When I perceive a tree, there is not, on the one hand, an intentional tree deprived of reality and existing only in my perception, and, on the other hand, a real tree which I rejoin through the intentional tree. The very purpose of the doctrine of intentionality is to avoid this ruinous distinction, the pitfall of all psychologism" (208).

In defense of Ingarden, I simply make the following observations. Admittedly, in Husserl there is no such entity as a purely intentional object when one immediately intends an ontically autonomous object. This is the case in Dufrenne's example, where one perceives a real tree. But Ingarden's thesis concerns not the perception of ontically autonomous objects, but of correlates to meaning-units, that is, to language. Husserl's treatment of the derived intentionality characteristic of language is very different from his treatment of immediate intentionality. In fact, Ingarden faithfully reflects Husserl's position, which is that language can project "mere intentions." The second equivocation laid at Ingarden's door is that "intentional object appears only through the phenomenological reduction." The phenomenological reduction requires the bracketing out of the ontological question. The phenomenological reduction involves a refusal to ask whether the intentional object is real, unreal, or whatever. How then can Ingarden make "intentionality" an ontic status? How can there be an "intentional being"? Here I must agree with Dufrenne, and grant that intentionality cannot be in itself an ontic mode. I would insist, however, that there is an ontological difference between a "mere intention," as we find it in the reading of literature, and an intention fulfilled by an autonomous object.[5] However, the ontological question must be asked prior to and outside of phenomenological reduction, and the term *purely intentional being* is inappropriate. On the other hand, one must not be forced by Dufrenne into a necessary choice between real and ideal. There may very well be a third status which characterizes represented objects. Ingarden has made a convincing case for this third status, but the term applied to it should be more felicitous.

Dufrenne continues, "Does the mere correlation of an object with an intending act certify its heteronomy? If this were so, it would be necessary to attribute heteronomy both to the perceived object, which implies a special perceptual intention, and to the real object, which implies a thesis of reality." In my opinion, it should be clear (despite what Dufrenne says) that Ingarden is not just repeating the truism that an object is not known until a conscious act intends it, and that on this score, all objects are heteronomous. An unintended represented object is not only unknown: it also ceases to exist. An objectively ideal or real entity, on the contrary, exists even when it is unknown. Surely, everyone would have to grant that in this sense there is an ontological difference between represented objects and autonomous objects. Nor is Ingarden claiming that "the mere correlation of an object with an intending act" certifies its (ontological) heteronomy. His point is just the opposite: that real and ideal objects correlate without being ontologically heteronomous whereas represented objects require this correlation to exist at all. Dufrenne closes with the enigmatic remark that "even in the literary arts, the aesthetic object, far from being a represented object, or . . . an intentional object, is still a perceived object." Though some of the confusion between Ingarden and Dufrenne arises from their disparate Husserlian sources (the former uses the *Logische Untersuchungen* and the latter the *Ideen*), I still cannot understand how, in Husserlian terms, a perceived object is not an intended object.

After short examinations of Boris de Schloezer and Waldemar

Conrad, Dufrenne continues his ontology of the aesthetic object. He asks, "From where do the meaning and being of the perceived object come? Does the being reduce to the meaning which it has for me? Does it have a meaning through itself or through the idea which gives me a grip on it? Is its being independent of the representation which I have of it—is it grounded in itself or, on the contrary, on this very representation"(218)? Answers to these questions, says Dufrenne, reduce to either idealism or realism, and he is unwilling to accept the constitutive idealism of Husserl's *Ideen*. Rather, "perception calls on us to conceive of a relation between subject and object such that the one exists only by means of the other—such that the subject is relative to the object in the same way that the object is relative to the subject." The above repeats Merleau-Ponty's formulation, of course, and Merleau-Ponty claimed to derive it from what were the unpublished and last works of Husserl himself. Dufrenne accepts this formulation, wherein the reconciliation of subject and object takes place in the human body: in the human person "the body as lived [subject] and the body as object are identified." Furthermore, Husserl's phenomenological reduction is anathematized: "No one can abstract himself from the world so long as he is in it, and the prereflective relationship with the world is always already given." Gestalt form is not the impression the object makes on the subject, but the "totality that the subject forms with the object" (221). Perception, adds Dufrenne, is precisely the expression of this totality. Besides, perception "never ceases returning to the initial experience in which the assuring presence of the object is given to it, because in this experience object and subject are not yet distinguished."

From the above, it at first seems that Dufrenne is about to identify meaning with the mutual implication of subject and object—a monistic formulation very close to Heidegger's own in *Sein und Zeit* (as we shall see). But all along Dufrenne has been the uncompromising realist, stressing the priority of the aesthetic object over perception, so that the latter is no more than a docile receptivity. He is not going to give up the ship now. While paying lip service to monism (because he doesn't want to sound like an empiricist), he actually deepens the rift between idealism and realism; in fact, he delivers himself as an old-fashioned realist.[6] As we now move through his development of an ontology, I shall make special efforts to quote the incriminating passages. The perceived object, says Dufrenne (following Merleau-Ponty) is an "in-itself-for-us." The perceived object (and *a fortiori*, the aesthetic object) holds the status of an in-itself because it "has an objective being which we are not able to grasp absolutely, because all knowledge begins with perception and because this in-itself cannot avoid being for us" (221). The perceived object is an object "refusing the complicity which binds it to me in perception and urging on me an objectifying attitude which upholds the truth of its objective being." For this reason, "the object thus claims the very distinction between subject and object which sanctions its autonomy." An authentic theory of perception "must accord priority to the in-itself over the for-us."

In a sub-section entitled "The aesthetic object and form," Dufrenne claims that the formula "in-itself-for-us" involves two propositions. First, the aesthetic object is a thing, and cannot be reduced to the being of a representation. Second, the thingly being of the aesthetic object is dependent on perception. The aesthetic object is the art-work as perceived, and thus needs perception to exist. Perception, however, does not contribute meaning to the art-work. On the contrary, the art-work "governs" perception. So much is this the case that "far from being simply for us, it is we who are for it [that is, for the art-work]." Meaning is not in the perceiver, but is "both immanent in the sensuous and proper to it." This meaning is sensuous form, and as the correlate of "feeling," is a for-itself. Thus the aesthetic object both as in-itself and as for-itself stands over and against us as perceivers, but the aesthetic object is still for-us.

Part two, "Analysis of the Work of Art," announces it is "going to move from the aesthetic object back to the work." In other words, Dufrenne will not here consider the art work as esthetically perceived, but rather as it is in itself (much as Ingarden examines the literary work which stands prior to concretization). Interestingly, Ingarden devotes most of *Das literarische Kunstwerk* to this "objective" enterprise, and Dufrenne gives it short shrift. Dufrenne's part two is the shortest part of his book. (As for Heidegger, he would of course deem such an "objective" stance at worst impossible, and at best useless.) Dufrenne's first three chapters of the "analysis" deal with what he calls the temporal and spatial arts. Though his point is that all arts are both temporal and spatial to a degree, he chooses to discuss only the extreme cases, that is, music and painting as temporal and spatial arts respectively. Consequently I shall with haste pass over to chapter four, which engages "The Structure of the Work of Art in General," and thus comports subject-matter relevant to literature as well as the other arts. Suffice it to say that the first three chapters draw some ideas from Heidegger and many from Kant (the Kantian concepts of "inner sense" and "outer sense" are the examples outstanding).

Chapter four penetrates in succession three aspects of structure—matter, subject, and expression. By "matter" Dufrenne means that which constitutes the sensuous nature of art. The matter of poetry, for instance, is "that particular sound which is the spoken word" (301). Every art work "involves harmonic schemata which elaborate with precision the unique language in which the work will be expressed." Note that "language" here simply means the form of matter, and "harmonic schemata" are the principles in control of the form; note, too, that the schemata exercise two functions:

> . . . Schemata serve to articulate the materials which serve as a language for the work, although this language is never perceived as language or independent of sense. These schemata fulfill two functions. First, they define and classify the elements of this esthetic language. . . . The act of selecting these elements and putting them in order constitutes a scale or spectrum of possibilities. . . . The second function of harmonic schemata follows immediately from the first. They establish accents in, and thus organize, the kind of scale just described. These accents also confer upon the work its particular allure (306, 307).

By "subject," a second aspect of artistic structure, Dufrenne means the "represented object" signified by the sensuous. "Representation" occurs "whenever the aesthetic object invites us to leave the immediacy of the sensuous and proposes a meaning in terms of which the sensuous is only a means and essentially unimportant" (312). Certainly not all arts are representational, says Dufrenne, but some, such as literary prose, definitely are. Just as we would expect, Dufrenne proceeds to downgrade representations: ". . . Whenever art becomes most forcefully conscious of itself and thus becomes most specifically art—this is, whenever it invents its own language of sound, color, form, and even its own poetic vocabulary—it also becomes conscious of the danger posed to it by representation." Novels and short stories, however, are so universally accepted as masterworks of art that Dufrenne must somehow acknowledge them. He does so by saying "the danger posed to the work by representation is perhaps the ransom for a unique advantage." An art work's "material base," such as the color of a canvas or a "word as a word written on paper" is often "concealed." As a result, the sensuous must "attach itself to a new support," namely, the represented object. Dufrenne is saying here that the sensuous *needs* the represented object in order to gain substantive coherence. The represented object magnetizes the sensuous, so the reader is drawn towards sensuous form. Of course, the latter statement clearly contradicts what Dufrenne just said before—that high art does not need representation. Hermeneutical dialectic is one thing, and downright contradiction is another. In this instance, as in others, I think Dufrenne is merely contradicting himself.

If the first role of the subject is to satisfy "an irrepressible urge on the part of perceptions to know the sensuous as the sensuousness OF something," the second role of the subject is to focus "expression" (314). By "expression," Dufrenne means the affectivity of the author (and this affectivity is somehow duplicated by the sensuous). True enough, "Rouault does not paint a Christ but a pictorial equivalent, through the depicted Christ, of what Christ signifies for Rouault" (316). To put it another way, in sensuous form Rouault duplicates his own affectivity (which involves a feeling toward Christ). But Dufrenne's precise point is that the duplication could not occur without a necessary support—the representation of Christ. This supportative role of subject affords Dufrenne a welcome transition: he next develops the third structural aspect of the art work, namely, "expression" itself. Though expression is "inseparable" from subject and the sensuous, it is to be distinguished from them. Expression, as the author's affectivity embodied in the sensuousity of the work, is earmarked by its special "depth": a remarkable characteristic of the aesthetic object is "that it offers a plurality of meanings which are not juxtaposed but, rather, superimposed on each other hierarchically. This plurality testifies to its depth" (319). There are two kinds of ambiguity, one bad and one good. The bad kind is ambiguity "by default," that is, uncertainty that arises from confusing significations. (Did not Dufrenne say earlier that expression does not signify? Isn't he garbling "subject" and "expression" here?) The good kind of ambiguity occurs "by excess," through a "superabundance of meaning." As we shall see, the latter situation is much like what I call the "surplus of Being" assumed by Heideggerian literary theory. Dufrenne, like Heidegger, concludes that in authentic ambiguous literature, "all interpretations are true at one and the same time." Unlike Heidegger, however, Dufrenne does not describe how multiple interpretations can materialize. In this same section Dufrenne also takes a feather from Ingarden's cap. The Frenchman says the aesthetic object "allows us a presentiment of a religious dimension of meaning," and this sounds much like the revelation of "metaphysical quality" Ingarden posits.

Dufrenne's next thesis is also borrowed, though he executes a clever *pas de deux* with it. Alongside Merleau-Ponty and the Geneva School, Dufrenne says that expression is a pre-reflective project of the universe and of the self. Furthermore, the reader's "comprehension of the work consists in a dialogue which we take up with its creator" (326). Objects in the world are inexhaustible, all right, but they are also opaque (because of their *en-soi* quality). The inexhaustibility of real objects becomes available only in art, because only therein are objects saturated with humanity (the author's *pour-soi*), and consequently opened up to human readers. Thus returns a familiar theme: the art work is a "for-itself of the in-itself." Part two closes with the statement that its analysis, just as all aesthetic analysis, must acknowledge limits. Expressivity is ultimately unanalyzable. The true aesthetician experiences the work and then talks about the work. In his "talking about," he describes "expressive traits." But these traits "are not schemata capable of engendering expression through their own development or their synthesis" (329). One is always driven back to perception. Thus Dufrenne undertakes part three, which describes the "perceiving spectator."

Dufrenne begins part three with the declaration that "the phenomenology of the aesthetic object must now give way to the phenomenology of aesthetic perception." A general theory of perception, he says, distinguishes among "three successive moments of perception: presence, representation, and reflection" (333); the reader will later see these have some affinity with Heidegger's "understanding," "interpretation," and "assertion." Dufrenne continues, "These moments parallel the three elements of the aesthetic object: the sensuous, the represented object, the expressed world." Dufrenne goes on to diminuate the parallel of "reflection" and "expressed world" (as indeed he must, given his premises), and he does so (clumsily) by substituting "feeling" for "reflection": feeling detects the expressed world, though feeling may be conjoined with reflection. As opposed to the Parisian Structuralists, Dufrenne maintains "the object is meaningful by itself, bearing its meaning within itself, *before* the relation constitutive of signification is shown and made explicit" (336). This is in contradistinction to

Ingarden, too, of course, since Dufrenne denies that meaning is conferred by a bestowing act of consciousness. Like Ingarden, however, though through a different mechanism, Dufrenne indicates that the author's "sense" controls meaning: "The experience of the spectator exists in the image of the creator's experience" (340). Most interesting is Dufrenne's next point, that the perceiver's body (the "corporeal cogito") first experiences and mediates the "presence" of the aesthetic object. And on the pre-reflective level of bodily presence, the distinction between subject (perceiver) and object (art work) has not yet crystallized.

Chapter twelve, "Representation and Imagination," concerns the second moment of perception. The image, or represented object, mediates the "brute presence" of the sensuous art work and the "idea" of that work developed by thought (there's some Kantianism here, though *sotto voce*). Imagination is "transcendental" because it participates in the spacing and timing of a possible representation, and imagination is "empirical" in that it accounts for the meaningfulness of an actual work: "As transcendental, the imagination sees to it that there is a given; as empirical, imagination makes certain that this given, enriched by possibilities, possesses a meaning" (348). Dufrenne next contradicts the Sartrean notion that imagination denies the real. Rather, says Dufrenne, "the essential function of imagination is to preform the real in an act of expectation which allows us not only to anticipate and recognize the real (as Alain showed) but also to adhere to it" (355). But Dufrenne again gives with one hand and takes with the other: imagination, he says, is less important in aesthetic perception than ordinary perception, because "the represented object is not truly imagined" (365). It seems he means that the imagination, when properly controlled, is confined to the appearances of the aesthetic object, whereas in ordinary perception the imaginative faculty has much freer rein.

Dufrenne next interpolates some remarks on time in literature. I shall just point out that his conclusions are the opposite of Ingarden's. Ingarden, you may recall, says that in real time the present has an ontic advantage over the past and future, whereas in literary time the present does not. Dufrenne says instead that literary time is like the "pure present of contemplation"; literary past and future are "immanent" and "given immediately" in the present. Ingarden also says that represented objects are "schematic" formations with "spots of indeterminacy" which must be concretized by the reader's conscious acts; the reader's imagination, in particular, imparts a "substantive fullness" to literature, and literature without concretization remains merely "skeletal." Since Dufrenne wants to argue that imagination is not very important in aesthetic experience, he takes the opposite tack. He says the "essential" is all the author means to say, and therefore all that should concern us. The author has deliberately sacrificed details, "but such sacrifices of detail impose no sacrifice on the spectator, for what has been eliminated is of no help to him anyway" (368). Dufrenne continues, saying we betray the author "if we do not accept a certain asceticism on his part, for otherwise our look will reintroduce into the work impurities from which it has already been cleansed." And then comes the clincher, which insists once more on the primacy of perception: when we read literature, "we have the right to know what happened, but we do not need to imagine it, since it will be shown to us."

Chapter thirteen considers the third moment of perception, namely, reflection and a concomitant "feeling." After showing that the third moment needs the second moment and vice versa, Dufrenne proceeds to the heart of this chapter, a section called "From Understanding to Feeling." I have already said that Dufrenne's conjunction of reflection and feeling is terribly unclear. Unfortunately, this new section does nothing to ameliorate matters. "Reflection" seems to mean in this context "a type of reflection on feeling through which feeling itself is fully realized" (377). Reflection "plays a role with respect to feeling similar to that which representation plays in regard to presence." As for the definition of feeling, it is "a new immediacy" which knows expression. Feeling is "a capacity of receptivity, a sensibility to a certain world, and an aptitude for perceiving that world." And the "world" in question, as I said, is expression, that is, affectivity inviscerated in sensuous style. Such a definition makes "feeling" sound like a return to the first moment—"presence" itself. But Dufrenne gives three reasons why this is not the case. First, "feeling reveals an interiority" while presence reveals the sensuous. Second, feeling implies "a new attitude" on the part of the subject: "I must make myself conform to what feeling reveals to me and thus match its depth with my own." And third, feeling presupposes that "representation has been exhausted and surpassed toward something else." Since presence is adequated to the appearance of the art work, and feeling coordinated with expression, Dufrenne concludes the chapter with a distinction between appearance and expression: "Appearance brings about the knowledge of an object, and expression that of a subject or quasi-subject. An appearance is a sign, while an expression makes a sign—gestures—to us" (379).

In chapter fourteen Dufrenne advances to an elaborate treatment of "Feeling and the Depth of the Aesthetic Object." Just as he moved from subject to expression when analyzing the art work's structure, he now moves from reflection to feeling when describing aesthetic perception. There are, he announces, two kinds of reflection, one analytic and one "adherent" or "sympathetic." Analytic reflection in turn comprises two types: "There is, first, the sort of reflection which treats of the *structure* of the aesthetic object. Then there is the sort which treats of the *sense* of the represented object" (388). But next Dufrenne asks whether this second type is merely "a ploy to introduce the conceptual into what properly pertains to the perceptible [*le sensible*] and to find a meaning in a formal flourish, a melodic line, or a patch of color?" He continues, and with fine rhetorical gesture:

> Is it not true that the literary arts, whose raw material [*matière*] is laden with thought, are the only arts blessed with an immediately communicable meaning? And even the word ceases to have a meaning explicable through reflection once it undergoes a poetic transformation. We become all the more convinced of the correctness of this objection if we believe that the ultimate access to the work lies in feeling (390, 391).

Yes, reflection on sense is a ploy, concludes Dufrenne, but then he adds in a characteristic Dufrennian *volte-face:* "Still, no one really comes to grip with feeling who has not undergone the experience of reflection."

Having covered the two types of analytic reflection, the sequence of this chapter next presents the kind of reflection that is adherent: "It is possible to distinguish between a reflection which separates us from and a reflection which makes us adhere to the object." Like the Geneva School, Dufrenne explains that "by means of adherent reflection, I submit myself to the work instead of submitting it to my jurisdiction, and I allow the work to deposit its meaning within me" (393). It seems to me this is practically a reversal of Ingarden's theory of perception: Dufrenne in effect attributes the intentional act to the art work and makes of the perceiver an intentional object. Dufrenne can maintain this, of course, because the aesthetic object is for him a "quasi-subject" and therefore can possess the *virtus* of intentionality. And because the aesthetic object is quasi-subject, he can argue later that adherent reflection "culminates in feeling." As a further consequence, Dufrenne takes the opportunity to exclude critical research from the extrinsic "intention of the creator, the influence of a tradition, or some other circumstance which may bear on the creator's intention." Like the Geneva critics, he considers the relevant intentionality of the author already transubstantiated into art—so one need not look beyond the work proper.

Dufrenne has said that adherent reflection culminates in feeling. His next two sections define feeling as "being-in-depth." One should keep in mind that feeling, or being-in-depth, characterizes both the aesthetic work (where the feeling is the author's) and the perceiver (whose feeling "lives" that of the work). Depth is not to be identified "with the hidden or the involuntary, that is, with the past and the unconscious" (so much for Freudianism). Nor is depth "quantitative" and a "matter of extension" (400). Rather, depth is best described as follows:

> To possess depth means to situate oneself on a certain level where one becomes sensitive throughout one's being, where a person collects himself together and commits oneself. . . . To possess depth means to reject the idea of being a thing, which is always external to itself and is dispersed and practically dismembered in the passing of time. It means being capable of an inner life, collecting oneself within oneself, and acquiring an intimacy (403, 404).

Dufrenne conflates some ontology at this juncture:

> The world of the aesthetic object is a world which it is, but it is an unreal world. It is an unreality internal to the reality of the aesthetic object of which it is the meaning, instead of being an external world which is a reality external to the unreality of a consciousness of which it is the intentional object (414).

Earlier, Dufrenne had argued that the world of the aesthetic object is real, precisely because expressivity (which is feeling embodied in art, after all) is real. Now, suddenly, the world of the aesthetic object, and meaning itself, have become unreal!

Chapter fifteen discusses "the aesthetic attitude," compares it to attitudes towards the true and the lovable, and finds several differences among these attitudes. Logical truth is acquired by intense effort, whereas the beautiful freely "happens" to us. Truth is treated "in the mode of having," so that we possess the true; but the beautiful, on the contrary, possesses us. Logical concepts are assimilated into the mind and acquire a universal character: art is always specific and effectively controls us only when in our presence. The difference is ultimately that "between knowing and feeling—feeling is nourished only by concrete presence" (429). Finally, we gain access to the true by renouncing the self's "depth"; the aesthetic attitude requires the opposite—we operate within our "depth" in order to sense the "depth" of the art work. Then, Dufrenne says there is another kind of truth which is available in art—metaphysical truth. As opposed to logical truth, metaphysical truth is intuitive, subjective, and particular, so that it has meaning only for the individual perceiving it. Dufrenne's debt to Ingarden, who also advances a theory of metaphysical truth, is obvious, even though Ingarden's truth is not subjective (and probably not particular). As for attitudes towards the lovable and the beautiful, one similarity and one difference are outstanding. When confronting both the lovable and the beautiful, one may recognize "the power of the other and our acquiescence in his or its rights." However, "Love requires a kind of union which is not needed by the aesthetic object, because the latter acts on the spectator and holds him at a distance." Having shown the uniqueness of aesthetic experience, Dufrenne now poises himself for part four, wherein he will search out the *apriori* structures which inform "the reading of expression by feeling" (434).

Part four, the "Critique of Aesthetic Experience," shows that aesthetic encounter brings into play various *apriori* of affectivity. "Just as the *apriori* of sensibility and understanding," says Dufrenne, "are the conditions under which an object is given or thought, so the affective *apriori* provide the conditions under which a world can be felt" (437). Affective *apriori,* moreover, are not vested in a Kantian transcendental subject, "but a concrete subject capable of sustaining a vital relationship with a world." I intervene here, saying that despite Dufrenne's remonstrances, his "subject" is just as transcendental as Kant's, since it is universal, and apparently precedes experience. If it were not to precede individual experience, why use the term *apriori* at all? In any case, Dufrenne defines the *apriori* as "a certain affective quality which lies at the origin of the world of the object." What's more, the affective quality is constitutive, in that it constitutes the aesthetic object. The several chapters of part four, declares Dufrenne, will answer baffling questions that relate to this thesis. If "the affective designates a certain mode of being which belongs to the subject, how can it qualify an object to the point of being an *apriori* for it?" (439) Furthermore, is affective quality also an *apriori* for the real world? What is the relationship between the world of the aesthetic object and the real world? And what is the truth of the aesthetic object?

Chapter sixteen begins with the proposition that just as the Kantian "*apriori* of understanding is rational in character," so too is the affective *apriori* affective in character. Feeling as such is "only a certain way of knowing an affective quality in the structure of an object," and again in parallel with Kant's notion of Taste, feeling "is disinterested in spite of the sort of proposition it presupposes" (441). Dufrenne goes on to reject the Kantian thesis that "It is the subject who bears the *apriori*." Instead, Dufrenne depends on the Heideggerian idea that subject and object are grounded in a unified Being. With considerable cleverness, *The Phenomenology* makes Being (and not just the subject or just the object) constitutive of affectivity, and of the feeling which carries affectivity. In Dufrenne's words, "To be at once a determination of subject and object, the *apriori* must be a characteristic of being, which is anterior to subject and object and makes their affinity possible" (455). Nor, for Dufrenne, is affectivity alone *apriori;* there are also *apriori* operative at the levels of presence and representation. As for the affective *apriori,* it is both existential and cosmological. It is existential as "the irreducible factor by means of which a concrete subject is constituted." It is cosmological in two senses: first, it constitutes the object, and second, it arises out of an ontological field (namely Being) that is the ultimate *real.*

In chapter seventeen Dufrenne reveals a theory of "pure aesthetics," that is, a theory of an *apriori* knowledge of affectivity (a knowledge which precedes empirical investigation). As Dufrenne says, "Just as we know of space before it is articulated in geometry, we must have some acquaintance with the affective *apriori* before they are revealed to us by feeling" (464). *Apriori* aesthetic categories are not as rigorous as those of geometry or physics, however, and they are not values. Dufrenne seems to accept the aesthetic categories (such as the Noble, the Sublime, the Pathetic, and so forth) postulated by Etienne Souriau, but, unlike Souriau, he considers these categories *apriori* instead of *aposteriori.* (Later, curiously, *The Phenomenology* will deny the possibility of tabulating aesthetic categories.) The aesthetic categories are "human categories," so "*apriori* knowledge of the different countenances which the world may assume is also an *apriori* knowledge of the different attitudes that can be adopted by man" (475). I interject here that such a theory of aesthetic categories could be used to justify a practice of the

Geneva School I explained in Part One: the Geneva critic "checks" the validity of both symbols and experiential patterns against his own similar experiences. Though I would not wish to do so, this testing for validity could obviously be explained as a testing against *apriori* aesthetic categories shared by all men. But back to Dufrenne's thesis. A category is a general idea, while we know feeling "arises in the presence of a singular world and subject." How then can we recognize a particular work by means of a general idea? After dismissing what he considers the fallacious solutions to this problem advanced by "intellectualism" and "conceptualism," Dufrenne proposes his answer (a solution neither surprising nor innovative). Something general, he tells us, "resides at the heart of the singular. . . . We mean that each man possesses a certain way of being himself which makes him similar to other men" (479). This whole issue gives rise to one last vexation: can we construct a definitive table of affective categories, as Kant does for the *apriori* of representation? No, responds Dufrenne, because the affective categories are general, but not generalizable, and they are necessarily "tied to the singular."

Chapter eighteen delves into the truth of the aesthetic object. Is the aesthetic object true? And if it is true, does this not require that the aesthetic object be real? Is there a Being "which grounds both nature and art and assures their affinity" (502)? Is art more than a "game," a Kantian "playing at" reality? Then comes the answer. Yes, "art is true for two reasons: because the signification of the aesthetic object transcends the subjectivity of the individual who expresses himself in it; and because the signification bears finally on a real world which is the locus of our judgments and decisions." This answer is curious because it implies the existential is real only if it is also cosmological. But the formulation Dufrenne used earlier, a purely Heideggerian formulation, judges the existential, or subjective, to be just as real as the cosmological, and to be inseparable from it. In any case, Dufrenne goes on to demonstrate the aesthetic object is true in three senses. First, "the work is true with respect to itself. The work is true in that it is finished, discourages every idea of erasure or correction, and asserts itself sovereignly." Second, the work is true in relation to the artist—"the work is what he *had* to do and what was expected of him." In an argument that could be used by the Geneva School, which also insists on the relative constancy of experiential patterns, Dufrenne says "The work manifests not only a formal necessity but also an internal one, namely, the necessity at the heart of the artist who creates in terms of what he is. For this reason, a given artist will always say the same thing" (505). The above two senses in which the aesthetic object can be considered true are, however, irrelevant in terms of chapter eighteen's overall concern. Dufrenne must show the aesthetic object is true in relation to the *real*, and not only in relation to itself or the artist (these two latter he considers somehow less real or unreal). When Dufrenne shows this relation to the real, he does so in two ways. First, in a mitigated sense the art work is true because it represents or imitates the real world. But second, the art work is true because it expresses affectivity, and affectivity, you will recall, is cosmological as well as existential. There remains a final question. How can the relation between the cosmological and the existential be explained, and from where arises meaning as such? In the last section of chapter eighteen Dufrenne argues that the objective world, or the real, receives its meaning (and therefore its truth) from subjectivities. The real "is an inexhaustible matrix of significations, but only because it has no signification of its own" (531). And again, "The unity of the world does not arise from the unity of the real but from the unity of the look which settles on the real. . . ." Have we come all this way for such a conclusion? Out and out subjective idealism? Not really, because Dufrenne bails himself out in chapter nineteen, "The Ontological Signification of Aesthetic Experience."

The subject (or "anthropological" or "existential") bestows meaning on the real (the "ontic" or "cosmological"), and does so especially through art, but the meaning is both pre-objective and pre-subjective. The meaning, in short, is Being, and Being compels man to utter meaning: "By assigning an ontological signification to aesthetic experience, we are admitting that the cosmological and existential aspects of the affective *apriori* are grounded in being, that is, that being is the bearer of a meaning or sense which it stamps on reality and which it also forces man to utter" (539). Thus even "anthropological bestowal of meaning" is a deceptive phrase: man really discovers meaning in himself and in the real. Furthermore, without the aesthetic object the meaning of the real does not even appear: ". . . reality needs the aesthetic world in order to appear as real." The aesthetic object is an expressivity (or affective dimension of Being) which "lays open" meaning both in and outside of man. As a result, "to the authenticity of the artist who strives to bespeak the real must correspond an authenticity in the real itself which seeks to be spoken in art" (543). The real even imitates art, in that art teaches the real to discover truth, that is, to discover reality's own ground. I add here that this formula is much more "realist" than Ingarden's, for whom the literary work is at most "quasi-judgmental." Ingarden says that literature, and especially "realistic" literature, is true in that it imitates the "objective consistency" of the real world. But clearly, this imitation is just a "playing at" the game of reality. For Dufrenne, on the other hand, literature and all the arts are true because they *are* the real world, the world of affectivity. Mikel Dufrenne ends *The Phenomenology of Aesthetic Experience* with a Heideggerian-style tribute to the inexhaustible surplus of Being and Being's meaning: "Perhaps absolute knowledge lies in the realization that there is no absoluteness in knowledge, but that there is, rather, a will to the absolute in man—a will attested precisely in the deep concern for the aesthetic which we find in the spectator as well as in the artist. Perhaps the last word is that there is no last word" (556).

# chapter 4

# A Heideggerian
# Theory of Meaning

In the very fecund section thirty-two of *Being and Time*,[1] Martin Heidegger offers a theory of meaning which justifies multiple interpretations. The theory, furthermore, accounts for the respective demands of perceiver and text. In this section, Heidegger is at the work of describing all legitimate hermeneutical activity. I shall now attempt a close exegesis of section thirty-two, but my exegesis will automatically adjust Heidegger's description (which is more general) to the literary work as such. The start of the hermeneutical process, begins Heidegger, is the projection of *Dasein* (the individual existent) towards the possibilities "laid open" by the text. Significantly, "these possibilities, as disclosed, exert their own counter-thrust [*Rückschlag*] upon *Dasein*" (188). This counter-thrust ensures the mutual implication of interpreter and literary work, so that both belong to the same ontological field. In the first stage of hermeneutical activity, the critic is *at one with* the text. Next Heidegger says that the "development of the understanding" is "interpretation" proper. Though he will shortly describe this development more clearly, it suffices now to point out that by "understanding" he means the unitary ensemble wherein critic and text are one; and by "interpretation" he means the phenomenological description of this understanding. Heidegger attaches an admonition: "Nor is interpretation the acquiring of information about what is understood; it is rather the working-out of possibilities projected in understanding" (188, 189). By all of this, he intends to place the essence of hermeneutical activity at the level of understanding (which is the level of primal Being), and not at the level of assertion or even interpretation. Assertion, in and of itself, is propositional thinking; it deals with "information," and therefore with *Seienden* instead of *Sein.* Hermeneutics, for Heidegger, is essentially ontology and not ontic study. Evident too is his ardent anti-Cartesianism. The subject-object dichotomy can produce assertion, but not ontological awareness.

Heidegger next attempts to ascertain what is common to all interpretation. Interpretation is the second level of hermeneutical activity and is descriptive (that is, phenomenological) rather than propositional: "In interpreting, we do not, so to speak, throw a 'signification' over some naked thing which is present-at-hand, we do not stick a value on it; but when something within-the-world is encountered as such, the thing in question already has an involvement which is disclosed in our understanding of the world, and this involvement is one which gets laid out by the interpretation" (190,191).

In this section, Heidegger's greatest contribution is a phenomenology of a phenomenology (that is, a description of the second level, which is itself a description of understanding). He finds that interpretative activity manifests three functions: the "As-question," the "As-which," and the "As-structure." *Apropos* the As-question, Heidegger simply means that an interpreter is never neutral, but always approaches a text with an implicit or explicit question, so that the answer given is shaped by the question asked: "As the appropriation of understanding, the interpretation operates in Being towards a totality of involvements which is already understood—a being which understands. When something is understood but is still veiled, it becomes unveiled by an act of appropriation, and this is always done under the guidance of a point of view, which fixes that with regard to which what is understood is to be interpreted" (191). The next function of interpretative operation is the As-which (or aspect) that the problem offers up in answer to the question: "That which is disclosed in understanding—that which is understood—is already accessible in such a way that its 'as which' can be made to stand out explicitly" (189). Any given As-question by its very nature selects and illuminates the corresponding aspect which is "there" in the text. The third function of hermeneutical knowing is the As-structure, also called the taking of "something-as-something" (189). The As-structure is the Articulation (here meaning description) of the "lock" an As-question has on an As-which and vice versa. The As-structure is the interpretation (or Articulation) proper: "That which is understood gets Articulated when the entity to be understood is brought close interpretatively by taking as our clue the 'something as something';

and this Articulation lies *before* [*liegt vor*] our making any thematic assertion about it" (190). Again, logical concatenation (the activity of the third level) plays no role at the interpretative level.

To recapitulate, then, understanding is a prereflective at-oneness of critic and text; interpretation is the phenomenological description of understanding, and consists of an As-structure which is the *interface* of As-question and As-which; and finally, assertion is logical language which abstracts from interpretation, and classifies interpretation into concepts (it therefore breaks interpretation down into subject and object). We can proceed now to Heidegger's next percept, that of "fore-structure." When using the word *fore*, he means that a kind of structure antedates encounter with text,[2] and in part determines how the text will be understood; and that the structure meshes with a text before the interpreter even knows this is the case. It is worth noting that Hans-Georg Gadamer, a quite faithful Heideggerian, echoes the notion of fore-structure, and attacks Husserl (who argues for a presuppositionless, contextless viewpoint): "Nevertheless this receptivity is not acquired by an objectivist 'neutrality': it is neither possible, nor necessary, nor desirable that one put himself in parentheses."[3]

Heidegger continues, saying that fore-structure is characterized by three kinds of fore-awareness, namely fore-having, fore-sight, and fore-conception. Fore-having equates with the first grasp a critic has on a problem at the level of understanding (and it occurs be-*fore* he or she consciously knows it has). Recalling that interpretation is grounded in understanding, Heidegger writes, "Interpretation is grounded in something we have in advance—in a fore-having" (191). Fore-seeing adequates to the first interpretative grasp that the second level has on the first, so that "this fore-sight 'takes the first cut' out of what has been taken into fore-having, and it does so with a view to a definite way in which this [the understanding] can be interpreted" (191). Fore-sight occurs before the interpreter knows he or she has seen anything, and is conditioned by the way of seeing the environment has encouraged. As you will notice, Heidegger's earlier treatment of the As-question anticipated much of what he says about fore-sight. Finally, there occurs in some instances a fore-conception, which is a set of pre-reflexive ideas that eventually become reflexive, and assume logical form. Fore-conception works upon the material of interpretation, and transmutes it into concepts. Heidegger says "Anything understood which is held in our fore-having and towards which we set our sights 'fore-sightedly,' becomes conceptualizable through the interpretation" (191). To rephrase it, fore-conception begins the process whereby the level of assertion conceptualizes the descriptive level.

Heidegger next takes up the question of "meaning" and the related percept of the hermeneutical circle. Keeping in mind that Articulation for Heidegger refers to the activity of the second stratum of awareness, one may conclude from the following that meaning is the facet of understood Being which can be described: "Meaning is that wherein the intelligibility [*Verständlichkeit*] of something maintains itself. That which can be Articulated in a disclosure by which we understand, we call 'meaning.' The concept of meaning embraces the formal existential framework of what necessarily belongs to that which an understanding interpretation Articulates" (193). Meaning, in other words, is an As-structure. The hermeneutical circle, in this context, refers to the circular movement from understanding to interpretation and back again: "Any interpretation which is to contribute understanding must already have understood what is to be interpreted" (194). Heidegger grants that the hermeneutical circle is indeed circular, and that "according to the most elementary rules of logic, this circle is a *circulus viciosus* [vicious circle]." Why so? Because in both traditional logic and "scientific proof, we may not presuppose what it is our task to provide grounds for." In his iconoclastic way, Heidegger continues, ". . . if we see this circle as a vicious one, and look for ways of avoiding it, even if we just 'sense' it as an inevitable imperfection, then the art of understanding has been misunderstood from the ground up." The understanding, or first stratum of awareness, operates on the pre-objective level; interpretation as such Articulates the understanding. Interpretation presupposes understanding, but through the very process of Articulating, interpretation provides grounds for understanding.[4]

Heidegger concludes section thirty-two with a discussion of "authentic" versus "fanciful" interpretation. Again, the notion of fore-structure is involved. According to the first sense of this term, fore-structure is the psychological apparatus the individual brings to the text: for example, one may think in terms of English language syntax, one may be a Freudian, one may be an archetypalist. Heidegger argues that without fore-structure, interpretation of any kind is impossible. Heidegger, however, most emphatically does not intend to deny the possibility of incorrect interpretations. Again, the crucial stratum is the interpretative stratum, which falls midway between the pre-objective awareness of the first stratum and the objective awareness of the third. The second stratum, in other words, does not dichotomize experience into subject and object as the assertive level does, but neither is it as unitary a phenomenon as the level of understanding. After all, as soon as one speaks of an As-question issuing from the interpreter and an As-which offered by the text, one is speaking in terms of a dichotomy. But the second level, in its *essential* construct, does *remain true* to the experiential unity found in understanding: the interpretation strictly defined, that is, the As-structure, is precisely the mutual engagement of critic and text. The interpretation is constituted simultaneously by an As-question and an As-which and thereby bridges the dichotomy of subject and object. The As-structure, in short, is a unitary phenomenon. *Apropos* authenticity, Heidegger says the following:

> To be sure, we genuinely take hold of this possibility [primordial knowing] only when, in our interpretation, we have understood that our first, last, and constant task is never to allow our fore-having, fore-sight, and fore-conception to be presented to us by fancies and popular conceptions, but rather to make the scientific theme secure by working out these fore-structures in terms of the things themselves (195).

This stricture applies not only to the interpretative level, but to contact between all three kinds of fore-structure on the one hand, and texts on the other. In fact, earlier Heidegger spoke of the same requirement in regard to conceptualization (fore-conception), warning the thinker not to "force the entity into concepts to which it is opposed in its manner of Being." Heidegger is saying that in a valid solution, fore-structure locks into an As-which that is *really there* in the text. (Thus a literary critic must "make a case" for his interpretation in terms of the aspects profiled in the work.) When such does not occur, just a "fanciful" or pseudo-interpretation materializes. Notice too that Heidegger intentionally ignores the author's sense here. Hans-Georg Gadamer, Heidegger's disciple, goes on to strictly exclude this sense. In *Truth and Method* Gadamer says, "The mens auctoris is not admissible as a yardstick for the meaning of a work of art."[5] And in another book, he repudiates the tradition of objective hermeneutics, and its quest for the author's sense: ". . . all that Schleiermacher and Romanticism report to us on the subjective factors of comprehension seems to us unconvincing. When we understand a text we do not put ourselves in the place of another, and it is not a question of penetrating the spiritual activity of the author. . . ."[6]

With its treatment of authenticity, section thirty-two comes to a close. Regarding literary interpretation, the section has engaged two issues that are very significant: first, the nature of meaning, and second, the legitimacy of multiple interpretation. I shall discuss both and append to the second issue a treatment of contradictory meanings. The first *punctum* defines the nature of meaning. The agenda is to review theories of meaning identified with other thinkers I have treated, and to counterpoise these theories against the Heideggerian position. In his essay, "Objective Interpretation," E. D. Hirsch sees meaning as an intentional object construed from the text. In chapters two and four of his book, *Validity in Interpretation*, he distinguishes between intentional object or "subject matter," and intentional act or "referring meaning." This second theory is an unpurposeful imitation of Husserl's own position, but what is important is that Hirsch insists the referring meaning should duplicate the author's meaning. Heidegger would answer here that in the normal run of things a phenomenology of interpretation shows no indication of an author's sense. The latter materializes only when an interpreter happens to bring authorial information to bear on textual aspects. But Heidegger's point is that such an As-question is by no means statutory. The author's sense is not an *arbitrium* built into the text.

In the *Logische Untersuchungen*, Edmund Husserl formulates the following proposition—that verbal expression (a kind of intentional act) places a sign to communicate a sense. The sign relates to a sense, or idea, or ideal "semantic essence," and this essence in turn relates to an object. Meaning is a function of the perceiver's intentional act, but his intentional act should repeat the intentional act of the speaker. Thus, though in a different way, Husserl reinforces Hirsch's central thesis—that the meaning of a verbal sign should be the author's meaning. Also of interest in this connection is the definition of aspects in the *Logische Untersuchungen*. In stark contrast with Heidegger's ideas, here matter is identified with aspect, so that aspect becomes part of the intentional act. The later Husserl, the Husserl of the *Ideen*, changes his position considerably. Within the field of consciousness, now rooted in a transcendental subjectivity, meaning is present both in the intentional act (*noesis*) and in the intentional object (*noema*). Ideal meanings or "abstract forms" inhabit the intentional object. As for aspects, they too are now embedded in the intentional object, or noematic structure.

The earlier position of Husserl, that meaning is a function of

the intending act, Heidegger finds untenable. In the Heideggerian
scheme, the object necessarily contributes to meaning. The Husserlian formulation, Heidegger would say, diminishes the authority of
the text, though an authentic phenomenology of reading vindicates
this authority. A dispassionate description of the literary experience
reveals that the text "proclaims" itself. It "shines forth," and thereby
donates to the phenomenon of meaning. Perhaps the Heideggerian
As-question is best considered a permutation of Husserl's noetic act.
Heidegger strips the latter of a "meaning-bestowing" function, but
retains the quality of "thrust": the As-question goes to meet the As-
which. The later Husserlian position, that meaning is in both *noesis*
and *noema*, is a bit closer to Heidegger's concept: at least here
Husserl restores some prerogative to the object. In Heidegger,
however, meaning is neither in the intending act of the critic nor in
the literary text (nor in both *per se*). Meaning is essentially *nexical*.
Meaning is precisely the engagement of subject and object, and the
engagement is a unified As-structure. The As-structure, furthermore,
is performative—it arises when reader and text participate in a joint
act. One further item is worth noting, and it is that both Heidegger
and the later Husserl agree on theory of aspects. Both thinkers place
aspects squarely in the object.

Roman Ingarden follows the *Logische Untersuchungen* quite
literally, but makes some crucial alterations. Meaning is again
consigned to the intentional act of the perceiver, though meaning is
no longer ideal; rather, it "belongs to" ideal concepts. The perceiver
aims to duplicate the intentional act of the author, since the author's
intentional act has passed over into the intersubjective "intentionality of the word." As the perceiver's purpose is to duplicate the
intending act of the author, the author's sense is again the
controlling factor. There is an outstanding difference from Husserl.
Husserl's intentional object *is* the ideal or real designatum, when
such exists. For Husserl, only the "merely intentional" object has no
designatum. Ingarden's intentional object is always "merely
intentional," though it correlates to real or ideal designata when
such exist. However, this difference between Husserl and Ingarden
does not affect theory of literature significantly, since literary objects
are "merely intentional" in any case (the only exceptions being
biography and the historical novel). In relation to Ingarden's key
thesis, Heidegger would again question why it is imperative to
duplicate the author's sense. Indeed, one could ask such an As-
question—"What is the author's sense?" But there are many other

questions equally valid. Textual aspects are made of language, and language functions apart from its erstwhile speaker. Language is "loose in the world," and its significations defined by the *langue* of the circumambient culture.

While the formulations of Hirsch, Husserl, and Ingarden are easily identifiable, those of Mikel Dufrenne are often amorphous. Through most of *The Phenomenology*, Dufrenne locates meaning in the intentional object. Meaning is the sensuous and is pre-given to perception. Aspects (as in Heidegger) are facets of this object. The sensuous materializes affectivity, but this affectivity is that of the author and must be understood accordingly. The perceiver's affective life submits to the control of the work's affectivity. However, in some sequences Dufrenne plays coquette with Heideggerian and Kantian ideas, thereby hamstringing his own committed position. Dufrenne tells us his notion of "presence" is pre-objective, and here he clearly mimes Heideggerian "understanding." Furthermore, Dufrenne's theory of the affective *apriori* places affectivity (which, for him, is meaning) anterior to the subject-object split. And elsewhere, he supports a Heideggerian theory of Being, which necessarily implies meaning is undifferentiated between subject and object. How then can Dufrenne maintain, consistently, his main formulation—that meaning is "in the object" (and not in the subject)? Isn't this to speak in terms of the Cartesian split? Such is the contradiction—a kind of amaurosis in the vision of *The Phenomenology*—and it is one Heidegger neatly avoids. Perhaps Dufrenne instinctively realizes that his level of "presence," like Heidegger's "understanding," cannot be meaning *per se*. Meaning, after all, must be a particularized and articulated phenomenon. To satisfy this latter requirement, Dufrenne places meaning in the intentional object. Yet he clings to the notion that meaning precedes subjectivity and objectivity. Heidegger, instead, formulates the concept of As-structure, a structure which is particularized and articulated. The As-structure is meaning, but because its structure unifies subject and object, it remains faithful to the unity of "understanding," and thus transcends the Cartesian dichotomy.

Progressing to the second *punctum*, the vindication of multiple interpretations, one meets at once the problem of ambiguity. The word *ambiguity* can be taken in two different ways: it can mean "ordered" aspects, so that two or more distinct interpretations come to stand alongside each other in the very same text; and it can mean "confused" aspects, in which two or more interpretations of the

same text become hopelessly entangled. Only the first kind yields
distinct multiple interpretations; when I use the word *ambiguity*, I
normally mean this kind. The second kind, though, can invite some
As-questions which can be successfully implemented. For example,
in the face of a confused text, one may ask: "Is life absurd, then?
Indecipherable? A riddle?" And the confused aspects of the text,
marshalled into one, adequate to such questions. (I have often seen
portions of Franz Kafka interpreted in this way.)

It is now time to review the ideas of Hirsch, Husserl, Ingarden,
and Dufrenne on multiplicity of interpretation. When the meanings
are not those of the author, Hirsch attacks the theory that the text
represents " 'an array of different *actual* meanings corresponding to
different actual interpretations.' "[7] He does so because such meanings become (in his opinion) indeterminate, and therefore unknowable and unshareable. Discussing theory of multiple meaning, he
writes, "Such a conception really denies the self-identity of verbal
meaning by suggesting that the meaning of a text can be one thing,
and also another; and this conception . . . is simply a denial that the
text means anything in particular."[8]

Heidegger would propose there are a plural number of aspects
in texts, but that each of these aspects is determinate and self-
identical (whether the author "willed" them there or not). To invert
Hirsch, the work means *many things* in particular. Hirsch's
perception of a text is remarkably flat: a text cannot have more than
one facet. The author's meaning excludes all others. Thus *Validity
in Interpretation* announces categorically: "It may be asserted as a
general rule that whenever a reader confronts two interpretations
which impose different emphases on similar meaning components,
at least one of the interpretations must be wrong. They cannot be
reconciled."[9] But why must this be the case? The often-used analogy
with a diamond is appropriate here. Our interpretative glance at the
diamond can contact one or more facets, and each is really part of
the diamond. But let's take a verbal example—the word *cleave*,
which has two opposing definitions. *Cleave* can mean *to separate* or
*to adhere*. Let us say a given text describes a God who descends in
blinding theophany, and utters to his hushed disciples, "Men and
women, cleave!" Let us assume furthermore that the verbal context
is of no help. But, and this is of utmost importance, let us take it as
given that all authorial evidence points to one interpretation as the
author's own—that he willed, let's say, "cleave" to mean "separate."
Does this authorial data make the alternative interpretation, that to

"cleave" is to "adhere," less determinate and self-identical? Both significations (to "separate" and to "adhere") are held firm by the syntax and lexic of the *langue,* which gives them shareability and particularity. What further determinacy is needed? For a Heideggerian, Hirsch's argument remains patently spurious.

Husserl copes with ambiguity in his sequences on "equivocation." In the case of "occasional expressions," for example, the perceiver should see the expression in relation to the author's intent. Husserl tells us, "If we read the word without knowing who wrote it, it is perhaps not meaningless, but is at least estranged from normal sense. . . ." As for "objective expressions" which are equivocal, one is told, "It may be that a glance at the speaker and his situation may help. . . ." Husserl tries, in short, to resolve multiplicity by recourse to the author. It is important to keep in mind, however, that Husserl is speaking here of ordinary communication. For the Heideggerian, literary language is extraordinary. It is the sanctum where the "Fourfold" powers dance, the sanctum where World and Thing play. Literary language dissolves its author, and goes on to live its own being. When Husserl and Heidegger talk about communication, they are not talking about the same thing.

Of all four thinkers, Roman Ingarden addresses most attention to multiplicity. In the section on "actual and potential stock" of word meanings, he makes textual context the sole criterion for exegesis: context determines which meanings of an ideal concept are in fact actualized. Stripped of its idealism, such a position approximates that of Heidegger. The Heideggerian critic must make a case for an interpretation in terms of semantic value (or aspect), and the value is determined by textual context. But Ingarden's section on "opalescent multiplicity" contrasts dramatically with the Heideggerian formulation. For Ingarden, a sentence which is ambiguous or contradictory in meaning content projects a purely intentional correlate characterized by opalescent multiplicity. (By ambiguity, he means both of the two types we have mentioned.) Ingarden's whole point is that the real world does not permit the aforesaid ambiguities, nor does it permit contradiction; but that literature does, since literature is not real but "purely intentional." Heidegger, on the contrary, sees literature as a revelation of the real, so that the literary word can be ambiguous or contradictory *because* Being is; or more accurately, he sees literature *as* the privileged real, so that the ambiguity of the universe is "solidified" therein.

Ingarden's next discussion of ambiguity appears in his sections on "schematic formation." Here the perceiver should "concretize" schematic formations in a way consistent with possible meanings of the word units involved. The foregoing sounds somewhat like Heideggerian As-structure, but Ingarden's concretizations are strictly distinct from both intentional object and intentional act. Furthermore, Ingarden insists that the schematic aspects concretized should be those "predetermined" by the author. Later still, Ingarden again takes up a question relevant to ambiguity. When does a concretization so change a work that a new work results? He answers that the same work survives if the predetermined aspects of the work are not contradicted. If the aspects leave open a variety of possible concretizations, any of these can be effected by the reader without violence to the "same work." Ingarden's notion of predetermination remains unclear, so a comparison with Heidegger is difficult. If a predetermined aspect is "built into" the literary work as an As-which, certainly Heidegger would respect it. If it is not an As-which, but just part of the author's unrealized "purpose," Heidegger then judges it irrelevant. If evidence of the author's "purpose" is available, and if Heidegger ignores it, Ingarden might protest that Heidegger is forming a "new work." But Heidegger would answer that he remains faithful to the As-which formations of the text, so the work in this case has *not* changed. Ingarden makes another point: that history can change the meaning of individual words, so that the work partially changes. For Ingarden, whether in this instance the work becomes a new work depends on the degree of change. As long as there is no "significant deviation," the same work persists. Heidegger would agree with the above in principle. If one analyzes Heidegger's stance toward change, the following principles emerge. First, as long as the As-which formations of a literary work remain the same, the work remains the same. This is not to say the meaning stays the same, since every As-question is different, and every As-question contributes toward As-structure. Second, portions of the *langue* which supported a text may be lost. A new *langue* may impute new significations to a text's As-which formations. If these substitutions are sizable, the work can be called a new work.

As for Mikel Dufrenne, the fourth theorist, he says the least about multiplicity of meaning. In chapter two of his part one he speaks of the "life of a work through history." A work "waxes or wanes, is enriched or impoverished, according to the warmth of our devotion to it, and the meaning we discover in it." The reader's "performance" (like Ingarden's "concretization") should submit to the anterior "demands" of the text. The demands originate in the work's "depth," which is the coefficient of the author's affectivity. A given tradition "sometimes guides, if not alters, our judgment by imposing too exclusive an image on the aesthetic object." A given tradition of performances, in sum, can distort the meaning of an art work. In chapter four of part one, Dufrenne says ambiguity appears when the meaning is undefinable, or when the reader is inattentive. In either case, "It is not that the meaning is concealed but that we ourselves are blind." Apropos the undefinability of meaning, a Heideggerian prefers to say there is simply no meaning in such an instance. The reader is unable to construct an As-question which adequates to the aspects of the text. In regard to the "blindness" of the reader, this is only one alternative. It may be that the literary work is defective: perhaps its aspects do not let Being "shine." Whether this is the case or not can be revealed by an immanent phenomenology of the experience of the text. Dufrenne's last word is that the text has inexhaustible "possibilities," but these activate only when the reader discovers and articulates them. The foregoing proposition derives in part from Ingarden and in part from Heidegger. According to the latter, it is Being's infinity which accounts for the inexhaustible nature of the text. One must keep in mind, however, that any one meaning is particular and determinate.

Heidegger's theory of multiple interpretation depends on a multi-faceted text, and on an array of As-questions. The Jungian asks an archetypal question of the work, and if the work displays a corresponding aspect, an As-structure solidifies—the text appears *as* an archetypal document. The Freudian asks a psychoanalytic question, and if an appropriate As-which presents itself—the text appears *as* an erotic document. Though he or she can only be partly successful, the historical critic may approximate a nineteenth-century fore-structure and bring such a fore-structure to bear on a nineteenth-century text. And, as already suggested, a biographical critic may ask questions involving an author's intention and construe the aspects of the text accordingly.

Let us take the example of Nathaniel Hawthorne's short story, "My Kinsman, Major Molineux." Set in revolutionary days, the story recounts a visit to the city of a boy named Robin. His mission is to obtain employment through the patronage of his important uncle, Major Molineux. He at last finds his uncle, a Loyalist, led in angry procession by a crowd of American revolutionaries. Tarred and feathered, the uncle is jeered by the onlookers. To his own dismay, Robin joins in the abuse. A Jungian may read the story as a boy's archetypal discovery of sin (in himself and others), so that the visit to the city becomes a "baptism into evil." The leader of the revolutionaries, a man with face half black and half red, becomes the archetypal Fiend. The Freudian critic may allude to a dream Robin has before he meets his kinsman: Robin dreams that his father locks him out of the family house. According to a possible Freudian interpretation, the uncle then becomes a surrogate father-figure, and Robin works his vengeance on his father by ridiculing Major Molineux. A Marxist may read the story in terms of class struggle. At the beginning of his journey Robin is dependent on nepotism, but learns at the end to make his own way in the world. Since they are struggling against colonialism, the revolutionary crowd and its leader represent the forces of good. Finally, a biographical critic can refer to Nathaniel Hawthorne's own purpose: some evidence shows he felt guilt over atrocities committed against Tories. And support for Hawthorne's pro-Loyalist sympathies can be found in the text. Each of these interpretations asks a different As-question, and each can prove its conclusions by way of the work itself. Because it will be of later use, let us introduce here a further sophistication in terms. The words of the story "My Kinsman, Major Molineux" are the "significations" or "verbal aspects" (rhythm, rhyme, and so forth are other kinds of aspect). For want of a better term, the qualities imparted to lexic aspects (Molineux as surrogate father-figure, for example) are "qualitative values." The latter, it should be clear, emanate from As-questions. In a valid interpretation, then, qualitative value accords with lexic and other aspects.

I can now append a word on contradictory interpretations *per se* and Heidegger's justification of them. Here I call upon a quotation from Heidegger's essay, "What are Poets For?":

> If Being is what is unique to beings, by what can Being still be surpassed? Only by itself, only by its own, and indeed by expressly entering into its own. Then Being would be the unique which wholly surpasses itself (the *transcendens* pure and simple). But this surpassing, this transcending does not go up and over into something else; it comes up to its own self and back into the very nature of its truth. Being itself traverses this going over and is itself its dimension.

> When we think on this, we experience within Being itself that there lies in it something "more" belonging to it, and thus the

> possibility that there too, where Being is thought of as the venture, something more daring may prevail than even Being itself, so far as we commonly conceive Being in terms of particular beings. Being, as itself, spans its own province, which is marked off (*temnein, tempus*) by Being's being present in the word.[10]

In the above passage, Heidegger gives one the wherewithal to justify the simultaneous validity of contradictory interpretations. Individual beings are often contradictory, yet according to Heidegger all beings share in the transcendent Being which is at their heart. The "surpassing" which is Being enters "into its own." It follows then that the "more" which is universal Being subsumes all contradictions into itself. What are logical contradictions on the level of "assertion" are organized into a holistic formation at the primal level of "understanding." Consequently, contradictions (as unique entities) can be simultaneously valid—since they are emanations, if you will, of the one Being. This paradox, furthermore, finds its privileged locus "in the word," where Being is "present." If I may attach an *additum*, however, I would like to make the point that ontology is not even necessary to justify contradictory senses. Whether or not human life is contradictory in ontological terms, it is often experienced as contradictory. Literature is an expression of human life, and as such, its role is to enverbalize human contradiction. Literary interpretations can be valid but contradictory because experience seems that way.

The critic's audience adjudicates the validity of his interpretation. This notion educes the issue of intersubjectivity, and the concomitant issue of change in the literary work. Regarding these questions, an extrapolation from Heidegger's section thirty-two produces the following conclusions. We have seen that meanings change because As-questions differ. But the work itself also changes, and this because its As-which formations, or aspects, change. A famous instance is provided by René Wellek in his *Theory of Literature*.[11] In the seventeenth century, Andrew Marvell's phrase "vegetable love" meant "vegetative love." That is, the signification or verbal aspect of "vegetable" was "vegetative." And according to the scholar Louis Teeter (quoted by Wellek), the usual qualitative value imparted to the expression "vegetable love" at the time was "life-giving principle." But in the twentieth century, "vegetable" signifies "edible plant" (with all its connotations), and this signification opens the way to a new qualitative value: "vegetable love" symbolizes "slow or stifled love" (love as an "erotic cabbage," as

Teeter says). In short, lexic aspects have changed. And with them the work. And with them the qualitative values.

Hirsch, in his discussion of the above example,[12] advances the following argument. Wellek's very thesis, that the modern interpretation is also viable, assumes the distinction between the author's sense and subsequent senses. In order to avoid a relativism, a chaotic flux of meanings, it is absolutely essential to distinguish between author's sense and other possible values. Thus the necessary distinction between "meaning" and "significance." Heidegger would answer that he too sees distinctions among significations (how could he not?). However, he refuses to attribute an exclusivity to the author's sense. What Hirsch calls "meaning" and what Hirsch calls "significance" both arise from an interaction of As-question and aspect. Thus the same validity obtains for both. In sum, both share the same axiological status. By this Heidegger does not mean to deny the importance of historical criticism. Ideally, signification and meaning sediment historically. Indeed, the notion of ecstatic temporality depends on tradition. And Heidegger has also asked the authorial question; that is, he has used biographical data to frame an authorial As-question, and he has adequated this question to textual signification derived from the author's own cultural period. (As I shall demonstrate, it is cultural *langue* which imputes signification to text.) But Heidegger's point here is that one need not generate meaning in this way. Modern As-questions and significations are just as legitimate. Hirsch's *riposte* is that such a formula reduces to pure relativism. In answer, I postulate there is a constancy adduced by Heideggerian theory—the constancy imparted by inter-subjectivism.

I shall begin with an example. In Henry James's novella *The Turn of the Screw*, a governess struggles to protect her two young charges against diabolical ghosts. It so happens that nineteenth-century critics brought a traditional Christian fore-structure to the text, and saw the governess as an integrated and wholesome personality, fighting the war of a Christian heroine against Satan. Freudian critics of the twentieth century have seen the governess as a neurotic personality, perverting the children through her malign fantasies. If one were to perform a phenomenology of critical dialogue, one would find each critic trying to make a case for a private interpretation (of course, this does not preclude learning from others as well). Each critic would try to "convince" the others. But "convincing" can take place only to the extent that the critics share values in common. In the above example, Freudians would convince those sympathetic to Freud; traditional Christians would convince Christians. In short, intersubjective values provide the constant whereby a work can be judged. And for Heidegger, this kind of constancy suffices.

At issue here is change in the literary work and not just in As-questions. To be sure, intersubjectivity controls the qualitative values which inform an As-question. But intersubjectivity also controls the As-which formations of the text. The Heideggerian critic hypothesizes an As-which and must show this As-which is "really there" in the text; in the case of significations, this is done by appealing to his culture's *langue* (which is an intersubjective constant); in the case of ethical values, by invoking intersubjective ethics. Culture, in other words, imparts signification and value to the text. Nineteenth-century critics did not and could not see neurosis (a kind of ethical definition) in the governess. For them, a neurotic aspect was not "really there." Twentieth-century Freudians can in part understand the Christian interpretation (available to them through the process of sedimentation), but they can also "find" the psychoanalytic interpretation. Enter Hirsch, who argues here that a cultural constant is a myth, since values change from moment to moment and individual to individual. The rebuttal to Hirsch's argument is succinct. Without constants people could not talk and could not share intersubjective values. Surely, intersubjective constants shift (indeed, Heidegger makes much of this point), but at any time in history there are constancies. There was, for example, a prevailing medieval attitude towards sex (an attitude we can never wholly understand), and the medieval attitude was different from that prevailing in modern America. A pluralistic society, such as our own, produces subcultures, or various sets of constancies. In literary study, this pluralism accounts for the amazing multiplicity of critical schools. When in contradiction, these schools have simply fought with one another. Heidegger is saying that contradictory interpretations (and the schools which project them) can all be valid, and can be accepted as such without ontological embarrassment. Nor is this relativism, since the latter would "found" its truth on the values of the believing group pure and simple. Heidegger, on the other hand, founds truth on Being, and this truth is only mediated through the values of the group. Different critical schools can reflect different facets of Being. Nor does Heidegger imply that one must accept every critical school that arises in history. One may be convinced a given school does not reflect Being. But Heidegger is saying that we can accept contradictory schools and interpretations, and that he has given us the theoretical means to do so.

Now let me submit the notion of *langue* to further examination, putting my conclusions to the test of the extreme case. At the outset, I assume the original significations of a text have been lost completely. In other words, the *langue* has been lost. In terms of the twentieth-century interpreters and their culture, the text may make no sense or perhaps some sense—the latter through chance alone. The marks on the page happen to make sense in a language known by the interpreters, even though their language is different from the language of the author (and the author's culture). Let me turn the screw another spiral. Through a fortuitous happening, the text makes complete sense in the second language. Attention, Hirsch: one cannot appeal to the author's sense now! Yet by chance perhaps an exquisite poem has arisen. Whence come the significations? They can only come from the language of the *interpreter's* culture. Recall Heidegger's exaltation of *die Sprache* in his later work. Language more than any other phenomenon bespeaks the humanity of a people. Language is the precious resource whereby the poem brings forth the world of *Dasein* and the realm of Things. But one should also account for the alternative option of the extreme case. If the text in question makes no linguistic sense in terms of available *langue,* the text is then no longer a cultural phenomenon but a natural one. A natural entity, when engaged by a fore-structure, may participate in meaning, of course. However, a natural entity is not saturated with humanity. In the case of a cultural phenomenon, a human interpreter meets the humanity of the phenomenon. In the case of a natural entity, the human meets the non-human. The text deprived of sense can no longer participate in literary meaning. Finally, it should be apparent from the above treatment that the hermeneutical enterprise involves signification derived from the interpreter's *langue* (though the *langue* may include knowledge of the author's *langue).* The author's sense, derived from the author's *langue,* need not come into play.

In sum, this chapter has described the structure of literary experience (including interpreter and interpreted). It has described the nature of meaning, and the norms of validity. In the light of the foregoing, it has commented on Hirsch, Husserl, Ingarden, and Dufrenne. The chapter has demonstrated, furthermore, that multiple and contradictory interpretations can be simultaneously valid.

And finally, it has discussed intersubjectivity, and the nature of change in the literary work. I end this book with some stanzas from Heidegger's poetry. To write about literary art and about the phenomenology of this art has been confounding. One meets the ineffable face to face. To write has often been ecstatic. But often my purpose has slipped into the fissures between words. Perhaps even this has been good. Being proclaims itself through the spoken, but also through the unspoken. Let Heidegger say it:

> Thinking's saying would be stilled in
> its being only by becoming unable to
> say that which must remain unspoken.

> Such inability would bring thinking
> face to face with its matter.

> What is spoken is never, and in no
> language, what is said.[13]

# *notes*

## Preface

1. *The Critical Moment: Literary Criticism in the 1960s—Essays from the London Times Literary Supplement* (New York: McGraw-Hill, 1964), p. 1.
2. Unless otherwise indicated, translations from French and German are my own.

## Part One

## Chapter One

1. Joseph J. Kockelmans, "What is Phenomenology?" in *Phenomenology: The Philosophy of Edmund Husserl and Its Interpretation*, ed. Kockelmans (New York: Doubleday, 1967), p. 25.
2. For more details, see Quentin Lauer, *Phenomenology: Its Genesis and Prospect* (New York: Harper and Row, 1965), chs. 2 and 4; and William A. Luijpen, *Existential Phenomenology* (Pittsburgh: Duquesne University Press, 1963), pp. 79-88.
3. See Maurice Natanson, *Literature, Philosophy, and the Social Sciences: Essays in Existentialism and Phenomenology* (The Hague: Nijhoff, 1962); and Natanson, *The Journeying Self: A Study in Philosophy and Social Role* (Reading, Mass.: Addison-Wesley, 1970).
4. Consult the section on Heidegger in Herbert Spiegelberg, *The Phenomenological Movement: A Historical Introduction*, 2 vols. (The Hague: Nijhoff, 1965), vol. 1.
5. René Wellek, "Ästhetik," *Lexicon der Weltliteratur im 20. Jahrhundert* (Freiburg, Basel, Vienna: Herder, 1964), col. 267.
6. René Wellek, *Concepts of Criticism* (New Haven and London: Yale University Press, 1963), p. 362.
7. Jean-Pierre Richard, *L'Univers imaginaire de Mallarmé* (Paris: Seuil, 1961), p. 37.
8. Roland Barthes, "Les Deux Critiques," *Essais critiques* (Paris: Seuil, 1964), pp. 246-51.
9. Wellek, *Concepts*, pp. 362-64.
10. René Wellek and Austin Warren, *Theory of Literature*, 3rd ed. (New York: Harcourt, Brace and World, 1956), pp. 81-93.
11. *Theory of Literature*, p. 149.

*193*

12.  Jean-Paul Sartre, "Une idée fondamentale de la phénoménologie de Husserl," originally published in January 1939; reprinted in Sartre, *Situations, I* (Paris: Gallimard, 1947), pp. 31-35.

13.  Jean-Paul Sartre, *Situations, II: Qu'est ce que la littérature* (Paris: Gallimard, 1948), pp. 67 and 69, respectively.

14.  Spiegelberg, 2:511; the quotation below is from p. 510.

15.  Jean-Paul Sartre, *Literary and Philosophical Essays*, trans. Annette Michelson (New York: Collier, 1962), p. 87.

16.  Ibid., p. 92.

17.  Eugene Kaelin, *An Existentialist Aesthetic: The Theories of Sartre and Merleau-Ponty* (Madison: University of Wisconsin Press, 1962); Kaelin has also developed his own interesting phenomenological aesthetic in *Art and Existence* (Lewisburg: Bucknell University Press, 1970).

18.  Consult Philip E. Lewis's "Merleau-Ponty and the phenomenology of language," *Yale French Studies* 36/37 (October 1966), wherein appears a more detailed study of Merleau-Ponty's influence on linguistics.

19.  The word *naive* is not by any means a pejorative; the word indicates a pre-reflective stratum of living which is, if anything, more authentic than conceptual behavior.

20.  Richard E. Palmer, *Hermeneutics: Interpretation Theory in Schleiermacher, Dilthey, Heidegger, and Gadamer* (Evanston: Northwestern University Press, 1969).

21.  Published in the Hague by Mouton and Company, 1963.

22.  Marvin Farber, *The Aims of Phenomenology* (New York: Harper and Row, 1966); quotations are from pp. 144 and 145, respectively.

23.  Ernest Cassirer, *Language and Myth*, trans. Susanne Langer (New York and London: Harper, 1946), p. 99.

24.  Susanne Langer, *Feeling and Form* (New York: Scribner's, 1953), p. 374.

# Chapter Two

1.  See Mikel Dufrenne, "Critique Littéraire et Phénoménologie," *Revue Internationale de Philosophie* 68-69 (1964): 193-208; Jean-Pierre Richard, "Quelques aspects nouveaux de la critique littéraire en France," *Filologia Moderna* (April 1961), p. 3; Paul de Man, "Modern Poetics: French and German," *Encyclopedia of Poetry and Poetics*, ed. Alex Preminger (Princeton, N. J.: Princeton University Press, 1965), p. 520; Vernon W. Gras, "Introduction," *European Literary Theory and Practice*, ed. Gras (New York: Dell, 1973), pp. 1-23; Robin Magowan, "Jean-Pierre Richard and the Criticism of Sensation," *Criticism* (Spring 1964), p. 156; Roland Barthes, *Essais critiques* (Paris: Seuil, 1964), pp. 246-51.

2.  Published in Cambridge, Mass., by Harvard University Press, 1968.

3.  Lawall, pp. 25, 29.

4.  Lawall, p. 8; I might add that Lawall uses the term *literary existentialism* in a very broad sense.

5.  Lawall, p. 75.

6.  Lawall, p. 223.

7.  Gras, ibid., pp. 11, 12.

8.  Preminger, ed., ibid., p. 520.

9. J. Hillis Miller, "The Geneva School," *Critical Quarterly 8* (1968); Lawall, p. 122.

10. Georges Poulet, *La Conscience critique* (Paris: Librairie José Corti, 1971); the page references to this book which follow are enclosed by parentheses in the body of the text after each quotation.

11. Georges Poulet, *The Interior Distance,* trans. Elliott Coleman (Baltimore: Ann Arbor paperback, University of Michigan Press, 1964); this quotation and the preceding one are from p. 233.

12. In Jean Starobinski, *L'Oeil vivant* (Paris: Gallimard, 1961), pp. 9-27.

13. Emil Staiger, "Time and the Poetic Imagination," in *The Critical Moment: Literary Criticism in the 1960s* (New York: McGraw-Hill, 1964).

14. Eva M. Kushner, "The Critical Method of Gaston Bachelard," in *Myth and Symbol: Critical Approaches and Applications,* ed. Bernice Slote (Lincoln: University of Nebraska Press, 1963), p. 48.

15. Poulet, *La Conscience critique,* p. 208.

16. Richard, "Quelques aspects," p. 12.

17. Paul Brodtkorb, *Ishmael's White World* (New Haven: Yale University Press, 1965), p. 3.

18. Fakhir Hussain, *Le Jugement esthétique* (Paris: Minard, 1967), p. 111.

19. Jean-Pierre Richard, *L'Univers imaginaire de Mallarmé* (Paris: Seuil, 1961), p. 19.

20. Roman Ingarden, *Das literarische Kunstwerk,* 3rd ed. (Tübingen: Niemeyer, 1965); English translation, *The Literary Work of Art: An Investigation on the Borderlines of Ontology, Logic, and Theory of Literature,* trans. George G. Grabowicz (Evanston, Ill.: Northwestern University Press, 1973)

21. Ingarden, *Literary Work of Art,* p. 30.

22. Georges Poulet, however, uses fragments of an author's correspondence and other informal writings when they are stylistically rich enough to qualify as "literature." For a good discussion of this problem, see Jean Rousset's *Forme et Signification* (Paris: José Corti, 1962) p. xix.

23. In his later writings, Dufrenne becomes more Heideggerian, and adjusts his interests accordingly. The self-world relation of the author is still present in the work through "expressivity," but it is the "world" pole of this polarity which receives quite exclusive attention. The "world" reveals itself in the work, and the author's selfhood seems no more than a funnel.

24. Ingarden also points to the intentionality operative between literary work and reader (here the work is the object, and the reader the subject). The literary work has "spots of indeterminacy" and "schematized aspects" which await fulfillment from the selfhood of the reader.

25. Terminology for these patterns varies from critic to critic.

26. Richard, *L'Univers imaginaire,* p. 17.

27. Ibid., p. 19.

28. Ibid., p. 27.

29. Ibid., p. 36.

30. J. Hillis Miller, *Charles Dickens: The World of His Novels* (Cambridge, Mass.: Harvard University Press, 1958), p. viii.

31. Brodtkorb, *Ishmael's White World,* p. 3. By *subjectivity,* Brodtkorb means the intentionality (subject-object relationships) of the subject. He is not using the term *subjectivity* in a Cartesian sense.

32. Poulet, *La Distance intérieure (Etudes sur le temps humain, II),* (Paris: Plon, 1952), p. 5.

33. Merleau-Ponty, *Sens et non-sens* (Paris: Nagel, 1948), p. 51.

34. This subject is well treated by J.-Claude Piguet in his phenomenological work *De L'Esthétique à la Métaphysique* (The Hague: Nijhoff, 1959), pp. 143-45.

35. Jean-Pierre Richard, *Littérature et sensation* (Paris: Seuil, 1954), p. 13.

36. Miller, *Charles Dickens*, pp. ix, x.

37. Emil Staiger, *Die Kunst der Interpretation*, 3rd ed. (Zürich: Atlantis, 1961), p. 13.

38. Ibid., pp. 14, 15.

39. Staiger, "Time and the Poetic Imagination," p. 134.

40. Leo Spitzer, *Linguistics and Literary History* (Princeton, N.J.: Princeton University Press, 1948), p. 18.

41. Ibid., p. 13.

42. Rousset, *Forme et Signification*, p. xviii.

43. Leo Spitzer, *Essays on English and American Literature* (Princeton, N.J.: Princeton University Press, 1962), p. 194.

44. Emil Staiger, *Die Zeit als Einbildungskraft des Dichters* (Zürich: Atlantis, 1953).

45. Brodtkorb, *Ishmael's White World*, p. 9.

46. Ibid., ch. 2.

47. Roland Barthes, *Sur Racine* (Paris: Seuil, 1963), p. 33.

48. *Apropos* time and space, their true natures have been at the center of controversy among phenomenological philosophers. Some would consider time and space to be modes of consciousness, whereas others would regard them as content categories. Designation of them as modes in this book is merely a practical choice. Whether time and space are modal or not does not really affect the practice of literary criticism, and philosophical discussion of the matter is beyond our present purpose. It is enough for us to remember that time is mutually implicated in Self and World, and so is space.

49. An excellent collection of essays relevant to the modes is available in Nathaniel Lawrence and Daniel O'Connor, eds., *Readings in Existential Phenomenology* (Englewood Cliffs, N.J.: Prentice-Hall, 1967).

50. Justification for this can be found in Eugene Minkowski's article, "Imagination," *Revue Internationale de Philosophie*, vol. 14, no. 51 (1960): 3-31.

51. For a discussion of content categories, consult J. H. Van Den Berg's *The Phenomenological Approach to Psychiatry* (Springfield, Ill.: Thomas, 1955).

52. See Jean-Paul Sartre, *Esquisse d'une théorie des émotions* (Paris: Hermann, 1939).

53. Rousset, *Forme et Signification*, p. 48.

54. Consult Merleau-Ponty, *The Phenomenology of Perception*, trans. Colin Smith (New York and London: Routledge and Kegan Paul, 1962), pt. 1, ch. 6; and Philip Lewis, "Merleau-Ponty and the phenomenology of language," *Yale French Studies* 36/37 (October 1966), p. 32.

55. For a good discussion, see Eugene Kaelin, "Aesthetics as a General Theory of Linguistics," in *An Existentialist Aesthetic: The Theories of Sartre and Merleau-Ponty* (Madison: University of Wisconsin Press, 1962).

56. The special quality of concrete expression in literature is examined by Merleau-Ponty in *Sens et non-sens*, the chapter entitled "Le roman et la métaphysique."

57. This is a possible psychological basis for the phenomenon of metaphor.

58. I think the school can even describe the ego of a structuralist writer such as Jorge Luis Borges or Alain Robbe-Grillet, even though these writers attempt to dissociate their personal sensibilities from language.

59. See *Die Zeit*, pp. 9-14.

60. J. Hillis Miller, "The Literary Criticism of Georges Poulet," *Modern Language Notes* (December 1963), pp. 486.

61. René Wellek also espies the a-historicism of the early Staiger and the historicism of his later work. See Wellek's *Concepts of Criticism* (New Haven and London: Yale University Press, 1963), p. 207; and Wellek's article "Literaturkritik und Literaturwissenschaft," *Lexicon der Weltliteratur im 20. Jahrhundert,* col. 204.

62. Staiger, *Die Kunst,* pp. 28, 29.

63. Of course, it would be my own position here that the Geneva School implies a general theory of history, though not a very particularized one.

64. I owe this example from Spitzer to Jan Brandt Corstium's *Introduction to the Comparative Study of Literature,* p. 131 *et seq.*

65. Richard, *L'Univers imaginaire,* p. 23.

66. Cleanth Brooks and Robert Penn Warren, *Understanding Fiction,* 2nd ed. (New York: Appleton-Century-Crofts, 1959), p. 688.

67. Ibid., p. 682.

68. Jean-Pierre Richard, *Onze études sur la poésie moderne* (Paris: Seuil, 1964), p. 10.

69. Miller, *Charles Dickens,* p. xi.

70. Ibid., p. ix.

71. See Richard, *L'Univers imaginaire,* pt. 4, secs. 1, 2, 5, and 6.

72. Staiger, *Die Kunst,* p. 11.

73. Richard, *L'Univers imaginaire,* pp. 24, 25.

74. Ibid., p. 28.

75. To *L'Univers imaginaire.*

76. Ibid., pp. 25, 26.

77. Jean Starobinski, "Présentation," in *Montesquieu par lui-même* (Paris: Seuil, 1953), p. 27.

78. Gaston Bachelard, *La Poétique de l'Espace* (Paris: Presses universitaires de France, 1964).

79. Richard, *L'Univers imaginaire,* p. 95.

80. Richard, *Littérature et Sensation,* pp. 125, 194.

81. Miller, *Charles Dickens,* p. 333 and *passim.*

82. Jean-Paul Sartre, *Literary and Philosophical Essays,* trans. Annette Michelson (New York: Collier, 1962), pp. 96, 97.

83. Marcel Raymond, *Senancour* (Paris: José Corti), p. 89.

84. Roman Jakobson, "Closing Statement: Linguistics and Poetics," *Style in Language,* ed. T. Sebeok (Cambridge, Mass.: M.I.T. Press, 1960), p. 368.

85. Michael Riffaterre, though not a phenomenologist, exposes the inadequacies of Jakobson's approach; see his "Describing Poetic Structures: Two Approaches to Baudelaire's 'Les Chats,'" *Yale French Studies* 36/37 (October 1966), pp. 206-212.

# Chapter Three

1. All my references are to the English translation: Martin Heidegger, *Being and Time,* trans. John Macquarrie and Edward Robinson (New York: Harper and Row, 1962).

2. Ludwig Binswanger, "Ibsen's *The Masterbuilder,*" in *European Literary Theory and Practice,* ed. Vernon Gras (New York: Dell, 1973), p. 185.

3. Binswanger, "Heidegger's Analytic of Existence and Its Meaning for Psychiatry," *European Literary Theory and Practice*, p. 54.
4. *Being and Time*, p. 437.
5. Binswanger, "Heidegger's Analytic," p. 51.
6. Hart Crane, *The Complete Poems of Hart Crane* (Garden City, N.Y.: Doubleday Anchor, 1958), p. 3.
7. Ibid., p. 30.
8. *Being and Time*, p. 37.
9. Though it evaluates them in a radically different way from my own, I still recommend the description of contemporary German critics written by L. L. Duroche, *Aspects of Criticism: Literary Study in Present-Day Germany* (The Hague and Paris: Mouton, 1967).
10. Good examples are Joseph J. Kockelmans, ed. and trans., *On Heidegger and Language* (Evanston, Ill.: Northwestern University Press, 1972); Calvin O. Schrag, "The Transvaluation of Aesthetics and the Work of Art," *The Southwestern Journal of Philosophy* 4 (1974): 109-24; and Hans Jaeger, "Heidegger and the Work of Art," in *Aesthetics Today*, ed. Morris Philipson (Cleveland and New York: World, 1961), pp. 413-31.
11. These two essays appear in the original German as "Heimkunft / An die Verwandten," and "Hölderlin und das Wesen der Dichtung," in Martin Heidegger, *Erläuterungen zu Hölderlins Dichtung* (Frankfurt: Klostermann, 1951).
12. Martin Heidegger, *Existence and Being*, introd. and analysis by Werner Brock (Chicago: Gateway, 1965).
13. Martin Heidegger, *Poetry, Language, Thought*, trans. Albert Hofstadter (New York: Harper and Row, 1971).
14. The respective German originals are *Aus der Erfahrung des Denkens* (Pfullingen: Neske, 1954); *Der Ursprung des Kunstwerkes*, Universal-Bibliothek Nr. 8446 / 47 (Stuttgart: Reclam, 1960); "Wozu Dichter?" in *Holzwege*, 1st ed. (Frankfurt am Main: Klostermann, 1950); "Bauen Wohnen Denken," in *Vorträge und Aufsätze* (Pfullingen: Neske, 1954); "Das Ding," also in *Vorträge und Aufsätze;* "Die Sprache," in *Unterwegs zur Sprache* (Pfullingen: Neske, 1959); and "dichterisch wohnet der Mensch," in *Vorträge und Aufsätze*. Throughout the pages that follow, page references to the essays in Brock and Hofstadter will appear in the body of the text, enclosed in parentheses and preceded by either a B (the Brock collection) or H (the Hofstadter collection).
15. David Steindl-Rast, Monk of Mount Savior Monastery, "Christian Confrontation With Buddhism and Hinduism," private monograph, p. 6.

# Chapter Four

1. Paul Ricoeur, *Le Conflit des interprétations* (Paris: Seuil, 1969), p. 85.
2. Ibid., p. 34.
3. Paul Ricoeur, "Lecture II," lecture series delivered in English at Wheaton College, Ill., 1969 (unpublished mimeographed text). The quotations which follow are from "Lecture I" and "Lecture II."
4. *Pourquoi la nouvelle critique?* (Paris: Mercure de France, 1966), p. 36.
5. Ricoeur, *Le Conflit*, p. 256.
6. Roland Barthes, *Elements of Semiology*, trans. A. Lavers and C. Smith (New York: Hill and Wang, 1968), pp. 42, 43.

7. Roland Barthes, *Essais critiques* (Paris: Seuil, 1964), p. 268.

8. Barthes, *Essais critiques*, p. 255.

9. Doubrovsky, "Critique et existence," *Les Chemins actuels de la critique* (text of the Cerisy-la-Salle symposium), director Georges Poulet, ed. Jean Ricardou (Paris: Plon, 1967), pp. 261-87.

10. "Language and French Critical Debate," *Yale French Studies* 45 (1970), pp. 154-65.

11. Tzvetan Todorov, *Poétique de la prose* (Paris: Seuil, 1971).

12. Barthes, *Essais critiques*, p. 214.

13. See the "Introduction" to *Introduction to Structuralism*, ed. and introd. Michael Lane (New York: Basic Books, 1970), pp. 25, 26, 35, 36.

14. For a good example of this kind of work, see Todorov, "Poétique," *Qu'est-ce que le structuralisme?*, dir. F. Wahl (Paris: Seuil, 1968), pp. 132-47.

15. Barthes, *Essais critiques*, p. 272.

16. Roman Jakobson, "Closing Statement: Linguistics and Poetics," *Style in Language*, p. 358.

17. Todorov, *Poétique de la prose*, p. 248; the discussion of "description" is on pp. 246, 247.

18. *Poétique de la prose*, p. 40.

19. Ibid., p. 186-96.

20. Ibid., p. 252.

21. Ibid., p. 248.

22. Ibid., p. 247.

23. Ricoeur, *Le Conflit*, p. 13.

24. Ibid., p. 34.

25. See n. 14.

26. Ricoeur, *Le Conflit*, p. 51.

27. "Poétique," *Qu'est-ce que le structuralisme?*, p. 153.

28. Ricoeur, *Le Conflit*, p. 34.

29. Ibid., pp. 60 and 59, respectively.

30. *Structuralism*, trans. C. Maschler (New York: Basic Books, 1970). All quotes from Piaget which follow are from p. 122-25.

31. Barthes, *Essais critiques*, p. 220.

32. In *Yale French Studies* 45 (1970), pp. 113-26.

33. Poulet, *La Conscience critique*, p. 267.

# Part Two

## Chapter One

1. E. D. Hirsch, "Objective Interpretation," *PMLA* (September 1960); the essay reappears as Appendix I in Hirsch, *Validity in Interpretation* (New Haven: Yale University Press, 1967).

2. Hirsch, "Objective Interpretation," *Validity in Interpretation*, p. 218.

3. Ibid., p. 219.

4. *Validity in Interpretation,* pp. 57, 58.

5. Ibid., p. 134.

6. All references are to the English translation, Edmund Husserl, *Logical Investigations,* trans. J. N. Findlay, 2 vols. (New York: Humanities Press, 1970); original German edition, *Logische Untersuchungen* (Halle: Niemeyer, 1900). The quotation is from *Logical Investigations,* p. 559.

7. Ibid., p. 565.

8. Ibid., p. 578.

9. Ibid., p. 269.

10. Ibid., pp. 276, 277.

11. Ibid., p. 287.

12. Ibid., p. 293.

13. Ibid., p. 588.

14. Ibid., p. 589.

15. Ibid., p. 590.

16. Ibid., p. 284.

17. Ibid., see pp. 288, 292.

18. Ibid., pp. 314, 315; the quotations which follow are from the same source.

19. Husserl, *Ideas: General Introduction to Pure Phenomenology,* trans. W. R. Boyce Gibson (New York: Collier, 1962), p. 153; the German original, *Ideen zu einer reinen Phänomenologie und phänomenologischen Philosophie,* was published in 1913. All subsequent references are to the English edition.

20. *Ideas,* p. 345.

21. Ibid., p. 334.

22. Ibid., p. 319.

23. Ibid., p. 320.

24. Ibid., p. 229.

25. Ibid., p. 338.

26. Ibid., p. 340.

27. Ibid.

28. Ibid., pp. 341, 342.

29. Ibid., p. 337.

30. Ibid., p. 346.

31. Ibid.

32. Ibid., pp. 336, 340-345.

# Chapter Two

1. All references are to the English edition, *The Literary Work of Art: An Investigation on the Borderlines of Ontology, Logic, and Theory of Literature,* trans. George G. Grabowicz (Evanston, Ill.: Northwestern University Press, 1973), a translation of the third edition of *Das literarische Kunstwerk* (Tübingen: Max Niemeyer, 1965). Page references are enclosed within parentheses in the body of the text.

2. In the apparently ambiguous sentence, consultation of the sentence's textual context resolves the ambiguity.

3.  This section of Ingarden is unusually abstruse. I have tried to introduce order, sometimes by rearranging the sequence of the argument.

4.  Of course, in the face of such a charge, Ingarden might quote those passages, described above, wherein he says the ontic status of metaphysical qualities in literature is heteronomous and purely intentional (and thus apparently not ideal). Actually, Ingarden is quite obscure in section forty-nine, suggesting in some places that the very same ideal metaphysical qualities are realized in the real world and only revealed in literature (so that all metaphysical qualities are ideal, and only their manner of concretization varies); and in other places, suggesting that two kinds of metaphysical qualities are involved, ideal ones for the real world and purely intentional ones for the literary world.

5.  After the last chapter appears an appendix entitled "The Functions of Language in the Theater."

# Chapter Three

1.  All page references, again indicated within parentheses in my text, are to the English translation, *The Phenomenology of Aesthetic Experience*, trans. E. S. Casey, A. A. Anderson, Willis Domingo, and Leon Jacobson (Evanston, Ill.: Northwestern University Press, 1973); the original French version is *Phénoménologie de l'expérience esthétique* (Paris; Presses Universitaires de France, 1953).

2.  Dufrenne falls back into dichotomy—for example, when he says that we exist in the work, but the work doesn't exist in us (59).

3.  Certainly Dufrenne is dependent on Heidegger's notions of *Vorhandenheit* and *Zuhandenheit* here.

4.  Which is a "duplication" or "reactualization" of the author's original meaning-bestowal.

5.  In this context, I equate the terms *ontic* and *ontological*.

6.  Earlier I said Dufrenne is at times more an idealist than Ingarden himself. Here Dufrenne is an absolute realist. This contradiction runs throughout *The Phenomenology*.

# Chapter Four

1.  Section thirty-two runs from p. 188 through p. 195 of *Being and Time*, the English translation of *Sein und Zeit*. Page references are again inserted into the body of the text.

2.  Take care not to confuse "fore-structure" with "As-structure."

3.  Hans-Georg Gadamer, *Le Problème de la conscience historique* (Louvain and Paris: Publications universitaires de Louvain, and Editions Béatrice-Nauwelaerts, 1963), p. 75.

4.  This hermeneutical circle finds an analogous operation in the practice of the Geneva School. The Geneva critic, still in a naive state, "experiences" the literary

work, and this experience founds the interpretation. The critic then returns to the initial experience of the work, and the interpretation he or she brings along helps to found the experience.

5.   Hans-Georg Gadamer, *Truth and Method,* translation edited by Garrett Barden and John Cumming from the second German edition (New York: Seabury Press, 1975), p. xix. Gadamer, in fact, is more rigorous than Heidegger in his negation of the author's meaning. As I shall demonstrate, Heidegger permits the author's meaning but does not make it a requirement for validity.

6.   *Le Problème de la conscience historique,* p. 68.

7.   E.D. Hirsch, *Validity in Interpretation* (New Haven: Yale University Press, 1967), p. 45.

8.   Ibid.

9.   Ibid., p. 230.

10.   Martin Heidegger, *Poetry, Language, Thought,* trans. Albert Hofstadter (New York: Harper and Row, 1971), pp. 131, 132.

11.   René Wellek and Austin Warren, *Theory of Literature,* 3rd ed. (New York: Harcourt, Brace and World, 1956), pp. 177, 178.

12.   *Validity in Interpretation,* p. 215.

13.   *Poetry, Language, Thought,* p. 11.

# index

*The text of* Phenomenology and Literature: An Introduction *was set in Baskerville typefaces, developed in England around 1752. John Baskerville designed the face in an attempt to improve the legibility of the Old Style faces then in use by increasing the contrast between the thick and thin strokes in the letters. Baskerville remains one of the most popular of the transitional faces. The typesetting was done on Addressograph-Multigraph phototypesetting equipment by ParaGraphics, Inc., of Bloomfield, New Jersey. Printing by offset lithography on 60-pound white Mead Text paper and casebinding in Columbia Millbank linen were by Thomson-Shore, Inc., of Dexter, Michigan. The main titles were set in Cancelleresca Swash. This phototype was hand modified by David Brannan, designer with the Purdue University Press. Mr. Brannan also designed the dust jacket, which was printed on 50-pound white Kromekote Cover by the Hollenbeck Press of Indianapolis. Diane Dubiel, managing editor, was editorial and production supervisor.*

# DATE DUE